GOOD PRACTICE in
Promoting Recovery and Healing for Abused Adults

Good Practice in Health, Social Care and Criminal Justice Series

Edited by Jacki Pritchard

This series explores topics of current concern to professionals working in social care, health care and the probation service. Contributors are drawn from a wide variety of settings, both in the voluntary and statutory sectors.

other books in the series

Good Practice in Assessing Risk
Current Knowledge, Issues and Approaches
Edited by Hazel Kemshall and Bernadette Wilkinson
ISBN 978 1 84905 059 3
eISBN 978 0 85700 252 5

Good Practice in Safeguarding Children
Working Effectively in Child Protection
Edited by Liz Hughes and Hilary Owen
ISBN 978 1 84310 945 7
eISBN 978 1 84642 894 4

Good Practice in Safeguarding Adults
Working Effectively in Adult Protection
Edited by Jacki Pritchard
ISBN 978 1 84310 699 9
eISBN 978 1 84642 825 8

Good Practice in the Law and Safeguarding Adults
Criminal Justice and Adult Protection
Edited by Jacki Pritchard
ISBN 978 1 84310 937 2
eISBN 978 1 84642 858 6

Good Practice in Brain Injury Case Management
Edited by Jackie Parker
ISBN 978 1 84310 315 8
eISBN 978 1 84642 508 0

Good Practice in Adult Mental Health
Edited by Tony Ryan and Jacki Pritchard
ISBN 978 1 84310 217 5
eISBN 978 1 84642 053 5

Good Practice in Health, Social Care and Criminal Justice

GOOD PRACTICE in
Promoting Recovery and Healing for Abused Adults

Edited by Jacki Pritchard

Jessica Kingsley *Publishers*
London and Philadelphia

First published in 2013
by Jessica Kingsley Publishers
116 Pentonville Road
London N1 9JB, UK
and
400 Market Street, Suite 400
Philadelphia, PA 19106, USA

www.jkp.com

Library of Congress Cataloging in Publication Data
Good practice in promoting recovery and healing for abused adults / edited by Jacki
Pritchard.
pages cm. -- (Good practice in health, social care and criminal justice)
Includes bibliographical references and index.
ISBN 978-1-84905-372-3 (alk. paper)
1. Sexual abuse victims--Services for. 2. Sexual abuse victims--Rehabilitation. I.
Pritchard, Jacki, editor.
HV6625.G66 2013
362.88'186--dc23
2012041886

British Library Cataloguing in Publication Data
A CIP catalogue record for this book is available from the British Library

ISBN 978 1 84905 372 3
eISBN 978 0 85700 723 0

Printed and bound in Great Britain

This book is dedicated to two very special
people – Vanessa and Nathan Pritchard (the
current Team P) – during a very important year

ACKNOWLEDGEMENTS

Editing a book is always so much harder than writing one of your own. I would never get to the end without the support I receive from particular people in my working life: Janice Ward, Louise Perry, Angela Sands and Mary Sarjeant. All of whom bring help, wisdom and laughter into my working day.

As I explain in the prologue, the idea and inspiration for this particular book came from past and current members of Beyond Existing. As in all my books, I want to acknowledge that everything I have learnt about abuse has come from the victims I have worked with over the years; I owe them so much and am extremely grateful.

This is a very special year, as the Good Practice Series becomes 20 years old, and I have had the privilege of being Series Editor since the beginning. So I would like to take this opportunity to thank everyone I have worked with in Jessica Kingsley Publishers since 1993, and especially Jessica herself, Dee Brigham and Stephen Jones.

Contents

PROLOGUE
LISTENING TO WHAT VICTIMS HAVE TO SAY
ABOUT RECOVERY AND HEALING

JACKI PRITCHARD

IDEA FOR THE BOOK

The idea for this book came after I fed back a discussion I had had with a professional about the term 'recovery' (which we defined very differently) to a group of abused women I was working with at the time. My own social work practice has been developed from and guided by what I have learnt directly from victims of abuse I have worked with over three decades. What occurred to me during this discussion about recovery was that many professionals across the sectors could hold views that are poles apart from how a victim of abuse may define it. I had been putting forward my definition of recovery, which has been developed from the work I have done with victims through the organisation I founded in 2000 – Beyond Existing: Support Groups for Adults who have been Abused. The main thread of my argument was that recovery is something very different to healing.

At the next Beyond Existing group meeting I talked about the differences in opinion I had encountered, and wanted to check out current members'[1] definitions regarding recovery and healing. Consequently, as often happens, we turned this into a group exercise where members are asked to discuss certain terms, saying what they mean to them. As a result of that exercise, together with other frustrations regarding the poor practice in regard to planning long-term healing work with victims of abuse, the idea for this book developed. The main comments from carrying out the exercise are summarised below, which seemed a fitting way to introduce the subject of this book.

---

1   'Member' is the term used for someone attending a Beyond Existing group.

RECOVERY AND HEALING

When a person gets hurt it is a normal human reaction to want to feel better, but sometimes things intervene along the way to impede the process of healing. A toddler may fall over and cut his knee; it stings for a while until it is cleaned and antiseptic cream is put on the injury. A cuddle from a trusted person (family member, teacher, nurse) and some verbal reassurances that it will get better help along the way whilst the cream works its 'magic'. However, if the cut is not tended to and dirt gets into the wound, infection can spread; it then becomes more painful and the healing takes longer. This is a very simplistic view of recovery and healing, but is a good analogy of how a person who has been abused needs help to recover and heal. The purpose in editing this book is to look at some of the different methodologies that can be used to help a person heal from the effects of abuse, whether it has occurred in childhood or adulthood.

A constant theme in my writing over the years has been about 'giving victims a voice'. I believe my own knowledge and practice is as it is because I have listened to and learnt from victims themselves – that is, from direct practice, not just reading books. Working closely with victims of abuse fuels my passion for promoting best practice – nothing less is good enough. So it is important that the introduction to this book includes what victims have to say about recovery and healing; and the book will also finish with their voices.

It is dangerous to promote one way of healing and make the assumption that a particular methodology is going to work for everyone. In-depth assessment is a necessity in order to find out how a person may be helped to heal; what works for one person is not necessarily going to work for another. It is vital to find out the best way to help a person work their way through the healing process. Sometimes it can be trial and error because the person does not know what will help them. They may not have given any thought to themselves, as they feel they are not worthy of help; possibly because they feel that they are to blame – the abuse is their fault, so they deserved it. Victims of abuse have often been told they are 'worthless' or 'useless', so why should they deserve attention?

This book will focus on the word 'abuse'. We should not shy away from using it; if it makes people feel uncomfortable, then that is a good thing. People have to accept that bad things go on and the victims need help.

VICTIMS' VIEWS ABOUT RECOVERY AND HEALING

As explained above, the idea for this book really came from the views which have been expressed by victims from past groups (as well as the current one) and from the work undertaken with them. They see recovery as something which happens in the short-term and from something physical. Healing is seen as a more long-term process and dealing with emotional things rather than physical. The current members of Beyond Existing were asked to participate in an exercise which engaged them in discussion about defining the terms 'recovery' and 'healing'. The key statements which came out of the exercise were:

> *Recovery is immediately after something; healing is long-term.*

> *Recovery is negative; a struggle; a whirlpool. Healing is more positive; calmer.*

> *Healing is emotional, recovery physical.*

RECOVERY

Participants[2] tended to think of recovery as a 'medical term' and as recovering from something physical; the main things discussed were:

- damage to body (after rape, assault)
- bruises
- scars
- internal damage 'down there' (which lasts into the long-term).

It was acknowledged that in the short-term there was also psychological damage, which resulted in needing help in the longer term to deal with:

- shock
- bad nerves
- lack of confidence
- low self-esteem
- walking on eggshells
- withdrawal
- avoidance
- fear
- anxiety
- panic attacks
- lack of trust
- stigma.

---

2   This term will be used to refer to those who took part in the exercise.

Some participants said that through taking part in the exercise they realised now (i.e. years later) what they needed to recover from:

You realise that the dynamics in the family are not as they should be. It's recognising it's not you it's other people to blame who are at fault.

I blame myself for what other people have done. I think if I'd come forward it would not have happened to others. I have regrets. Could I have done something different?

Being weak. It's a British thing – have to have stiff upper lip – have to appear to be strong. It's historical: if you have a problem keep it to yourself; don't air your dirty washing in public. Abusers tell you that you are weak. You feel it yourself – you can't do anything against them. You always feel pathetic.

From the anger towards my abuser. Anger towards myself because of the length of time I tolerated things.

Hatred – what they have done. Hatred – who I have become; not recognising myself.

Loss of childhood and teenage years.

Although Beyond Existing is primarily concerned with helping people through the healing process, we have supported people during their recovery stage:

- older people (men and women) placed in emergency placements after being raped; assaulted; financially abused; burgled
- younger people after rape
- after suicide attempts
- after being sectioned
- escaping domestic violence
- people still living in domestic violence situations
- harassment – eviction
- women waiting to go to court to give evidence about historical child abuse – needing short-term help in the interim/short period.

HEALING

As has already been said, members see healing as more to do with their emotional state. Although Beyond Existing leaflets state clearly that the main objective is to help victims of abuse through the healing process, it is not uncommon for men and women to struggle during the first few sessions to identify how they may be helped. All they know is they 'want to get better'.

The exercise again proved that hindsight is a great thing. The majority of members who participated in the exercise were very clear as individuals about what healing should be and what it should achieve:

Acceptance – coming to terms with what's happened.

Soothing.

Peace.

Feeling good about yourself.

Healing gives you hope.

Not thinking about it [abuse] *all the time and what I have lost.*

Start having some pleasure in life.

Giving self treats.

Freedom.

Letting go – putting your emotions in the right place – not being angry with yourself.

Going over things what's happened physically tires you and stops you enjoying the rest of your life. Healing is about not using up that energy on the abuse issues.

Can think about the abuse without the same effects. Can still be upset but it's not destroying you.

Living in the moment.

TO FORGIVE OR NOT TO FORGIVE?

A major discussion took place during the exercise about whether 'forgiveness' is part of the healing process; and this is a debate which has come up in previous group meetings. One participant said:

I should be able to forgive my abusers because they are family.

Some participants were very quick to disagree and said in unison:

You don't have to.

The participant went on to explain that the uncle who had sexually abused her as a child was currently dying, and she said:

I must forgive him.

Several participants said:

Why should you?

Another said:

Why should he die in peace?

The participant went on to say that she did blame herself for the abuse happening and felt:

I need to be able to forgive myself; but I can't.

Ultimately it was agreed that the split in viewpoints about forgiveness was because:

It depends on your upbringing and religion.

It's how you view it: a way to move on or to let them [the abuser] *off – accepting what they did.*

One participant said her view of forgiveness had changed whilst going through the healing process:

I used to think I should forgive them [parents]. *I now think I don't have to forgive them. What they did was downright wrong.*

THE WORDS VICTIMS HATE

Another topic which was raised by participants during this exercise was about the words and phrases they absolutely hate being said to them:

You need to move on.

Pull yourself together.

Deal with it.

That's life.

Put it behind you.

It's the real world.

Put it in the past.

THE REST OF THE BOOK

In presenting in this prologue to the book the views of people who are actually going through the healing process, I hope to interest the reader in finding out more about how recovery and healing can be achieved in the chapters which follow. My aim was to put together a collection of chapters which would describe a variety of methodologies used by practitioners from different backgrounds and settings to work with recovery in the short-term and healing in the long-term. I felt it was very important to include chapters on male victims of abuse, because unfortunately they still are not given the attention they deserve. Throughout the book there are recurring themes about:

- the victim being given time to heal – not being rushed to fit agencies'/workers' timescales
- developing trust
- providing the right setting
- finding the right methods and resources to help the recovery and healing processes for the individual victim.
- welfare and self-care of the practitioner.

The book will also end with the views and voices of victims who clearly demonstrate that:

It is never too late to be what you might have been.[3]

---

3   This quotation is often attributed to George Eliot (1818–1880) but there is some controversy about its origin. Some cite its origin as being *A Life for a Life* by Dinah Maria Craik (1859).

CHAPTER 1

How Recovery and Healing Should Fit into the Adult Safeguarding Process

JACKI PRITCHARD

The aim in writing this chapter is to give some thought to how a victim of abuse should be helped to recover and heal as part of the adult safeguarding process. Nowadays there is so much emphasis on process and paperwork that it seems we can lose sight of the person who matters – that is, the victim[1] of abuse. I have been concerned for a long time that during adult safeguarding meetings not enough attention is given to in-depth planning for the possible therapeutic methods which will aid recovery and healing. Practitioners can often talk in what I call 'global terms' and do not explain verbally or in written records the exact methodology which will be adopted. Because resources are stretched to the limit, many workers are (quite rightly) involved in and focused on crisis intervention work; consequently the long-term work is often not considered in enough detail. It would seem that nowadays there is a lot of crisis intervention work rather than preventative work and therapeutic intervention. I have always believed that it is critical to develop good, detailed protection plans[2] for both short-term and long-term work; and much can be learnt and transferred from child protection practices past and present.

The necessity to follow procedures and work to targets seems to be killing off creativity in practice. I find it very sad when, on a training course, I give out examples of tools which might help promote best practice and a worker asks: 'Can we use this if it is not in the policy or been agreed by management?' There is a constant fear of 'getting

---

1   The term 'victim' will be used in this chapter to describe someone who has not yet gone through the healing process.

2   Some areas use the term 'safeguarding plan' rather than 'protection plan' in the local safeguarding adults policy. The terms are synonymous. In this chapter I shall use the term protection plan, because victims frequently tell me that they prefer the word 'protection' to 'safeguarding'.

things wrong' and being criticised for not doing things procedurally – especially in regard to completing the correct paperwork. I feel strongly that practitioners must be encouraged to think 'outside of the box' (the forms and templates) and not become robotic in their practice and recording skills. Another concern of mine is how I am constantly told that I 'talk about best practice all the time; we shall decide what is good enough'. Good enough for whom? The management perhaps; but certainly not the victim of abuse.

This chapter is based on my belief (and my own practice) that workers should distinguish between short-term (recovery) and long-term (healing) work. Planning for both types of work can be done by developing proper protection plans (both interim and full). I am very conscious of the fact that victims often tell me that they feel too many people are involved with them, so this should be borne in mind when thinking about who can help the recovery and healing processes. Victims should not feel overwhelmed, or that they are being forced to try some form of counselling or therapy. Before discussing this further I would like the reader to be conscious of the following problems which can exist in safeguarding meetings:

Common problems hindering recovery and healing work

- Focus of discussion is solely on the immediate issues regarding safety and capacity.
- Not enough planning for the long-term healing work.
- Pressure to close cases or pass them back to care management.
- Lack of knowledge about what/who is available locally for therapeutic work.
- Statutory bodies are too precious – not looking to the voluntary and independent sectors for resources which could aid recovery and healing.
- Not asking the victim for their views about how they could be helped to heal.
- Not involving the victim in the development of the protection plan.
- Not enough preparation work in relation to the protection plan before a meeting takes place.
- Lack of training regarding how to write a protection plan.

RECOVERY AND HEALING: FITTING INTO THE ADULT SAFEGUARDING FRAMEWORK

As a practitioner I have always felt it has been useful to think in terms of short-term and long-term work; it is probably because of the way I was trained a long time ago. Sometimes it is helpful to look back and see how things worked in the past and to pick out what might still be relevant and useful now. It is important for any worker to plan their work and to set clear objectives which can be reviewed at regular intervals.

The adult safeguarding process usually has the following distinct stages:

The stages in safeguarding adults work[1]

- Alert – someone is concerned that an adult is at risk of harm; the alerter could be a worker in an agency within the statutory, voluntary or independent sectors, or a member of the public
- Referral to adult social care (social services)
- Strategy discussion/meeting
- Investigation
- Case conference (initial)
- Review (case conference)

---

1   Terminology can differ in local area policies, e.g. regarding strategy discussions or meetings, planning meetings, case conferences; so please check the correct usage in your local policy.

Short-term work (recovery) can be defined as taking place up to the point where an initial case conference is convened; thereafter I would deem this to be long-term work (healing). Protection plans are a crucial part of the process – that is, demonstrating what work is being done to protect the adult at risk of harm/abuse.

GOOD PRACTICE POINT

An *interim* protection plan should be developed and formally written up at the strategy meeting stage for short-term work and a *full* protection plan should be developed at the case conference stage for long-term work.

There is now so much emphasis on passing cases back to normal day-to-day care management that it is imperative that detailed protection plans are written so that the abuse issues do not get lost. This framework and process can lend itself nicely to the definitions of 'recovery' and 'healing' as stated by victims.

Recovery is immediately after something; healing is long-term.

THE TERMS SAFEGUARDING AND ABUSE

I have always had concerns about the adoption of the word 'safeguarding' in working with adults. Nowadays so many things are deemed to be 'safeguarding issues', many of which could be dealt with in normal day-to-day work rather than going down the safeguarding investigation route. Instead workers and managers can spend an enormous amount of time agonising about whether to implement the safeguarding adults policy and about thresholds. This book is concerned with 'abuse', adults' experience of it and how to recover and heal from it. It is impossible to be accurate about the prevalence and incidence of abuse, but it would seem that a considerable number of adults who experience abuse in adulthood have also experienced abuse in childhood. Therefore, it may be helpful to the reader to be reminded of the definitions and categories of abuse here in the United Kingdom:

Categories of abuse[2]

Adult	**Child**
• Physical	• Physical
• Sexual	• Sexual
• Financial/material	• Emotional
• Neglect/act of omission	• Neglect
• Emotional/psychological	
• Discriminatory	

---

2 For more detail about the categories of abuse the reader should refer to *No Secrets* (Department of Health 2000) and *Working Together to Safeguard Children* (Department of Health, Home Office and Department for Education and Employment 1999; HM Government 2006 and 2010).

The key definitions in relation to adult safeguarding work are:

Definition of adult abuse

2.5 Abuse is a violation of an individual's human and civil rights by any other person or persons.

2.6 Abuse may consist of a single act or repeated acts. It may be physical, verbal or psychological, it may be an act of neglect or an omission to act, or it may occur when a vulnerable person is persuaded to enter into a financial or sexual transaction to which he or she has not consented, or cannot consent. Abuse can occur in any relationship and may result in significant harm to, or exploitation of, the person subjected to it.

(Department of Health 2000, p.9)

Definition of significant harm

2.18 'Harm' should be taken to include not only ill treatment (including sexual abuse and forms of ill treatment which are not physical), but also the impairment of, or an avoidable deterioration in, physical or mental health; and the impairment of physical, intellectual, emotional, social or behavioural development.

(Department of Health 2000, p.12)

LACK OF RESOURCES FOR HEALING

A problem in the current economic climate is that often there is a push to close cases because of a lack of resources. Securing funding to provide a service – especially therapy or counselling over a long period of time – can be a problem. Many agencies may deny this, saying they assess need based on eligibility criteria and offer a good quality service when appropriate. However, the reality is that with heavy caseloads workers in the statutory sector often do not have enough time to undertake in-depth assessments over a long period of time. Also they might not have researched in advance which therapeutic resources are available locally, and consequently they are not able to plan long-term work properly. Many victims of abuse tell me that they feel *passed around the professionals because they don't know what to do with me'*. Workers may suggest that other people get involved without knowing much about the services offered and methods used. Dealing with abuse is a specialist area of work, and workers who may be involved in investigations need to understand that healing needs to be planned properly, undertaken by someone else, and cannot be rushed.

LEARNING FROM CHILD PROTECTION

I believe we can learn and take a lot from child protection work, whilst fully acknowledging that there are differences between children and adults. It is very easy for the media and others to criticise agencies when things go wrong, but actually a lot of good work is done where positive outcomes are achieved. When things do go wrong it is usually because of lack of communication, which is highlighted as a key finding in most inquiries or serious case reviews (children and adults). We know that adult protection work has always lagged behind child protection, so it is important that lessons are still learnt and transferred from work with children. The way protection plans are developed is one such example.

I have seen frequently at the end of an adult safeguarding strategy meeting or a case conference that the protection plan is written in the form of bullet points and is sometimes merged with the decisions and recommendations – that is, it is not a stand-alone document. Or there is a pro-forma in place which does not allow for creativity or flexibility in developing a plan for an individual which includes recovery and healing interventions. It seems many templates are designed to suit the local software package rather than meet the needs of the workers who use them. During the course of an investigation it is important to discuss needs and options in relation to recovery and healing with the victim; choices should be offered before going to a case conference. A protection plan is something you develop *with* the victim – it is not something you can force them to adopt or adhere to. This is why it is crucial that the victim attends any safeguarding meeting whenever it is possible or appropriate to do so – that is, s/he is part of the process.

GOOD PRACTICE POINTS

- A protection plan is something you develop with a victim – it is not something that can be imposed on them.
- Whenever possible the victim (or their advocate) should attend any adult safeguarding meeting so they can be involved in the development of the plan.
- Resources for recovery and healing should be discussed before a case conference takes place.

I think it can be helpful to look at guidance which has been used in child protection and to transfer some of the good practices. The original guidance about developing protection plans under the Children Act 1989 is particularly useful:

> 5.17.1
>
> A written plan will need to be constructed with the involvement of the carers/parents and in the light of each agency's statutory duties and will identify the contributions each will make to the child, to the family members and the abuser. It will make clear the part to be played by parents, what expectations they may have of agencies and what expectations agencies may have of them. This is separate from the plans required under the Arrangements for Placements Regulations but will need to be consistent with them.
>
> 5.17.2
>
> Once the plan has been agreed, it will be the responsibility of individual agencies to implement the parts of the plan relating to them and to communicate with the keyworker and others as necessary. The keyworker will have the responsibility for pulling together and co-ordinating the contributions of different agencies.
>
> 5.17.3
>
> The production of the protection plan must include consideration of the wishes of the child and parents, local resources, the suitability of specialist facilities, their availability for addressing the particular needs of the child and his or her family. Special attention will need to be given to ensuring the services provided under the plan are co-ordinated, structured and ethically and culturally appropriate for the child and the family, with built-in mechanisms for programme review and crisis management.
>
> 5.17.4
>
> Children and parents should be given clear information about the purposes and nature of any intervention together with a copy of the plan. Every effort should be made to ensure that they have a clear understanding of the objectives of the plan, that they accept it and are willing to work to it. If the families' preferences about how the work to protect the child should be conducted are not accepted, the reasons for this should be explained, as should their right to complain and make representations.
>
> (Home Office *et al.* 1991, p.32)

When an adult has capacity, they can choose to live their lives as they wish to do; and, like all of us, they will at certain times in their life make unwise choices and decisions. The Children Acts 1989 and 2004 give workers statutory powers to intervene whilst acting in a child's best interests, but it is more complicated when working with adults. The starting point is to assume that an adult has capacity to make decisions; where there is concern about capacity, the task is to prove that a person actually lacks capacity in relation to a specific issue. This has massive implications regarding how a protection plan for an adult at risk is developed and implemented – especially if s/he lacks capacity in regard to some aspect of their life.

GOOD PRACTICE POINT

A person has the right to live their life as they wish to do.

THE OBJECTIVE IN WRITING PROTECTION PLANS

The objective of any protection plan is clear in its title: to protect the person from future harm. A thorough risk assessment should have been undertaken before any protection plan is developed. Risk assessment is an integral part of all adult safeguarding work; it should underpin any actions taken and all decision-making. However, the reality is that at the alert and strategy meeting stages information may be scant and emergency measures may need to be taken very quickly. So the plan cannot always be written in as much detail as it should be. Risk management should be used to measure and sustain the effectiveness of a protection plan, which has been developed to minimise the risk of harm occurring in the future. Risk management is an on-going process, and one of the main objectives should be to help the victim of abuse through the healing process.

In day-to-day work it is the task of a worker to predict whether a person is going to be harmed by, first, predicting any dangers (the negative outcomes) and then predicting the *likelihood* of those dangers occurring. A care plan is then developed to demonstrate how the risk of harm occurring will be minimised; that is, what resources will be put in. In safeguarding work (whether children or adults) it is necessary to predict the likelihood of significant harm (see definition on page 20 above) occurring. A protection plan will have the same objective as a care plan – to minimise harm occurring. In this chapter we are concerned with minimising the reoccurrence of abuse, but also helping the victim through the healing process.

GOOD PRACTICE POINT

The main objective of a protection plan is to demonstrate how the risk of abuse and harm occurring will be minimised. It is the **goal-setting stage** of the risk assessment process.

WHAT A PROTECTION PLAN SHOULD INCLUDE

GOOD PRACTICE POINTS

A protection plan should be explicit about:

- *who* is going to do *what* and *when*
- what is going to be monitored and how (frequency and duration)
- how and where this will be recorded.

I have already stated my concern about protection plans not being detailed enough. So I now want to discuss how plans should be developed and written, both in the short-term (interim protection plan) and the long-term (full protection plan), in order to aid recovery and healing. It is essential that all workers are trained on how to write protection plans properly. As discussed above, many policies include a template for protection plans. As with any form, a template can be too generalised (to be meaningful to the worker who may have to complete it without guidance or training); or conversely too long and prescriptive. Every abuse case and individual victim is different, and a template/form needs to allow for a worker to think, reflect and write freely.

GOOD PRACTICE POINTS

- Workers need written guidance and training on how to write a good protection plan.
- Any template needs to give the worker freedom to write creatively after reflection.

STRATEGY MEETING STAGE AND RECOVERY

Risk assessment actually starts as soon as anyone has a concern that an adult is being harmed. Many experienced workers will automatically risk-assess in their heads, but it is important to formalise the thinking into a written format. When a victim is in immediate danger, then something may be done straightaway and recorded later. During a strategy discussion or meeting it is important to formalise the risk assessment, record it and write an interim protection plan (which may include actions already taken, e.g. securing medical attention; removing a person to a place of safety).

There may be many things to discuss in a strategy meeting which are procedural issues, and these are not the subject of this particular chapter. However, the emphasis on following procedures can result in neglecting the emotional needs of the victim. Participants in a strategy meeting will discuss the safety of the victim, but rarely is the concept of 'recovery' part of the agenda or discussed in therapeutic terms.

Key Question

Have you ever heard 'recovery' being discussed in a strategy meeting?

Remembering that victims see recovery as being from something *physical* in the short-term, all sorts of situations may have to be considered when writing the interim protection plan.

Typical situations where help with recovery is needed

- Physical attack
- Sexual violence/rape
- Injuries
- Self-harm
- Over-medicated by someone/ overdose
- Suicide attempt
- Withdrawal of medication
- Alcohol/drug misuse
- Money stolen

- Debt
- Not enough food/drink, malnutrition/dehydration, underweight
- Force feeding/overfeeding/ overweight
- Lack of heat/lighting
- Inadequate clothing
- Eviction/homelessness

At this early stage in the process it is not always possible to problem solve and resolve issues immediately. However, in regard to some of the above, the following resources may be used to aid recovery.

Resources needed for recovery

- Visit to hospital, doctor, nurse for:
  - medical examination
  - medical treatment
  - surgery
  - bed
  - psychiatric assessment.
- A person with experience who can:
  - listen
  - answer questions
  - give clear explanations
  - give advice.
- Police, for:
  - reporting incidents
  - a helping presence (e.g. to gain entry, get belongings)
  - dealing with alleged abuser.
- Accommodation – place of safety:
  - refuge
  - hostel
  - bed-and-breakfast establishment
  - care home.
- Provision of basics:
  - food
  - drink
  - clothing
  - warmth
  - heat
  - light.
- Money.
- Freezing of bank accounts.

Bearing in mind the emphasis in the chapter is about writing explicitly in protection plans about recovery and healing, the reader might like to undertake the following exercise before reading on.

. . . .

EXERCISE 1.1

1. Re-read the list of resources above.

2. Write down where you would find/access these resources in your local area.

. . . .

It is important to acknowledge that although victims see recovery as something more physical, there will be emotional needs to consider as well; the victim may be experiencing:

- fear
- doubt
- self-blame
- guilt
- depression
- low self-esteem
- lack of confidence
- need to feel safe
- need to be loved
- need to be believed
- mistrust of people.

. . . .

EXERCISE 1.2

1. Re-read the list of emotional needs above.

2. How might these needs be met in the short-term (remembering that this is before an investigation has taken place or been completed)?

. . . .

The reality is that at the strategy meeting stage sometimes information is scant, has not been verified or is not available. This is one of the many reasons why the alleged victim should be present at least for some part of the meeting. A victim can express their views about being interviewed (i.e. helping to plan the investigation; preferred gender of investigating officers; address any cultural issues; special needs; location and time of interview[s]), and also talk about their immediate needs; recovery should be part of this discussion. I am certainly not suggesting the victim is interviewed in the meeting, but it is about including them in decision-making. Below is a list of subject areas which should be included in an interim protection plan; these are not exhaustive and not all of them will be relevant to each case/victim.

Subject areas for an interim protection plan

- Objectives of the plan
- Categories of abuse alleged
- Any emergency measures already taken
- Categories of abuse to be investigated
- Named investigating officers (who will be the keyworkers for the plan whilst the investigation takes place)
- People to be interviewed (who, when, where)
- Any special needs/measures for interviewees
- Other types of evidence to be collected (gaining access to e.g. medical records; medication sheets; rotas; bank records)
- Timescales
- Resources for the victim (whilst the investigation takes place) – which should include addressing any recovery issues
- Other issues which need attention

CASE CONFERENCE STAGE AND HEALING

Whilst I was working on the original research project 'The Needs of Older Women' and the follow-up project 'The Needs of Vulnerable Adults', I read many case files which included the minutes of meetings and protection plans. It was very clear that in many cases the investigating officers had not spent enough time with the victim discussing options and what might be included in a protection plan before the case conference. The case conference should not be seen as a professionals' meeting; if a person has capacity it is crucial that they are involved in developing their plan. As noted earlier, we do not have the same powers as in children's work; we cannot make an adult accept a protection plan.

Investigating officers are obviously concerned with gathering evidence to prove whether abuse has happened or not, but it is equally important to discuss the feelings and wishes of the victim; and this must include talking about healing. It is much easier to focus on how physical harm can be remedied, rather than emotional harm. Workers must not get into avoidance. The investigating officer needs to have knowledge about:

- resources available locally to help a victim heal
- the local experts in abuse – counsellors, therapists
- specialist organisations.

I suggest that workers need to build resource files (before the need for a resource arises), but before that they need to have some understanding of the different types of counselling and therapies which exist and how they might work for a victim of abuse. I am back to making the point that workers should be aware of theories and methods, which can be explained in a protection plan.

GOOD PRACTICE POINTS

- Workers need to be proactive in making a resource file so they know what/who is available before the need/crisis arises.
- The resource file needs to list specialist workers or organisations who can work with victims of abuse.

Key Questions

Key questions any worker should ask him/herself are:

1. How much do you know about the following terms and ways of working with a victim of abuse?

- counselling
- therapy
- one-to-one work
- person-centred
- group work

- psychodynamic approach
- gestalt
- transactional analysis
- cognitive behavioural therapy
- creative writing
- art therapy
- drama therapy
- music therapy.

2. Do you understand the differences in the way counsellors and therapists practise the above?

3. Who offers these services in your local area?

Before a case conference takes place, an investigating officer should have spoken to the victim about their needs and wishes for the future; this is where discussion about the healing process is crucial. The worker needs to have the knowledge and ability to explain how healing works. Some victims may have had enough of talking at this stage and may not want to engage with even more professionals to talk about their past experiences. Nevertheless, it is important that the victim knows what help can be made available, immediately or in the future. The discussion should include explanation regarding the following aspects:

- what healing is
- how it can be done and by whom
- the length of time it takes to heal is different for every victim
- some victims take breaks from the healing process and come back to it
- a person has to feel it is the right time to engage in the healing process.

After an investigation has been completed, the findings should be presented to an *initial* case conference. The investigating officer's report should include the findings, a risk assessment and recommendations for the future, which will be discussed in full by all participants at the conference. It must be noted that if a criminal investigation has taken place and prosecution is being pursued, advice must be taken regarding what counselling and therapy a victim can engage in before a case proceeds to court (Ministry of Justice 2011).

Subject areas for a full protection plan

- Objectives of the plan
- Categories of abuse which have been: (i) substantiated; (ii) not substantiated; (iii) inconclusive
- Keyworker for the plan, i.e. who is responsible for co-ordinating the plan and ensuring it is implemented correctly
- Named people (with job titles or relationship to the victim) who will actively have a role in the plan (these would form a core group)
- Clearly state the objectives, roles, responsibilities and tasks of each individual involved
- Explanation about methodologies to be used
- Frequency of contact
- Timescales – what will be achieved by when
- Monitoring tools (being explicit about what is being monitored and how)
- Recording the monitoring processes (which will form the basis for the review of risk management)
- Contingency plans if something goes wrong or does not work in practice
- Set date for review

Review case conferences should be convened in order to review the protection plan which will involve the reassessment of the risk of harm occurring.

CASE STUDIES TO ILLUSTRATE RECOVERY AND HEALING ISSUES

Two case studies are given below which illustrate the different recovery and healing issues for the victims involved. They can be used for training purposes using the following exercise:

• •

EXERCISE 1.3

1. Read the case study you have been given.

2. Discuss how you would work with the victim to address: (i) recovery issues; (ii) healing issues.

3. Write down and be explicit about: (i) methods to be used; (ii) how you would find and access local resources.

• •

CASE STUDY 1.1

Victim of abuse: Gita Udin
Age: 19

Background information
Gita came to England to live with her aunt and uncle when she was 18 years of age; this was after her parents had died in Pakistan. She married Ravi, aged 50, one month after arriving in the country. Five months after the marriage Ravi took Gita to see his own GP and said he thought his wife might be pregnant. The GP made a referral to the local hospital and the pregnancy was confirmed, but Gita did not attend for any appointments so she never had a scan. A midwife, Janet, had tried on two occasions to see Gita at home, but each time she had called Ravi had said: 'It is not a good time.' On the third attempt Ravi did let Janet in; probably because Gita was in the early stages of labour.

The alert
Janet called an ambulance immediately and Gita was admitted to hospital, where her baby was stillborn. Janet made the alert to social services.

Strategy meeting stage – recovery issues
A strategy meeting was held within one day. Janet and the GP were the only people who had any information about Gita. Gita could not speak English, so her husband had acted as interpreter. It was evident that Gita did not understand what her husband had been saying to her and Janet suspected that Gita might have some learning difficulties. When Janet had tried to ask Ravi some questions about Gita and her background, Ravi said it was none of her business.

There were many areas of concern, but the recovery issues in this stage of the process were as follows:

- Loss of the baby.
- Recovery from the birth.
- Gita was malnourished and dehydrated; she had sores on her body.
- Loss of freedom – possible imprisonment: Gita had been confined to one room. Janet heard Ravi unlock the door before showing Janet to the room, which was full of junk and very dirty. There was a mattress in one corner of the room and a bucket.
- Lack of light: the room did not have a window and there was no bulb in the light fitting.
- Gita had scars on her wrists.
- Need for clothing.

Case conference stage – healing issues
After leaving hospital, Gita went to stay in a refuge for Asian women. A very long and complex investigation took place because there were concerns about forced marriage. Information about Gita and her family had to be sought from Pakistan. Gita did have very mild learning difficulties; her reluctance to communicate was due to fear.

The healing issues in this stage of the process were as follows:

- incarceration
- neglect
- violence
- dignity
- loss of parents
- loss of baby
- loss of home, country, familiar surroundings, culture.

CASE STUDY 1.2

Victim of abuse: Alfie
Age: 78

Background information
Alfie lived alone in a semi-detached house, which he and his second wife, Betty, bought 40 years ago. Betty has Alzheimer's disease and now lives in a care home. Alfie had a stroke two years ago, which has caused mobility problems for him, so he does not go out very often. Home care workers go in three times a day because Alfie's daughter, Stella, lives 15 miles away and only visits once a week to collect 'her post'. Stella was made redundant two years ago and she persuaded her father to borrow money against the house so she could set up her own business.

The alert
The home care workers, Ailsa and Jan, became concerned when Alfie started getting a lot of cuts and bruises. When asked about the injuries he always said: 'I have had another fall.' Ailsa and Jan always thought it odd that a lot of post came to the house for Stella. Alfie said it was because she moved flats a lot. An alert was made when Alfie was found on the floor badly injured and he disclosed that Stella had attacked him when he refused to give her money. Alfie was admitted to the local hospital.

Strategy meeting stage – recovery issues
Being seriously assaulted by Stella was the trigger for Alfie to give a full disclosure about the abuse he had been experiencing from Stella for some years. The alleged categories of abuse were: physical, emotional and financial. The police were invited to the strategy meeting and an investigation was planned under the local safeguarding adults policy and procedures.

The recovery issues in this stage of the process were as follows:

- Alfie needed urgent medical attention, as he had sustained serious external and internal injuries during the assault.
- Alfie had recurring nightmares about being assaulted.
- Alfie was frightened that Stella would come onto the ward.
- Alfie said he did not want to return home because Stella had keys to his house.

- Stella had Alfie's debit and credit cards in her possession.

Case conference stage – healing issues

Alfie remained in hospital while the investigation took place. He was interviewed by the police (who brought a mobile camera unit to tape the interview) and a social worker. During the interview Alfie disclosed how Stella had been financially abusing him (taking money from his bank and savings accounts; obtaining credit cards in Alfie's name; using Alfie's address to get credit cards in her own name). Stella was arrested and subsequently charged with various offences related to assault, theft and fraud.

The healing issues in this stage of the process were as follows:

- Alfie needed to talk about the abuse he had experienced from Stella.
- The violence from Stella had triggered memories of the abuse he had experienced from his mother (physical and neglect) in childhood. The recovered memories included severe beatings, being hungry and being locked in a coalshed.
- Alfie had also been physically abused by his first wife.
- Nightmares and flashbacks.
- Alfie felt shame about being abused by three women in his life.
- Alfie described himself as 'weak and pathetic'.

VICTIMS IN COMMUNAL SETTINGS – THE OPPORTUNITY TO RECOVER AND HEAL

Where adults have been abused by staff in communal settings the investigation quite rightly focuses on getting evidence and considers what to do with the members of staff (e.g. suspension, prosecution, etc.). The main objective is to ensure the safety of service users. However, once the investigation has taken place, there can be recommendations about what should happen to the staff, if it has been substantiated that abuse has taken place, and there may well be recommendations regarding practices within the communal setting. The service users who have been the victims often 'get lost' again because of the focus on the perpetrators. How often is the following question asked in either a strategy meeting or a case conference?

Key Question

What needs to be done to help the residents recover and heal from this?

Best practice would suggest that each victim should have an individual protection plan developed for them, and it has to be acknowledged that this could be very time consuming. Below is an example of good practice where group work can be used to help the healing process.

||||||||||||||||||||||||||||||||||||||||||||||||||||||||||||||||||||||||||||||||||||||||||||||||||||||||||||||||

CASE EXAMPLE 1.1

The communal setting

The Redhouse Care Home has 60 residents of mixed dependency. Some residents have perfect mental capacity; others have cognitive problems, some being Alzheimer's disease.

The original alert

Beatrice Wagner, aged 80 years, was a resident in the care home. She told her daughter, Mary, that two care workers had hit her. She had cuts and bruises on the trunk of her body. Mary telephoned the social worker who had originally placed Mrs Wagner in the home to say that her mother had been injured.

The investigation

A formal investigation took place under the local safeguarding adults policy and procedures. Beatrice was interviewed by the social worker and a police officer. She gave a clear account of what the two care workers had done to her and said this had not been the first time. She also went on to disclose about what they did to other residents. Beatrice alleged that physical, emotional and financial abuse was taking place. The two members of staff were suspended. A second strategy meeting was convened and a larger investigation took place; this involved other residents being interviewed.

Findings

It was proven that the two members of staff had been threatening residents and systematically stealing money and other possessions from both residents and staff.

Actions

- After a criminal investigation had been undertaken by the police the case was referred to the Crown Prosecution Service.

- It was reported to the case conference that many residents were extremely upset to find out that two members of staff whom they trusted had, unbeknown to them, been stealing from them. A recommendation was made that all residents should be offered the opportunity to participate in group work to talk about how they felt.

- A simplified protection plan was developed for each resident.

The groups

Not all the residents wanted to participate in a group and some did not have the cognitive ability to understand the purpose of the groups. However, 30 residents did participate.

- Three groups were formed.

- Each group met for three sessions.

- Duration: an hour per session.

- Purpose: to vent their feelings.

- Emotions talked about: anger; feeling let down.

IIIIIIIIIIIIIIIIIIIIIIIIIIIIIIIIIIIIIIIIIIIIIIIIIIIIIIIIIIIIIIIIIIIIIIIIIIIIIIIIIIIIIIIIIIIIIIIIIIIIII

REFERENCES

Department of Health (2000) *No Secrets: Guidance on Developing and Implementing Multi-agency Policies and Procedures to Protect Vulnerable Adults from Abuse.* London: Department of Health.

Department of Health, Home Office and Department for Education and Employment (1999) *Working Together to Safeguard Children: A Guide to Inter-agency Working to Safeguard and Promote the Welfare of Children.* London: Department of Health.

HM Government (2006 and 2010) *Working Together to Safeguard Children: A Guide to Inter-agency Working to Safeguard and Promote the Welfare of Children.* London: Department for Children, Schools and Families.

Home Office, Department of Health, Department of Education and Science and Welsh Office (1991) *Working Together under the Children Act 1989: A Guide to Arrangements for Inter-agency Co-operation for the Protection of Children from Abuse.* London: HMSO.

Ministry of Justice (March 2011) *Achieving Best Evidence in Criminal Proceedings: Guidance on Interviewing Victims and Witnesses, and Guidance on Using Special Measures.* London: Ministry of Justice.

The Children Act 1989. London: HMSO.

The Children Act 2004. London: The Stationery Office.

CHAPTER 2

RECOVERY AND HEALING FROM COMPLEX TRAUMA

CHRISTIANE SANDERSON

While much has been written about trauma and post-traumatic stress reactions, many professionals are less aware of the impact of *complex trauma*, which occurs within close or intimate relationships in which the victim may be dependent on the abuser. When such abuse is systematic and prolonged as in childhood physical abuse (CPA), childhood sexual abuse (CSA), domestic abuse (DA), institutional abuse and elder abuse it can lead to and activate a range of trauma reactions. These can be so pervasive that they require longer-term therapeutic intervention in which the therapeutic relationship becomes the medium for recovery and healing.

This chapter will examine what is meant by complex trauma and how this impacts on the individual. It will identify the effects of complex trauma in terms of trauma reactions which occur outside conscious control and reset the body's alarm system. In addition, it will highlight how complex trauma affects everyday functioning, in particular perceptions of reality, of self and others, and how this manifests in relationships, including the therapeutic relationship.

To enable professionals and practitioners to be most effective in working with survivors of complex trauma, the chapter will highlight core therapeutic goals and how these can be achieved through safe trauma therapy. The focus will be on the necessity of going beyond recovery or symptom relief towards healing, in which reparative work on trust, self-identity and relational worth is facilitated to allow for post-traumatic growth. In essence, the dehumanisation inherent in complex trauma, in which the individual has been objectified, can only be undone in the presence of a human relationship.

Finally, working with survivors of complex trauma can be demanding and challenging. Professionals need to be aware of how working with survivors of complex trauma impacts on them and how they can minimise the effects of vicarious traumatisation by ensuring that they look after themselves in order to avoid 'burnout'. This enables them to facilitate post-traumatic growth, which can be transformative for both client and practitioner.

TRAUMA AND COMPLEX TRAUMA

Trauma is usually defined as an overwhelming threat to life, serious injury or physical integrity involving intense fear, helplessness or horror (American Psychiatric Association 2013).[1] Trauma can consist of a single event or multiple and repeated traumatic events. The overwhelming nature of trauma activates a cascade of chemicals and primitive defences such as withdrawal, numbing and dissociation. This is accompanied by alterations in perception of self, others and the world, and systems of meaning. While only one-third of survivors of trauma develop post-traumatic stress disorder (PTSD), many survivors develop post-traumatic or acute stress reactions such as persistent re-experiencing of the trauma in the form of flashbacks, intrusive memories and recurrent nightmares, leading to avoidance of trauma cues. As these are often triggered by internal or external cues, survivors tend to avoid any thoughts, feelings, activities, places or people associated with the trauma. Some survivors split-off or dissociate from the trauma, leading to a sense of numbness, detachment and estrangement, while others experience increased arousal, including exaggerated startle response, irritability, extreme mood swings, difficulties in concentration and hypervigilance. As these reactions are activated outside of conscious control, they can be extremely terrifying and reinforce the sense of lack of control, which is reminiscent of the abuse experiences.

Symptoms included in criteria for PTSD

1. **Intrusion symptoms:** intrusive distressing memories; recurrent distressing dreams; dissociative reactions such as flashbacks, through to complete loss of awareness of present surroundings; intense or prolonged psychological distress at exposure to internal or external cues that symbolise or resemble the traumatic event(s); marked physiological reactions to reminders of the traumatic event(s).

---

1   This definition is from the draft proposed criteria for the new *Diagnostic Statistical Manual V* due to be published in May 2013, and may be subject to change.

2. **Avoidance symptoms:** avoidance of distressing memories, thoughts or feelings associated with the traumatic event(s); avoidance of external reminders (i.e. people, places, conversations, activities, objects, situations) that arouse distressing memories, thoughts or feelings associated with the traumatic event(s).

3. **Alterations in cognitions and mood:** dissociative amnesia for important aspects of the traumatic event(s); persistent and exaggerated negative beliefs or expectations about oneself, others or the world; distorted blame of self or others about the cause or consequences of the traumatic event(s); persistent negative emotional state (e.g. fear, horror, anger, guilt or shame); diminished interest in significant activities; feelings of detachment or estrangement from others; persistent inability to experience positive emotions (e.g. unable to have loving feelings, psychic numbing).

4. **Alterations in arousal and reactivity:** irritable or aggressive behaviour; reckless or self-destructive behaviour; hypervigilance; exaggerated startle response; problems with concentration; sleep disturbance.

(Adapted from American Psychiatric Association 2013)

In the case of complex trauma these symptoms become chronic as they begin to affect the very core of the self. Complex trauma is commonly seen in people who have experienced systematic and prolonged sexual or physical abuse, or torture. It is also more likely to develop when the abuse is perpetrated by a significant other such as a parent, close relative or partner. When abuse masquerades as affection and love, internal and external reality is compromised. This, alongside the betrayal of trust and dehumanisation, renders all relationships as dangerous, even therapeutic ones, making it difficult to seek support or help. The accompanying secrecy and paralysing shame prevent many survivors from naming their abuse experience, and as a result they are unable to legitimise it. In the absence of a voice to 'speak the unspeakable', abuse experiences cannot be processed and become 'ossified as a nub of despair' in which self and others cannot be trusted (Sanderson 2010a).

Like PTSD, complex trauma results in high levels of arousal, and strong out-of-control physical reactions. It also impacts on perception of self and others, how survivors feel about their body, and how they relate to others. In addition, complex trauma can result in the distortion of reality, stigmatisation, and a deep sense of shame. To manage such strong reactions can lead to an avoidance of all feelings, even pleasurable ones, and a withdrawal from others, leading to social isolation and an abyss of traumatic loneliness.

Symptoms of complex trauma

1. **Impairment in regulating emotional impulses:** in particular anger directed at both self and others.

2. **Chronic self-destructive behaviours** such as self-mutilation, eating disorders or drug abuse.

3. **Alterations in attention and consciousness** leading to dissociative episodes, amnesia or depersonalisation; Dissociative Identity Disorder.

4. **Alterations in self-perception** manifested by a chronic sense of guilt, shame or inflated sense of responsibility.

5. **Alterations in relationships** with others, primarily evident in the inability to trust and enjoy emotional intimacy.

6. **Complaints of diffuse somatic pain and dysfunction** for which there is no medical explanation.

7. **Alterations in systems of meaning** such as loss of faith in existing belief systems or the value and meaning of one's unique life.

(Adapted from Sanderson 2010a)

UNDERSTANDING THE IMPACT OF TRAUMA AND COMPLEX TRAUMA

Irrespective of whether the trauma was a single event or systematic and prolonged, involving several perpetrators, the impact of trauma will vary from person to person and depend on:

- the type of trauma
- age
- the frequency of the abuse
- the duration of the abuse
- the relationship to the abuser(s)
- degree of resilience.

What is common to all are trauma reactions which act as *the body's alarm system* to aid survival. In the presence of danger the brain releases a cascade of chemicals which start a complex chain of bodily reactions, outside of conscious awareness and not under voluntary control. These chemicals prepare the body for fight or flight. If the danger is inescapable, as in CPA, CSA or DA, the only option is to freeze, which prevents these powerful chemicals from being discharged, so they become trapped in the body. When such danger is repeated and prolonged, the alarm system remains on high alert, making it harder to shut off (Sanderson 2010b). This gives rise to many of the post-traumatic stress reactions, such as hyperarousal and hypervigilance, seen in survivors of CSA and DA (Sanderson 2010a; van der Kolk *et al.* 2005). As these trauma reactions are biologically mediated they occur outside conscious awareness and are perceived to be outside of the survivor's control. This leads many survivors to believe they are 'going crazy', which generates further anxiety.

This in turn prevents the processing of the trauma, keeping it 'online' with the same vividness and intensity as when the actual assault happened. Not being able to process the experience will make it harder to store memories of the experience and lead to incomplete or fragmented memories of the trauma. High levels of circulating stress hormones can also impact on physical well-being, leading to:

Physical symptoms associated with complex trauma

- Hypertension
- Physical exhaustion
- Chronic fatigue syndrome (CFS)
- Sleep problems
- Digestive problems
- Respiratory problems
- Endocrine problems

In addition, chronic fear reactions and high levels of adrenaline can result in tsunami-like anger which cannot be expressed for fear of consequences. Hyperarousal also affects concentration levels and impairs the processing of information, making it hard to gain meaning from the trauma experience.

Psychological symptoms associated with complex trauma

- Difficulty in regulating emotions
- Dissociation
- Lack of reflection
- Reduced concentration
- Reduction in processing of information
- Inability to make sense of experiences
- Distorted reality, perceptions and core beliefs
- Shame and self-blame
- Self-harm
- Self-medication and substance misuse
- Lack of self-agency
- Relationship difficulties
- Withdrawal and traumatic loneliness

When the alarm is on high alert the regulation of emotions is compromised. In order to manage overwhelming trauma reactions many survivors resort to self-injury or self-medication through food, alcohol or substance misuse, work, sex or gambling to either numb or release the emotional or psychological pain. These are commonly accompanied by chronic feelings of ineffectiveness, sense of being out of control, lack of efficacy, shame, hopelessness and feeling permanently damaged. In addition, distorted perceptions result in negative thoughts such as self-blame, as well as loss of previously valued beliefs. The loss of trust in others can lead to defensive tactics such as avoidance or hostility, and a lack of trust in a safe or benign world. Such alterations in perception of self and others commonly lead to relational disturbances and a need to conceal the self. Survivors of complex trauma learn that to be visible is dangerous, as they are likely to be attacked, so they feel compelled to become invisible, even though this threatens their very existence. This existential conflict pervades all future relationships, in which the survivor oscillates between 'approach and avoid' behaviours (Sanderson 2010a).

As the alarm system is reset to high alert the individual becomes hypersensitive and hypervigilant to any perceived threat. The sense of heightened danger is easily tripped by external cues that resemble the original trauma, or by internal triggers such as thoughts or feelings, even in the absence of external danger (Sanderson 2010a, 2010b). This accounts for associated traumatic reactions such as:

- irritability
- outbursts of anger
- flashbacks
- panic attacks
- nightmares
- intrusive memories.

IIIIIIIIIIIIIIIIIIIIIIIIIIIIIIIIIIIIIIIIIIIIIIIIIIIIIIIIIIIIIIIIIIIIIIIIIIIIIIIIIIIIIIIIIIIIIIIIIIIIIIIIIIIIIIIIIIIIIIIIIII

CASE EXAMPLE 2.1

A young woman who was sexually abused by her nanny was plagued by flashbacks and nightmares which would occur several times during the day and night. When having flashbacks she would be overwhelmed by images of the abuse with such intensity that she would have panic attacks. Her nightmares made her too scared to go to sleep at night, which meant that she rarely slept more than three hours a night. This led to such high levels of arousal, and her body being flooded by stress hormones, that she developed chronic fatigue syndrome, preventing her from working or managing even relatively simple daily tasks.

IIIIIIIIIIIIIIIIIIIIIIIIIIIIIIIIIIIIIIIIIIIIIIIIIIIIIIIIIIIIIIIIIIIIIIIIIIIIIIIIIIIIIIIIIIIIIIIIIIIIIIIIIIIIIIIIIIIIIIIIIII

Alternatively, the disruption to the alarm system can lead to complete shut-down, or hypo-arousal, in which the person becomes detached or dissociated from their surroundings and internal state to anaesthetise their pain, making it easier to survive emotionally. This is aided by compartmentalisation in which the abuse is split off, allowing the survivor to retain a positive image of the abuser (Sanderson 2010b). Such dissociation has been variously described as 'a separation of mental and experiential contents that would normally be connected' (Howell 2005, p.vii) and 'a failure of integration of ideas, information, affects and experience' (Putnam 1997, p.157). It is this lack of integration which prevents the integration of self-states in young children, or fragmentation of integrated systems of experiencing and decoupling of self-states in adults (Bromberg 1998). Dissociation can impair everyday functions, and practitioners need to be aware of the hallmark signs of dissociation and the cues that signal when survivors begin to tune out.

Dissociation

Hallmark signs

- **Loss of memory, or dissociative amnesia** for past and present events. Can be partial or complete. In the present no recollection of events, meeting familiar people, conversations or topics discussed, or what they have been doing.

- **Time loss** for hours or days at a time. Find themselves somewhere with no idea how they got there, and no recollection of where they have been or what they have been doing.

- **Time distortions** in which time passes extremely fast or extremely slowly; not sure where they are in terms of space or time.

- **Alienation or estrangement of self or body,** or depersonalisation – numb, blank, outside of body, exist solely 'in the head', no control over actions, on automatic pilot.

- **Alienation or estrangement from surroundings,** or de-realisation, in which familiar surroundings, family and friends appear unreal and strange.

- **Alternations between hypo-arousal,** in which survivors avoid feelings and therefore experience too little, and **hyperarousal,** in which they experience too much as a result of the intrusion of sensation, feelings, thoughts, memories.

Cues to dissociation in session

- Facial features, eyes unfocused, waxy, blank, zone out, glazed look
- Inability to speak the unspeakable, numb with terror, prolonged silence, become compliant and avoidant, helplessness
- Robotic language – repetitive phrases, details
- Long monologues characterised by stream of consciousness with no reflection or mentalisation
- Changes in narrative – unfocused, disorganised, incoherent
- Misinterpretation, miscommunication
- Somatic cues – jerky movements, changes in temperature, freezing
- Entering parallel worlds – 'beautiful and benign' fantasy world vs. 'terrifying and hostile' reality world
- Submissive, compliant, 'good client'
- Switching between submission and hostile aggression

When survivors dissociate they are no longer in the present and are not able to focus on what is happening in the here and now. This means that they are not able to concentrate on what is being discussed or process information. This can be dangerous, as they will not have understood vital instructions such as medical advice or skills to help them manage trauma reactions. In being unaware of their surroundings they may be at risk or put others at risk, such as vulnerable dependants or pets.

||||||||||||||||||||||||||||||||||||||||||||||||||||||||||||||||||||||||||||||||||||||||||||||||||||||||||||||||||||

CASE EXAMPLES 2.2

- A young client (aged 18) would frequently board a bus near home in one part of the city and find herself several hours later in another part of the city. She had no recollection how she got there or what had happened in the intervening time. This put her at considerable risk.

- A 28-year-old male would find himself in the middle of the night in another part of the country, with no recollection of how he had driven there.

- A client with a young child, who was two years old, would regularly dissociate, leaving the child at risk of dangers in the home, e.g. electrical appliances such as irons and hair tongs left switched on.

||||||||||||||||||||||||||||||||||||||||||||||||||||||||||||||||||||||||||||||||||||||||||||||||||||||||||||||||||||

Alongside trauma reactions, survivors of complex trauma often present with a range of interpersonal and relational difficulties which characterise their personal relationships; these can be healed through a reparative therapeutic relationship. The sense of shame and the betrayal of trust make it very hard for survivors to trust, as all relationships are seen as dangerous. This can lead to withdrawal and social isolation, making it hard for them to seek therapeutic help, as they fear being betrayed again.

As a result survivors often present with fierce self-reliance, invulnerability or self-sabotaging behaviours, making it hard to establish trust. This is compounded when survivors test boundaries by switching between compliance and aggression, submission and control. This must be understood as part of building trust and a relationship, rather than a personal attack on, or rejection of, the professional.

Conversely, some survivors trust too quickly and indiscriminately, which makes them more vulnerable to further re-victimisation. As a result survivors often test boundaries, which can create rupture in the therapeutic relationship. It is critical to see these as breakthroughs rather than a breakdown in the therapeutic relationship, as the survivor needs to test that they will still be accepted despite these ruptures.

||||||||||||||||||||||||||||||||||||||||||||||||||||||||||||||||||||||||||||||||||||||||||||||||||||||||||

CASE EXAMPLE 2.3

A very successful 38-year-old business woman was high-functioning in her career and yet found it difficult to succeed in her personal relationships. She would eagerly enter relationships in which she was initially very accommodating, only to find as the relationship became closer that she would switch between being submissive and controlling, which was confusing to her partners. She would often have inexplicable and explosive outbursts of anger, with no idea what prompted them. Her partners often ended relationships, saying that it was both confusing and exhausting being close to her and they felt unable to sustain a relationship, let alone have a family with her.

||||||||||||||||||||||||||||||||||||||||||||||||||||||||||||||||||||||||||||||||||||||||||||||||||||||||||

WORKING WITH SURVIVORS OF COMPLEX TRAUMA

The fear of being re-traumatised makes it hard for survivors to connect, which can lead to a range of therapeutic challenges that practitioners need to be aware of in order to create a secure base in which traumatic experiences can be integrated to facilitate healing and post-traumatic growth. A central component is the need for a secure base in which survivors feel validated and respected. To create such a secure base necessitates awareness of what constitutes safe trauma therapy in which the emphasis is on healing.

There is a range of therapeutic approaches that can be helpful when working with survivors of complex trauma, and counsellors may combine their own therapeutic model with more specific therapeutic interventions that have been found to be effective when working with survivors of sexual violence and DA, such as:

- prolonged exposure therapy (Foa and Rothbaum 2002)
- cognitive processing therapy (Resick and Schnicke 1993)
- dialectical behavioural therapy (Linehan 1993)
- eye movement desensitisation and reprocessing (EMDR) (Shapiro 1995)
- schema therapy (Young, Klosko and Weishaar 2003)

- management training and psycho-education (Kilpatrick *et al.* 2007).

The techniques employed in these models have been shown to be particularly helpful when working with survivors of CSA and DA, especially when conducted within a safe and secure base and a sensitively attuned therapeutic relationship (Sanderson 2008, 2010a) in which the client's willingness to risk trusting again despite repeated betrayals is honoured.

GOOD PRACTICE POINTS

- It is critical to pace the therapeutic work in a way that is manageable for the client and does not overwhelm them and re-traumatise them.
- Rushing the therapeutic work is reminiscent of the need to 'rush' through the abuse experiences and can trigger trauma reactions.

It is for this reason that longer-term therapeutic work within an integrative framework is seen to be most effective (Linehan 1993; Sanderson 2012). While some useful skills and techniques can be taught to manage trauma symptoms in short-term intervention, these need to be supported by longer-term work in which impaired self and relational dynamics can be healed. This takes time and is difficult to achieve in 12 one-hour sessions. Many survivors feel a sense of failure when they do not show expected improvements after short-term therapeutic intervention, which reinforces their belief that they are too damaged and beyond repair. As one survivor commented after her allotted 12 sessions: 'All this has proved to me that I am so flawed and damaged that I will never be cured.'

GOOD PRACTICE POINT

Repairing trust and relational worth can only be achieved through building a sensitively attuned therapeutic relationship which takes time to develop.

Practitioners who work with survivors of complex trauma, and specialist agencies (such as One in Four[2] in the UK) who work with survivors of CSA, tend to recommend a minimum of two years of therapeutic support (Sanderson 2010a). As the therapeutic work can revive trauma reactions it is essential to adopt a phased treatment approach in which external and internal safety is established to enable the survivor to restore control over overwhelming internal states before embarking on the trauma narrative.

One such model, Safe Trauma Therapy (Herman 1992a, 1992b; Rothschild 2002; Sanderson 2010a, 2012, 2013), can be combined with a range of therapeutic modalities whilst ensuring that the work progresses through three fundamental stages, as shown below.

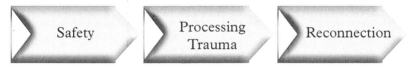

Figure 2.1: Safe Trauma Therapy
Sources: Herman 1992a, 1992b; Sanderson 2010a, 2013

Stage 1: Establishing safety and control
In Stage 1 the focus is on safety and stabilisation. The aim is to create a safe environment in which the client can restore control over unbearable internal states and trauma reactions through affect regulation. (For exercises for survivors see Sanderson 2010b.) This can be extremely empowering for survivors, as they regain control over their body, which has previously been controlled by trauma reactions. This allows them to gain mastery over their abuse experience and restore self-efficacy. Mastering affect regulation and control over trauma reactions has a cumulative effect in enabling survivors to take control of other areas of their lives, such as rest, exercise, diet and general well-being. From this they can develop more healthy ways of managing their distress, rather than self-harm, self-medication or substance misuse. Once safety is established and the survivor is more able to regulate emotions, s/he is able to reduce the intensity of trauma reactions, which enhances distress tolerance. This allows the survivor to manage a high level of arousal without resorting to self-medication or self-harm. Once the survivor has gained mastery over their physiological and emotional responses, the process of integrating the traumatic experiences can begin.

---

2   For contact details see the Useful Organisation section at the end of the chapter.

Stage 2: Processing the trauma narrative
During Stage 2 the focus shifts to exploring and processing the abuse experience, safe in the knowledge that the survivor has mastered affect regulation and has some control over trauma reactions. Through the improved regulation of distress, survivors are more able to explore the traumatic experiences and develop a more coherent narrative in which they can begin to gain meaning and make sense of their experience. In this process survivors will also need to grieve any losses associated with complex trauma (Sanderson 2010a) and explore psychological and social effects such as shame, self-blame, relational difficulties, social isolation and traumatic loneliness.

Stage 3: Reconnection
Once these losses have been mourned the survivor can move into the third stage and begin to reconnect to self. Throughout this stage they can begin to develop self-compassion and become more confident in trusting themselves and expressing feelings appropriately, which can enable them to build and rebuild relationships with others as a source of comfort rather than danger. This is the beginning of post-traumatic growth in which they begin to reconnect to others and the world with greater vitality and appreciation of life.

CORE THERAPEUTIC GOALS
It is critical, when working with survivors of complex trauma, to establish safety from the tyranny of out-of-control trauma-related symptoms such as hyperarousal, flashbacks, panic attacks and intrusive memories. This can be mediated through a combination of affect regulation and psycho-education in which physiological responses are linked to the complex trauma (Sanderson 2010b). Psycho-education reassures the survivor that flashbacks, intrusive memories and dreams are normal responses to trauma which signal unprocessed aspects of their experiences, and not evidence of loss of sanity. In the case of sexual abuse it is important that survivors understand the sexual arousal cycle, to reduce shame and self-blame if their body responded during the abuse (Preble and Groth 2002; Sanderson 2006).

The role of psycho-education is a powerful one in that it enables survivors not only to have a clearer understanding of their symptoms and lived experience, but also to develop greater understanding of their experiences.

GOOD PRACTICE POINTS

- Recognising that trauma reactions are biologically mediated and outside of voluntary control not only normalises symptoms but also relieves the survivor from feeling responsible, ashamed or inherently flawed in not managing the impact of their abuse experiences.
- This helps to restore self-esteem and self-worth, which is necessary to develop relational worth.

Given the relational damage sustained in interpersonal abuse, a fundamental goal is the building and maintenance of a therapeutic relationship in which the survivor can learn and practise relational skills. This is pivotal to rebuilding relational worth and discovering more authentic ways of relating in which needs, feelings and thoughts can be expressed without fear of being punished or humiliated. It is through the therapeutic relationship that the survivor can restore reality and challenge distorted perceptions, to develop renewed trust in self and others (Sanderson 2010a).

Core therapeutic goals

- Safety and stabilisation
- Create a secure base
- Restore control over trauma reactions
- Reflection and mindfulness
- Psycho-education and normalisation of symptoms
- Validation of existing coping skills
- Process traumatic experiences
- Restore reality and challenge distorted perceptions
- Rebuild relational worth through the therapeutic relationship
- Make sense of traumatic experiences
- Grieve losses
- Reconnect to self, others and the world
- Restore autonomy and self-efficacy
- Post-traumatic growth

CREATING A SECURE BASE

GOOD PRACTICE POINTS

- In order to work most effectively with survivors of complex trauma it is crucial to establish a safe, secure setting in which the client can pace their recovery and healing.
- It is critical to pace the work and encourage the survivor to take small, manageable steps that are under his or her control.

Restoring control and autonomy is essential to undo the control experienced during the abuse. This involves respecting the client's knowledge and survival so far, and validating existing coping skills and resources rather than seeing him or her as a passive victim. To have survived, survivors will have employed a range of active survival strategies to minimise the impact of the abuse (Sanderson 2010a). Counsellors also need to be flexible in permitting the survivor to pace the therapeutic process at a level that is manageable for them. Throughout the process practitioners must ensure they do not reinforce false beliefs that shame the survivor. Counsellors will also need to remain realistic and honest about what can and cannot be done, and be mindful of not making assurances that cannot be fulfilled.

Creating a safe therapeutic setting

- Safe and calm setting with no external distractions or loud noises.
- Clients need to see exit and have unobstructed access to door.
- Power and control needs to be restored to client to encourage self-agency.
- Boundaries of confidentiality, length of session, out-of-session contact and duration of therapy all need to be explicitly stated and supported in written or auditory form.
- Pacing of sessions needs to be client-led; some clients benefit from longer sessions of an hour-and-a-half, others need shorter.
- Preparing to leave is essential and should be started at least ten minutes before end of session so that clients are contained to go back into the outside world.
- Do not pressurise to talk – some clients need to settle in in the first ten minutes before they can go into material.

- Secure base of the therapeutic relationship that is well bounded and genuinely warm and human, predictable and consistent.
- Collaborative process.

Crucially, a collaborative therapeutic relationship will emphasise choices and provide opportunities to develop self-efficacy. To this effect it is important not to pressurise client's to adopt prescriptive solutions, but to explore what is best for the individual client. This is best achieved through open, honest communication to minimise the risk of confusion, distortion of reality, and to prevent mind-reading.

THE ROLE OF THE COUNSELLOR

In order to promote healing and not just recovery, practitioners working with survivors of complex trauma need to have comprehensive understanding of traumatic effects and the dynamics of complex trauma. Counsellors will also need a high level of awareness of their own beliefs around:

- gender
- power
- control
- domination
- submission
- sexuality
- interpersonal abuse.

To facilitate this, practitioners may benefit from attending specialist workshops or continuing professional development (CPD) in working with complex trauma. It may also be helpful to increase knowledge and understanding of sexuality to manage the sexual elements of CSA.

GOOD PRACTICE POINTS

- Counsellors must be able to talk about sex and sexual practices without embarrassment or shame, as this will make it easier to talk to survivors.
- Counsellors need to understand their own relational experiences, both past and present, and examine any interpersonal abuse they may have experienced.

This will enable counsellors to be more mindful of how these experiences might manifest when working with survivors of complex trauma, and understand any feelings of shame, sexual arousal or abuse fantasies that may be evoked in the therapeutic process (Sanderson 2006, 2010a).

Role of the counsellor

- Create secure base and sensitively attuned and human therapeutic relationship.
- Knowledge of dynamics and impact of complex trauma, shame, self-harm, sex and sexuality, power and control.
- Ability to talk about sex and sexuality without embarrassment.
- Awareness of own relational experiences in childhood, or any abuse or traumatic experiences.
- Able to identify own attachment style and how this impacts on the therapeutic relationship.
- Knowledge of transference and counter-transference reactions, somatic counter-transference, erotic transference and counter-transference.
- Counsellor self-care.

Counsellors also need to be aware of their own attachment style, to ensure that they provide a genuinely empathic therapeutic relationship in which they are fully present and engaged without blaming, recoiling, or hiding behind clinical protocols. To avoid replicating interpersonal abuse dynamics, counsellors need to be authentic and honest and not hide behind clinical façades. It is only through the warmth of human connection that brutalisation and dehumanisation can be undone and relational worth restored.

GOOD PRACTICE POINTS

The therapeutic stance should:
- be honest and transparent – counteract secrecy
- be explicit to counteract implicit nature of abuse and avoid need to mind-read
- not make promises that can't be kept
- be collaborative
- be non-judgmental
- show a genuine interest in helping and ability to convey that to the client
- be warm and caring
- validate experience
- set and maintain boundaries
- enable a flexible approach – not rigid but what works best for individual
- allow survivor some control e.g. pacing, not forcing, rushing
- not make assumptions.

THERAPEUTIC CHALLENGES

There are a number of therapeutic challenges that practitioners face when working with survivors of interpersonal trauma.

Therapeutic challenges

- Knowledge and understanding and enough time for reading and CPD
- Fear of re-traumatising survivors
- Having enough skills to manage the work without becoming overwhelmed
- Client hostility, rage or anger
- Client dependency needs
- Doubting the survivor's account of trauma

- Dissociation, altered states of consciousness, disembodied client or counsellor
- Fear of being aroused
- Fear of withdrawing, or distancing
- Witness guilt in which practitioner feels guilty for not having experienced trauma
- Over-identification – fear of triggering own abuse experiences
- Transference – client projections, acting out
- Counter-transference (CTR) – negative CTR, interplay between client's projection and therapist's own psychology
- Balance between knowing when to put the brake on and when to accelerate
- Need to remain contained and containing

A significant challenge is to be able to bear the pain of listening to abuse experiences without feeling overwhelmed or disconnecting from the survivor (Herman 1992a). While such responses are normal, practitioners need to ensure that they can manage their own responses and contain any fears that may emerge so that these do not impede or contaminate the therapeutic process (Sanderson 2010a). Counsellors also need to be sensitive to avoid shaming or alienating the survivor, or coercing the survivor toward their own preferred course of action. The survivor must be empowered to make their own informed choices, and counsellors will need to support the survivor in that decision and continue to remain supportive and engaged (Sanderson 2008, 2010a).

As each trauma experience is unique to each survivor, it is important to not make assumptions and to ensure that the survivor's individual needs are met. Rather than being prescriptive it helps to ask:

Key Questions

- What concerns you the most?
- What works best for you?
- What would you most like help with?

This will extend the necessary respect to the client and allow for full engagement. A survivor also needs to know that the counsellor can manage their anger, or negative emotions, without becoming defensive.

This will ensure that the client feels accepted, no matter how difficult or challenging they are.

GOOD PRACTICE POINTS

- Counsellors need to demonstrate that they have the stamina and staying power to not abandon the client when they are at their most challenging and most vulnerable.
- Counsellors need to be mindful that hostility, anger and aggression are often born of fear and are a defence, as are compliance and submissiveness.
- It is important to not personalise such defences, but to see them as evidence of how terrified or hurt the survivor feels.

In essence such defences signify a need for mastery, control and potency. Rather than engage in a power struggle, it is more beneficial to let the survivor take control in real terms, rather than pursue an illusion of control through negative behaviour.

Another common pitfall is doubt, or not believing the survivor. In such instances it is important to seek supervision as to the origins of doubts and seek advice on how to manage this. Some counsellors find that they become aroused when listening to the survivor's experiences, especially when they have experienced sexual violence or CSA. While this is natural, if it becomes too intense or overwhelming it is important to examine it in supervision. Practitioners must remain mindful that the felt arousal may not necessarily be sexual, but may have its origins in fear which has been eroticised. This mirrors the survivor's experience in which fear during sexual violence has become eroticised. It is crucial that such feelings are explored in supervision, and under no circumstance should sexual feelings be acted upon.

GOOD PRACTICE POINT

To minimise re-traumatisation, practitioners must guard against becoming over-involved or getting lost in the survivor's despair and hopelessness, as this can lead to over-identification.

This can lead counsellors to impose their own attitudes and beliefs onto the client. It is critical to remember that disclosure, confrontation and forgiveness are very personal things that only the survivor can choose to do. Counsellors must refrain from imposing their own beliefs on the client, as this is at best unethical and at worst abusive. Moreover, it is reminiscent of the abuser imposing his or her beliefs on the survivor. To truly respect survivors it is critical to help them to restore their own reality, reach their own conclusions, and make their own autonomous choices.

GOOD PRACTICE POINTS

- It is crucial to be clear around the process of therapy, what can be achieved and how the counsellor works.
- Being explicit is a strong antidote to the implicit messages associated with interpersonal trauma which generate confusion and distort reality.

Given the nature of CSA it is important to be explicit around boundaries and the therapeutic process. By being authentic, clear and transparent the practitioner can enable the survivor to counteract a history of subterfuge and deception and enable him or her to relate openly and honestly without fear. Through this, healing can take place.

VICARIOUS TRAUMATISATION AND COUNSELLOR SELF-CARE

GOOD PRACTICE POINT

Like the survivor, counsellors must make sure they remain connected to others and the world so that they can truly facilitate healing.

Working with survivors of interpersonal trauma can be extremely emotionally and physically draining and it is important to ensure practitioner self-care. Bearing witness to the destructive nature of complex trauma can be highly stressful, and can give rise to terror, revulsion and disbelief which can activate a need to detach, disengage or retreat into a rigid professional role, or hide behind prescriptive techniques or protocols. If this is not addressed it can lead to vicarious traumatisation, or secondary traumatic stress (STS), resulting in a range of post-traumatic stress reactions which can impact negatively on professional and personal functioning (Sanderson 2010a).

Impact of secondary traumatic stress

- **Trauma-like reactions:** hypervigilance, heightened physiological arousal, numbness.
- **Somatic reactions:** irritability, exhaustion, apathy, restlessness, changes in appetitive behaviours, nightmares.
- **Cognitive changes:** distorted perceptions, intrusive thoughts, ruminating over cases, preoccupation with abuse, uncertainty, impaired concentration, loss of meaning, shattered assumptions about the world.
- **Behavioural:** avoidance, disconnecting from others, adversarial, over/under-protectiveness towards own children, self-medication.
- **Emotional:** anxious, sense of powerlessness, helplessness, despair, loss of trust.

To minimise STS, counsellors need to ensure that they are adequately supported through appropriate training, regular discussion with colleagues and peers, supervision, and balancing the level of trauma work (Sanderson 2010a). Counsellors will also need to prioritise self-care by seeking regular connection with family and friends and by engaging in life-sustaining activities that are pleasurable and revitalising. To counteract the traumatic impact of the work, counsellors will benefit from physical exercise such as martial arts, tai chi or yoga to ensure that they remain embodied. To remain grounded, counsellors will benefit from making a commitment to take regular breaks and to engage in activities that are fun, stimulate all the senses, and enhance creativity and spirituality. It is through play, humour and laughter that counsellors can ensure that they maintain their vitality, hope and zest for life.

Counsellor self-care

- **Work:** supervision, consultation, mentoring, peer support, continued professional development, balance trauma work, regular breaks, set limits and boundaries.
- **Body:** physical health, diet, rest, relaxation, yoga, martial arts, play.
- **Mind:** reflection, sense of control and agency, recreational activities that stimulate, read for fun.
- **Emotion:** respect and nurture self, listen to music, watch films, see plays, laughter, humour.
- **Creativity:** allow for inspiration, write, draw, paint, sculpt, make music.
- **Spirituality:** beauty, nature, tranquillity, hope, optimism, passion.

Working with survivors of complex trauma is transformative for both client and counsellor and can lead to post-traumatic growth. In the presence of trauma and bearing witness to the depth of human resilience and dignity, counsellors can become more sentient practitioners who not only understand but come to 'know' their clients (Bromberg 1998) and truly appreciate what it means to be human and to be alive.

REFERENCES

American Psychiatric Association (2013) *Diagnostic and Statistical Manual of Mental Disorders* (5th edition). Arlington: APA.

Bromberg, P. (1998) *Standing in the Spaces: Essays on Clinical Process, Trauma, and Dissociation.* Hillsdale, NJ: The Analytic Press.

Foa, E. and Rothbaum, B.O. (2002) *Treating the Trauma of Rape: Cognitive Behavioural Therapy for PTSD.* New York: Guilford Press.

Herman, J.L. (1992a) *Trauma and Recovery: The Aftermath of Violence from Domestic Abuse to Political Terror.* New York: Basic Books.

Herman, J.L. (1992b) 'Complex PTSD: A syndrome in survivors of prolonged and repeated trauma.' *Journal of Traumatic Stress* 5, 377–392.

Howell, E.F. (2005) *The Dissociative Mind.* Hillsdale, NJ: The Analytic Press.

Kilpatrick, D., Amstadter, A., Resnick, H. and Ruggerio, K. (2007) 'Rape-related PTSD: Issues and interventions.' *Psychiatric Times* 7, 24.

Linehan, M.A. (1993) *Skills Training Manual for Treating Borderline Personality Disorder.* New York: Guilford Press.

Preble, J.M. and Groth, A.N. (2002) *Male Victims of Same Sex Abuse: Addressing their Sexual Responses.* Baltimore, MD: Sidran Press.

Putnam, F.W. (1997) *Dissociation in Children and Adolescents: A Developmental Perspective.* New York: Guilford Press.

Resick, P. and Schnicke, M. (1993) *Cognitive Processing Therapy for Rape Victims.* London: Sage.

Rothschild, B. (2002) *The Body Remembers.* New York: Norton.

Sanderson, C. (2006) *Counselling Adult Survivors of Child Sexual Abuse* (3rd edition). London: Jessica Kingsley Publishers.

Sanderson, C. (2008) *Counselling Survivors of Domestic Abuse*. London: Jessica Kingsley Publishers.

Sanderson, C. (2010a) *Introduction to Counselling Survivors of Interpersonal Trauma*. London: Jessica Kingsley Publishers.

Sanderson, C. (2010b) *The Warrior Within: A One in Four Handbook to Aid Recovery from Childhood Sexual Abuse and Sexual Violence*. London: One in Four.

Sanderson, C. (2012) 'Working with Survivors of Domestic Abuse and Rape.' In C. Feltham and I. Horton (eds) *The Sage Handbook of Counselling and Psychotherapy* (3rd edition). London: Sage.

Sanderson, C. (2013) *Unlocking Complex Trauma: A Skills Manual for Counsellors*. London: Jessica Kingsley Publishers.

Shapiro, F. (1995) *Eye Movement Desensitisation and Reprocessing: Principles, Protocols and Procedures*. New York: Guilford Press.

van der Kolk, B.A., Roth, S., Pelcovitz, D., Sunday, S. and Spinazzola, J. (2005) 'Disorders of extreme stress: The empirical foundation of a complex adaptation to trauma.' *Journal of Traumatic Stress 18*, 389–399.

Young, J.E., Klosko, J.S. and Weishaar, M.E. (2003) *Schema Therapy: A Practitioner Guide*. New York: Guilford Press.

SUGGESTED READING

De Zuletta, F. (2006) *From Pain to Violence* (2nd edition). London: Wiley Publishers.

USEFUL ORGANISATION

One in Four
219 Bromley Road
Bellingham
Catford
SE6 2PG
Telephone: 020 8697 2112
Website: www.oneinfour.org.uk

CHAPTER 3

THE WORK OF A SEXUAL ASSAULT REFERRAL CENTRE

BERNIE RYAN

INTRODUCTION

This chapter will explore the role of Sexual Assault Referral Centres (SARC) and in particular St Mary's Sexual Assault Referral Centre in Manchester and its role in the recovery and healing following sexual violence.[1] In considering the SARC response and the provision of immediate psychological support in the context of a forensic medical examination, it will demonstrate that the recovery and healing process is influenced at an early stage.

My interpretation of recovery and healing in the aftermath of one of the most intimate crimes against an individual has been informed by the experience of those who have been subjected to sexual violence, my own experience as a crisis worker and counsellor working with this client group, and working with other professionals in the field.

Recovery

Recovery from sexual violence takes into account the physical and psychological consequences of sexual assault. The physical aspects of recovery are often short-lived. Offering accurate information and explanation to the victim on what has been found on examination is key to recovery. The victim may feel that s/he should have sustained injury or significant harm to fit the 'stereotypical' belief that rape is a violent and aggressive act. Whilst this is true, violence may be not so much physical as psychological. Often the victim will submit without resisting, simply in order to survive the experience, in which case the

---

1   It is difficult to provide a descriptor for those who have experienced sexual violence, and the chapter refers to them as *victim, client* and *patient*. For purposes of confidentiality and understanding, these terms are used interchangeably throughout the chapter.

abuse may not involve explicitly physical violence. The perpetrator may suggest that if the victim does not comply, their life or that of their loved ones would be in danger.

White and McLean (2006) report that genital and/or body injuries are not routinely found in adolescents after an allegation of rape or sexual assault, even when there is no previous sexual experience. The absence of injury does not exclude the possibility of intercourse – with or without consent. Recovery can begin once the victim understands this, and in the cases where there are physical injuries, these are usually small and heal quickly.

Information, knowledge, empowerment, dignity and respect are important factors in enabling recovery in the immediate aftermath of sexual assault.

Healing

Healing is the longer-term process which clients often describe as a transition from being a 'raped person' to becoming a 'person who happens to have experienced rape' with the ability to integrate that experience into their lives. This is an individual journey and can be influenced either positively or negatively by the response of professionals and agencies. This creates a huge responsibility for practitioners to get it 'right'.

This chapter will demonstrate that there is no definitive approach; however, it will illustrate some key learning points for good practice which will assist practitioners in identifying how they can influence recovery and healing when working with victims of sexual violence.

ST MARY'S SEXUAL ASSAULT REFERRAL CENTRE

Sexual Assault Referral Centres (SARCs) have increased in number since the first SARC was established in Manchester in 1986. There are now 41 SARCs across England and Wales offering a range of services aiming to empower those who have experienced rape and sexual assault to begin the process of recovery and regain control over their lives. SARCs should meet the minimum elements of service in order to meet the expectations of service users (Department of Health, Home Office and Association of Chief Police Officers 2009).

SARCs emerged as one way to meet the needs of victims/survivors and the criminal justice system simultaneously in the immediate aftermath of rape (Lovett and Kelly 2004). The SARC in Manchester, St Mary's Centre, provides a range of services, including forensic medical, therapeutic medical,[2] support and counselling services to men,

---

2 Assessment and treatment of potential infections; emergency contraception and assessment of injuries if present.

women and children who have experienced this type of crime. The aim is to facilitate recovery from the trauma and support the beginning of the healing process at one of the most vulnerable times in the person's life. Whilst St Mary's Centre provides services to children, the focus of this chapter will be on adults (women and men).

McLean, Balding and White (2004) report that male-on-male rape and sexual assault comprise fewer than 10 per cent of such assaults reported to the police, which is reflected in the low number of male victims among SARC referrals. There were 1222 referrals to St Mary's in the year 2011–2012, 8 per cent of which concerned male victims (St Mary's SARC 2012). Often the alleged perpetrator is male, but in a small number of cases seen at the SARC the perpetrator is female. The SARC sees all age ranges, with the youngest case seen aged six weeks old and the eldest 96 years (St Mary's SARC 2011). In order to ensure that male victims have access to specialist support, the St Mary's SARC can refer to a male survivors' group[3] in Manchester, who provide support and counselling services specifically to male victims of sexual violence. Nevertheless, many men are happy to see a female worker (Chowdhury-Hawkins *et al.* 2008).

The St Mary's SARC is provided by a multidisciplinary team that includes forensic physicians,[4] crisis workers,[5] counsellors, independent sexual violence advisors (ISVAs)[6] and child advocates. The provision of a forensic medical examination, collecting forensic samples, documenting injuries, and medical care such as emergency contraception and post-exposure prophylaxis (PEP)[7] can be therapeutic in itself; however, immediate psychological support receives attention from the outset in an attempt to reduce psychological trauma.

SARC services can be accessed either by a direct police referral, or by self-referral for those who are either undecided about making a report or prefer not to report to the police, while wishing to access the SARC advice and support services.

The initial response to sexual violence is crucial in terms of recovery. Often victims feel that they will not be believed. Media, culture and

---

3 Survivors Manchester – for contact details see Useful Organisations at the end of the chapter.
4 A forensic physician is a doctor specialising in forensic medicine, in this case sexual offences.
5 A crisis worker is someone who supports the victim and can advocate on their behalf where they feel unable to represent themselves.
6 Independent sexual violence advisors provide on-going support (mainly to adults and young people) through the criminal justice process, and facilitate access to other services.
7 Medication given after potential exposure to prevent infection.

social context all have an impact on an individual's decision to either tell someone or make a report to the police. Kelly, Lovett and Regan (2005) report that powerful stereotypes function to limit the definition of 'real' rape. Victims often have their own preconceived ideas about sexual violence, which may impact on their ability to report the crime.

The way in which the initial disclosure is received will have a psychological impact. For example, if a victim feels judged in any way, this can reaffirm their feelings of low self-worth immediately after the assault. Victims are often confused and have a tendency to self-blame; they will frequently be hypervigilant and pick up any changes in anyone they come into contact with and the environment they are in (Lodrick 2007). They look to the reactions of others to demonstrate that they are being believed.

GOOD PRACTICE POINTS

Multi-agency training should address:
- myths and stereotypes in relation to sexual assault
- psychological response
- forensic medical issues.

The St Mary's SARC is committed to ensuring that people are treated with respect and dignity and are able to assert their choice and control over the services they receive to facilitate the recovery process. The opportunity for SARC services to contribute to that process is immense and should be taken into consideration when professionals are making a referral. Commissioners should take this into account when exploring the provision of sexual violence services to meet the needs of the population (Department of Health and Association of Chief Police Officers 2011).

IMMEDIATE RESPONSE

Rape is one of the most devastating personal traumas. Burgess and Holstrolm (1974) describe a cognitive, behavioural and emotional response to rape. Many victims feel that their lives are shattered and that they have been invaded and humiliated psychologically and physically. Typical reactions following rape include:
- feeling of shock
- disbelief, numbness

- fear
- anger
- guilt
- self-blame.

Other symptoms may include changes in behaviour, such as:

- social and/or emotional withdrawal
- sleep disturbances
- heightened sensitivity to real or perceived danger
- mood swings
- poor concentration
- lifestyle changes (this is usually dependent on the factors surrounding the assault – for example, victims may change the way in which they socialise/working patterns/mode of transport or journey, to avoid the location of the assault)
- avoidance (of intimate encounters, sexual difficulties, feelings of violation specific to the nature of the crime).

Victims who experience this type of crime will first consider who to tell. That person may be a family member or a friend, or the victim may consider making a report to the police. For some, telling someone about the assault entails much greater exposure than they feel they can cope with initially, and so they may not tell anyone for days, months or, in some cases, years. For others, telling a stranger (e.g. the police) is better than telling someone known to them, as this avoids the potential for facing that person on a day-to-day basis and feeling responsible for the other's feelings as well as their own.

GOOD PRACTICE POINT

Sexual violence is a significant breach of personal boundaries leaving the victim feeling violated. It is important that professionals model safe and consistent boundaries and do not act outside of their professional role.

The need for support in the aftermath of rape is obvious if the interpersonal relationship of the trauma is considered. Counselling provision for survivors, in order to help them attempt to come to terms with this experience, is considered vital by many survivors and those who work closely with them. Trauma destroys the trust relationship of the victim with themselves and the world (Newberry 2003).

There has been much debate about the response of the criminal justice system and the resulting impact on the victim in terms of recovery from the event. More than with any other crime, complainants experience reporting rape and the legal process as a form of re-victimisation (Kelly *et al.* 2005). The role of the police is to gather evidence and conduct an investigation. If approached in a sensitive manner this can feel supportive to the victim, and therefore impact positively on recovery (Her Majesty's Crown Prosecution Service Inspectorate 2007).

GOOD PRACTICE POINT

The recovery process starts from the point of the assault – therefore every contact following that will influence the recovery process.

In Manchester the police work closely with the SARC and engage in joint training to ensure that the response is appropriate. With any multi-agency response there needs to be mutual respect for the organisational pressures and demands. It is necessary to have a culture which allows · for challenge and discussion to constantly review and improve the joint response to the victim.

Following a report to the police, a specially trained officer is usually deployed to gain the initial details pertaining to the assault so that the investigation can commence, evidence can be gathered, and the victim can receive the appropriate medical treatment and support. The police will liaise with the SARC to arrange a forensic medical examination, where appropriate.

Should a forensic medical examination not be indicated, or where the victim declines the option, then the police must consider referral to the SARC or appropriate health care service to ensure that support can be provided and essential therapeutic medical treatment be considered. Some victims have an overwhelming fear of sexually transmitted infections or pregnancy as a result of the assault. If these fears are not addressed quickly, then the potential could become a reality and the psychological impact is exacerbated by physical consequences.

ENVIRONMENT

The St Mary's SARC provides services 24 hours a day, 365 days per year, in order to respond to the varying degrees of need. The SARC provides a forensic examination facility to assist in a potential investigation and prosecution. Therefore forensic integrity[8] is important. It involves the decontamination[9] of the forensic medical suite. To further ensure this, the examination suite is divided into pre-examination room, examination room and post-examination room and shower/toileting facilities so that each suite is self-contained (Faculty of Forensic and Legal Medicine 2007).

The psychological impact on the victim of forensic integrity measures should be considered. It is essential, when considering advances in deoxyribonucleic acid (DNA) identification techniques and the associated recommendations, outlined above, that the human response to sexual violence is not lost. The provision of this kind of medical intervention needs a very sensitive approach if the victim is not to experience the examination as a further trauma.

There are professionals who misunderstand or have poor knowledge in relation to the forensic medical examination, and the danger is that this ignorance influences their discussions with victims, which in turn influences the latter's decision to access the service. It is important that professionals seek advice and support from the SARC so that victims can make an informed choice and maximise their options for the future; particularly in the collection of forensic evidence for those undecided about making a report to the police.

Safety plays a major role in recovery. It is essential that the environment in which these services are provided feels safe and secure, and that access is discussed with the client at the earliest opportunity.

---

8   The reduction in risk of cross-contamination between cases.
9   Specialised cleaning to a specific protocol.

GOOD PRACTICE POINTS

Safety issues and measures:

- No-one can enter the building unless access is authorised – often the victim has paranoid feelings that the perpetrator is still out there and may have followed them to the SARC.
- Knowledge of custody status may be helpful; for example, the police will advise when:
  - the perpetrator has been held in custody
  - bail has been granted
  - terms of the bail conditions have been set.

CRISIS INTERVENTION

There are many interpretations of crisis intervention, which relate to a range of health services from mental health to accident and emergency. Crisis intervention in this context is the immediate emotional support provided to victims of sexual violence. This includes offering information and advice about what services can be accessed at the SARC and the process of the examination, so that the victim starts to understand and is therefore better able to make an informed choice about what happens next. The crisis intervention plays a huge part in recovery, as respect, choice and control and dignity are required for the process to begin.

Crisis workers provide immediate emotional support from the point of contact with the SARC, acting as advocate on behalf of the victim throughout the forensic medical examination, or when the victim or significant other accesses the out-of-hours telephone support helpline. One crisis worker describes her role:

> An advocate for the client is making sure they understand how we can help them and liaising with the police or doctor on their behalf. I explain it in a step-by-step approach. If they contact us on the phone and don't want police involvement then I will take the initial call, discuss the case with the doctor and make arrangements to meet at the centre.

The telephone support line is not a telephone counselling service. It provides a key contact for those who have experienced sexual violence to gain information quickly, so that they can begin to make a decision about what to do next. In some cases it might meet the need just to tell *someone*. The crisis worker will always outline the options available but the victim is then free to choose what happens next, if anything.

For some the act of telling will be sufficient to acknowledge what has occurred and enable them to take the next steps towards recovery. The St Mary's SARC takes on average 30 calls a day from victims and other professionals where a disclosure has been made.

When the victim is referred, or wishes to access the forensic medical service without making a report to the police, the crisis worker will again be the first point of contact. The crisis worker:

- meets and accompanies the victim from the point of their arrival at the SARC
- supports the victim through the examination
- provides support and advice on: what might happen next in terms of the criminal justice process; accessing follow-on health care services; support immediately after the examination.

GOOD PRACTICE POINTS

The crisis worker should explain what is happening at each step of the process:

- Ways in which the crisis worker might demonstrate that support, e.g.
  - ◦ 'Do you know where you are?'
  - ◦ 'Do you know why you are here?'
  - ◦ 'My role is...'
  - ◦ 'Does anyone know you are here?'
  - ◦ 'Do you need to let anyone know you are here?'
- The crisis worker will provide a safe and non-judgmental response to the early psychological response to rape and sexual assault, e.g.
  - ◦ 'This is not your fault.'
  - ◦ 'No-one can come in here unless we let them in.'
  - ◦ 'No-one is going to do anything to you here that you don't agree to.'
- During the examination the crisis worker continues to provide that support and observe the client for signs of distress, e.g.
  - ◦ 'I will be at the top end of the bed with you so that you can talk to me and let me know if you are uncomfortable in any way.'

It is important for crisis workers to have a non-judgmental attitude to sexual violence and to possess excellent communication skills. There is an opportunity to pull out attitudinal issues in relation to rape and sexual assault during the recruitment process. This work is not for everyone, and it is vital that the 'right' response is made to the victim at the time of crisis. For example, it would be inappropriate for the crisis worker to be shocked by or indifferent to what s/he hears from the victim. Victims sometimes feel that what they are about to say may be too difficult for the crisis worker to hear. The crisis worker must have (and demonstrate) empathy, rather than be so emotionally distressed by what the victim says that it detracts from the victim's own experience. This is true not just of crisis workers but of all professionals with whom the victim comes into contact. With this in mind, joint training and meetings are useful in challenging misconceptions of sexual violence, but also allow a space to discuss cases and the impact on the workers.

THE FORENSIC MEDICAL EXAMINATION

Where a SARC referral is made, the forensic physician will determine an appointment so that arrangements can be made to attend for a forensic examination. In considering the appointment the doctor will consider forensic issues such as the type of assault, time since the assault, and any actions the victim may have made since the assault. All these factors could affect the potential for forensic recovery. Also for consideration are other medical concerns or injuries which need urgent treatment. In considering timeframes for the examination, the victim may wish, for example, to make childcare arrangements, or to bring a change of clothing with them. If there is a delay in attendance for the examination the doctor may advise in relation to collection of early evidence, taking of mouth swabs and urine, or limiting bathing to reduce the risk of losing forensic evidence.

A significant delay would be unusual, however, consideration must be given to the victim's feelings around any potential delay. The crisis worker could have a key role here in keeping the victim (and police) updated on timescales and advice. A potential result of delay could be that the victim feels unworthy of SARC time and attention, which lowers self-esteem/self-worth even further in the early stages of recovery. The specially trained police officer will escort the victim to the SARC.

White (2010) describes the forensic physician as having a dual role. First is the forensic role: taking forensic samples by the collection of a series of swabs from anywhere the victim may have come into contact with the perpetrator (for example, anywhere they may have been kissed, licked, touched, or where anything has been inserted). The second role is a therapeutic one: considering emergency contraception; assessment of risk in relation to sexual health; safeguarding of children and vulnerable adults; self-harm and mental health. As previously mentioned, attending to physical symptoms or potential for disease could have a positive impact on recovery.

The forensic physician is an independent expert working on behalf of the courts, being non-partisan. The relationship between the forensic physician and the patient is different from the usual doctor–patient relationship in terms of confidentiality. The forensic doctor will be required to make a report to the courts.

The commencement of examination is determined by the client, following discussion with the crisis worker. During the examination phase the doctor and crisis worker will conduct risk assessments in relation to:

- domestic violence
- child protection
- self-harm
- mental health.

Where a specific risk is identified, actions required will be discussed and agreed with the client, ensuring those discussions and decisions are documented. For example, where the client has experienced domestic violence in the past and is at continued risk of experiencing current domestic violence, then a Domestic Abuse, Stalking and Harassment and Honour Based Violence Risk Assessment (DASH) (Co-ordinated Action Against Domestic Abuse 2009) will be conducted. A decision can then be made about the need for a social care emergency duty team referral and any necessary actions.

There are occasional conflicts between empowering clients by offering choice and making a decision about safety, particularly where children may be at risk and safeguarding concerns override autonomy. In these cases recovery is enhanced (despite the statutory requirements to make a referral) if the client is involved in the discussion and kept informed about what will happen as a result of the referral.

The examination process takes between two-and-a-half and three hours from arriving at the centre to leaving. In a small number of cases there may be extensive injuries, usually associated with a very violent attack. Consequently, the process may take longer, so it is important that the client is aware of this from the outset and is given the opportunity to stop the examination at any point.

The forensic physician will conduct the examination in a caring and sensitive way, supported by the crisis worker. The examination commences with the forensic physician introducing him/herself to the patient and making sure that the victim is able to give informed consent to the examination. In cases where capacity to consent is an issue the doctor may wish to consider the need for examination based on the best interests of the patient. Initial details of the assault will be taken from the police officer (this is conducted away from the client and whilst the crisis worker is with the client), or directly from the victim in the case of self-referrals. Any additional information or changes will be recorded on the forensic medical examination form, which is disclosable to the courts.

The information offered by the forensic physician may reiterate some of the crisis worker's discussions. This helps the client to absorb the information, and the recovery commences when understanding of the 'Whys?' and 'What ifs?' are addressed. It is also important to remember that information overload could impact on what the client remembers once s/he leaves the centre.

In the early stages following the assault it may be difficult to determine what information may be relevant as part of the investigation (e.g. a previous termination of pregnancy). The forensic physician may consider this to be sensitive information and enter it in the confidential medical record, which may be afforded greater confidentiality than the forensic medical records. This would be determined later by the courts, depending on other evidence available. The physician would discuss this with the client as part of gaining consent.

The client is shown into the medical room, and putting them at their ease as far as possible is the primary focus. The forensic physician will begin by weighing and measuring and explaining the reasons for this, affording the opportunity for the client to settle in a clinical environment.

GOOD PRACTICE POINT

Recovery is helped when the medical examination is not rushed or in the control of the clinician, as happens in so many medical settings. The client should determine the pace.

The client will be invited to undress and put on a gown. To ensure dignity, a curtain is pulled around. Once the client is ready, the crisis worker then joins the client to continue support and act as a chaperone for the physician. The physician will conduct the examination by looking carefully at one part of the body at a time. The client is never naked, so, for example, one arm is removed from the gown to be examined, then the other, working the way around the body, and a note is made of any marks or injuries.

It is important to note that very often there are no marks or injuries, which can be reassuring to the client. However, there are societal misconceptions that forced sexual contact results in visible injuries and signs of force. This can increase the victim's fears and anxiety about not being believed if there is no visual evidence. The forensic physician can help put the absence of injuries into context, not only for the client but also for the courts when providing expert evidence.

Once examination of external body surfaces is complete, the physician will explain the ano-genital examination,[10] which again is conducted in a very sensitive manner, the aim being to minimise the trauma of the examination so soon after the sexual assault. Forensic samples are taken in consideration of the latest forensic science guidelines (Faculty of Forensic and Legal Medicine 2012). The crisis worker and physician work as a team and remind the victim that s/he can stop the examination at any time if it becomes uncomfortable. One of the aims of the examination is to reassure that all is well; this can be very beneficial for recovery in itself.

Once the examination is complete the forensic physician goes through any other medical issues with the client. This may include assessment of human immunodeficiency virus (HIV) risk and involve the prescription of post-exposure prophylaxis (PEP)[11] (Benn, Fisher and Kulasegaram 2011). The assessment is complex and is conducted by the forensic physician, referring to the latest guidance and if necessary with the advice from a sexual health consultant.

The crisis worker will then offer the client the opportunity to meet basic needs:

- shower
- change of clothing
- food and drink.

The crisis worker will discuss the more practical issues related to the examination rather than the detail to avoid further distress, which assists in recovery:

- answer any questions of concern
- address questions from significant others.

It is important to try to limit the number of times the client talks about the assault, as this may increase the distress and therefore the trauma experienced. It could also generate conflict in evidential issues.

10 Examination of the genitalia and anus.
11 Medication to attempt to prevent disease.

At this stage the forensic physician is completing notes, labelling and bagging samples. On completion of this, the forensic physician will hand over all the samples to the police officer with a brief summary of findings.[12] The physician will have a final chat with the client to make sure they have understood everything, including discussion about any injuries that may have been found. It is important that where appropriate the physician has discussed the absence of injuries, to help put that information into context (White and McLean 2006). The physician will also ensure that the client is aware of any medication and follow-on services required, and finally see if the client has any specific questions for the doctor.

When all is complete the client leaves with the police officer, who transports the client home for some rest. Occasionally the police will request to undertake a video interview[13] (Ministry of Justice 2011). In most cases this would be inappropriate, given the trauma of the assault, time taken for the examination process and lack of sufficient rest; however, the victim may wish to continue to 'get it over with'. If after consideration this is what the victim chooses, then it may go ahead and is the next stage in investigation. If the client requires rest, then this can be delayed to a more suitable time.

GOOD PRACTICE POINTS

The crisis worker will:

- make sure that the client has understood what has taken place during the examination phase
- offer information leaflets in relation to SARC services
- give the name of the forensic physician
- give the name of the crisis worker
- ensure the client has any medication prescribed by the forensic physician
- discuss details of follow-on appointments such as counselling or sexual health appointments.

---

12 Known as the 'This is not a statement' document; a formal section 47 statement will be requested at a later date should the investigation proceed further.

13 See pages 54–55 in the *Achieving Best Evidence* guidance (Ministry of Justice 2011) regarding recording interviews.

In addition the crisis worker will check:

- contact details of the victim
- whether contact by telephone is acceptable
- that the telephone number is correct
- if it is OK to leave a message
- if it is OK to say who has called
- the best time to call
- if written communication is acceptable.

INDEPENDENT SEXUAL VIOLENCE ADVISOR (ISVA)

The role of the ISVA is to provide practical support through the criminal justice process, although for some clients that is not the only route, as some may not wish to follow the case through to prosecution. In terms of recovery the immediate contact with the ISVA can address short-term issues such as housing or access to follow-up medical support. The progression through the criminal justice process can be complex and can take a long time.

Some may not wish to support an investigation and prosecution, and the reasons for this are usually very personal to the victim. Under these circumstances the ISVA can provide other support in relation to:

- access to other health care services
- housing
- education (e.g. where a child victim is having difficulty attending school because of counselling or follow-up medical treatment)
- other practical issues (e.g. arrangement for pets to be cared for whilst the client gets a break from the home environment).

The ISVA will undertake a support needs assessment to establish the level and type of support required. Practical support issues are individual to the client and will be considered as part of the needs assessment. Although the role is primarily in relation to supporting the client, the ISVA can also assist the police to support the client in an independent way, and provides a conduit between support and counselling.

In considering recovery and healing, clients are often confused in the immediate aftermath of the assault and find it difficult to navigate through systems and services. The ISVA helps them to do this until issues are resolved or the client feels empowered to continue without support.

In cases that proceed through the criminal justice process, the ISVA is unable to influence the police, Crown Prosecution Service (CPS) or courts, but s/he can advocate on behalf of the client – often liaising with the police or CPS. During the initial investigation stage there is often a flurry of activity in terms of access to the SARC and constant contact with the police. As the investigation continues the victim can often feel alone, which is where the ISVA can have a crucial role to play in providing continued support whilst the investigation progresses.

The ISVA is not a police officer and therefore can offer advice independently from the investigation process and can attend the pre-court visit with the victim. This is often reassuring, as victims sometimes think that the defendant will be there when they attend to give evidence – which is not the case, as the victim will be afforded the benefit of waiting in the witness suite. The court process can be one of the most intimidating and stress-provoking situations following the assault. The ISVA can alleviate this anxiety by keeping in contact and communicating what is happening each step of the way.

The recovery process is an individual experience, so there is no time limit on when the ISVA should end contact, but the practical and court issues are usually resolved within 18 months. It is possible to have longer ISVA support. For example, the St Mary's ISVA has had contact over a number of years where issues are on-going (such as adjournment of the court case or retrial, or where fresh evidence may have come to light which progresses the investigation in the future).

The nature of sexual violence, trust and relationship issues surrounding the assault often mean that the victim can become dependent on individuals providing support. It is important to discuss the potential for this upfront and to ensure the victim understands the reason for boundaries around any therapeutic relationship. This is not a matter of rejection but of creating independence and enabling the victim to begin to trust themselves again so that they can establish non-abusive relationships in the future. Practitioners often express concern about ending therapeutic relationships, and passing/referring victims on to another practitioner, but if co-ordinated and communicated well, this should not be an issue.

COUNSELLING

When we begin to discuss healing, the provision of a therapeutic relationship to deal with the psychological impact of the assault is essential. There are many counselling services which either shy away from, or do not prepare therapists sufficiently well to provide, pre-trial therapy (Crown Prosecution Service 2001). Delay in access to therapeutic approaches can exacerbate the psychological issues experienced by victims of sexual violence. The intention of providing therapy at the SARC is to ensure the continuum of services and to facilitate access to a therapist who is trained in sexual violence and trauma recovery in the context of a potential criminal justice process. Early access helps to begin the healing process before the psychological impact is exacerbated and longer-term mental health issues arise. Clients often have the sensation of losing their reasoning or ability to function. This is best described as a normal response to an abnormal event. Once clients accept that they will experience a psychological response to this type of trauma, they feel better able to discuss and engage in a therapeutic relationship and work through their own particular process.

The SARC counselling service is open-ended, but due consideration is given to boundaries, which are discussed at contracting. Sessions are held weekly for 50 minutes and are reviewed after six sessions, with the option for clients to continue. If a case is going through the criminal justice process, as previously discussed, clients may also benefit from the support of the ISVA in conjunction with the counselling service.

The aim of counselling is to help the individual to:

- understand their emotions at a time when they may feel out of control
- make sense of what has happened when there might be no apparent sense to be made
- move on in their lives.

For some this may take many years and contact with a wide number of agencies and professionals.

IMPACT ON PROFESSIONALS (VICARIOUS TRAUMATISATION)

It would be remiss not to mention the potential impact of this work on the workers. Clinical supervision is essential to monitor vicarious traumatisation[14] (Hedge 2002) and to ensure that workers at all levels do not become desensitised by what they hear and see, but can contain the distress so that clients have the space in which to experience their

---

14 Where the impact of the work creates emotional difficulty for the worker and impedes their ability to respond empathically.

own emotions. It is difficult to recognise the symptoms of burnout in oneself. Working with a supervisor and being open about what is explored in supervision will help. Ideally a supervisor should be familiar with the effects of vicarious traumatisation and burnout, and should be vigilant at recognising when a worker is 'stepping into' some form of trauma replay (Lodrick 2007).

It is possible that individual workers may not recognise this phenomenon themselves, or they might deny the symptoms, which could occur over time. The SARC should expect vicarious traumatisation to occur in the workforce at some stage and put measures in place and create an environment to support the team and facilitate access to support, should it occur. Tehrani (2007) suggests that if ways can be found to manage occupationally induced stress, this can directly benefit the health carers and indirectly, by reducing costs, benefit both the organisation and the clients.

CONCLUSION

The St Mary's Sexual Assault Referral Centre was established in the 1980s to bridge the gap in services for victims of sexual violence at that time. Since then there has been significant progress in the development of sexual violence services and a sea change in the way in which professionals, and in particular the criminal justice services, deal with such cases. For those affected by the crime, their individual experience is dependent on so many variables, including the ability of agencies and society in general to disregard misconceptions, have a sensitive approach and treat individuals with respect.

If a service or individual can give time to listen to someone, going at their own pace, and demonstrate respect, that can have a huge impact on that individual's recovery and healing. Clients often describe something positive coming out of something so negative. This demonstrates the capacity of human beings to recover from such a terrible ordeal. If we can be a part of that process of recovery and healing, then that makes the SARC service absolutely invaluable.

REFERENCES

Benn, P., Fisher, M. and Kulasegaram, R. (2011) 'UK guidelines for the use of post-exposure prophylaxis for HIV following sexual assault.' *International Journal of STI and AIDS 22*, 695–708.

Burgess, A. and Holstrolm, L. (1974) 'Rape Trauma Syndrome.' *American Journal of Psychiatry 131*, 9, 981–986.

Chowdhury-Hawkins, R., McLean, L., Winterholler, M. and Welch, J. (2008) 'Preferred choice of gender of staff providing care to victims of sexual assault in Sexual Assault Referral Centres.' *Journal of Forensic and Legal Medicine 15*, 6, 363–367.

Co-ordinated Action Against Domestic Abuse (2009) *CAADA-DASH Risk Identification Checklist (RIC) for MARAC Agencies*. Available at www.caada.org.uk/marac/RIC_without_guidance.doc. Accessed on 19 August 2012.

Crown Prosecution Service (2001) *Provision of Therapy for Vulnerable or Intimidated Witnesses Prior to Criminal Trial – Practice Guidance*. Available at www.cps.gov.uk/publications/prosecution/pretrialadult.html. Accessed on 19 August 2012.

Department of Health and Association of Chief Police Officers (2011) *Response to Sexual Violence. Needs Assessment (RSVNA) Toolkit*. London: DH.

Department of Health, Home Office and Association of Chief Police Officers (2009) *Revised National Service Guide: A Resource for Developing Sexual Assault Referral Centres*. London: DH.

Faculty of Forensic and Legal Medicine (2007) *Operational Procedures and Equipment for Medical Examination Rooms in Police Stations and Victim Examination Suites*. Available at http://fflm.ac.uk/upload/documents/1193757602.pdf. Accessed on 19 August 2012.

Faculty of Forensic and Legal Medicine (2012) *Recommendations for the Collection of Forensic Specimens from Complainants and Suspects*. Available at http://fflm.ac.uk/upload/documents/1341587308.pdf. Accessed on 17 October 2012.

Hedge, B. (2002) 'The Impact of Sexual Assault on Health-care Workers.' In J. Petrak and B. Hedge (eds) *The Trauma of Sexual Assault: Treatment, Prevention and Practice*. Chichester: Wiley.

Her Majesty's Crown Prosecution Service Inspectorate (2007) *Without Consent: A Report on the Joint Review of the Investigation and Prosecution of Rape Offences*. Available at www.hmcpsi.gov.uk/documents/services/reports/THM/Without_Consent_Thematic.pdf. Accessed on 19 August 2012.

Kelly, L., Lovett, J. and Regan, L. (2005) *A Gap or a Chasm: Attrition in Reported Rape Cases*. Home Office Research Study No. 293. London: Home Office.

Lodrick, Z. (2007) 'Psychological trauma – what every trauma worker should know.' *British Journal of Psychotherapy Integration 4*, 2, 18–28.

Lovett, J. and Kelly, L. (2004) *Sexual Assault Referral Centres: Developing Good Practice and Maximising Potentials*. Home Office Research Study No. 285. London: Home Office.

McLean, I.A., Balding, V. and White, C. (2004) 'Forensic medical aspects of male-on-male rape and sexual assault in Greater Manchester.' *Medicine, Science and the Law 44*, 2, 165–169.

Ministry of Justice (2011) *Achieving Best Evidence in Criminal Proceedings: Guidance on Interviewing Victims and Witnesses, and Guidance on Using Special Measures*. Available at: www.cps.gov.uk/publications/docs/best_evidence_in_criminal_proceedings.pdf. Accessed on 19 August 2012.

Newberry, J. (2003) 'Counselling provision as a response to the inadequacies of rape survivors: Support offered by the British Criminal Justice Service.' Unpublished paper.

St Mary's SARC (2011) *Annual Report 2010–2011*. Manchester: St Mary's Sexual Assault Referral Centre.

St Mary's SARC (2012) *Annual Report 2011–2012*. Manchester: St Mary's Sexual Assault Referral Centre.

Tehrani, N. (2007) 'The cost of caring.' *Counselling Psychology Quarterly 20*, 4, 325–339.

White, C. (2010) *Sexual Assault: A Forensic Clinician's Practice Guide*. Manchester: St Mary's Sexual Assault Referral Centre.

White, C. and McLean, I. (2006) 'History taking – adolescent complainants of sexual assault: Injury patterns in virgin and non-virgin groups.' *Journal of Clinical and Forensic Medicine 13*, 172–180.

USEFUL ORGANISATIONS

St Mary's Sexual Assault Referral Centre
Telephone: 0161 276 6515
Website: www.stmaryscentre.org
Visit the website for information on services; access to publications/training calendar; annual report.
Also available at www.stmaryscentre.org: Resource DVD 'Patients' Journey' and St Mary's SARC Clients' Voices.

Survivors Manchester
PO Box 4325
Manchester
M61 0BG
Website: www.survivorsmanchester.org.uk

CHAPTER 4

MALE SURVIVORS OF CHILDHOOD SEXUAL ABUSE
EXPERIENCE OF MENTAL HEALTH SERVICES

SARAH NELSON, RUTH LEWIS AND
SANDRA S. CABRITA GULYURTLU

This chapter outlines key mental health themes described by 24 adult male survivors of child sexual abuse (CSA) from varying backgrounds and ages (from 18 to 63 years). These men took part in a Scottish qualitative, life-history study which explored how they saw their own needs for care, protection and support throughout their lives, and what had proved helpful or unhelpful for their own lives in that quest.

All the men had experienced mental ill-health (often including severe symptoms, such as hallucinations or suicide attempts). Their responses about mental health services had many similarities to other studies (Dale 1999; Draucker and Petrovic 1997; Havig 2008; Hopkins, Loeb and Fick 2009; Nelson 2001), particularly in the finding that theoretical approach or qualification is less important than personal empathy and skills in the practitioner. They found most unhelpful disbelief, discomfort or a failure to recognise their abuse history; medical models of diagnosis and treatment; being re-traumatised through physical restraint; and lack of practical support.

What they found most helpful were understanding (especially of male survivor issues); belief, acceptance and consultation; noticing and asking about abuse; a safe, warm setting; respectful counselling; and practical support. Issues like safety, reassurance and environment set a trusting atmosphere, where distressing issues could be tackled with professionals skilled in working with victims of abuse.

Many studies (Jacobson and Herald 1990; Jacobson and Richardson 1987; Lab, Feigenbaum and De Silva 2000; Sorsoli, Kia-Keating and Grossman 2008; Valente 2005) have urged routine inquiry in mental health settings into a possible abuse history, and the need to work with CSA trauma. Yet progress is still limited, medical models predominate, and many mental health professionals still report feeling uncomfortable or unskilled about opening this 'can of worms'. With this further example of survivors' own clear preferences, a key question for practice remains: why are these still to be adopted in many psychiatric settings?

HEALING AND RECOVERY FROM CHILDHOOD SEXUAL ABUSE: ETHICAL DILEMMAS

Among those working with sexual abuse survivors, the significant emphasis on recovery and healing, rather than on prevention and deterrence, raises ethical problems. Childhood sexual abuse is a serious crime. When people suffer other serious crimes, although recovery programmes such as Victim Support may be one element of the response, most effort goes into convicting perpetrators and reducing their opportunities for further crime. Childhood sexual abuse is also a major public health issue. Most substantial advances in public health have come through preventive measures (such as providing clean water) and through attempts to eradicate, or greatly to reduce, serious diseases, not through accepting them as regrettably inevitable and putting the most effort into convalescence services.

Focusing efforts on recovery services may also lead to a comforting complacency: if people can recover, perhaps CSA is not too serious after all? This might reduce the impetus and funding for prevention and deterrence. It can obscure or deny the reality that many survivors of CSA will only ever make a partial recovery. The role of sexual abuse support organisations and agencies which had a campaigning role against sexual abuse in the 1980s has now largely turned into one of therapeutic support after abuse has taken place – losing, some would argue, a 'cutting edge' as a result.

On the other hand, however principled this position is, it does not assist the numerous people who struggle now with severe after-effects of CSA trauma. There remains relatively little therapeutic help (especially for males) available in the United Kingdom, and certainly little free or low-cost therapeutic help. Survivors of CSA deserve support to address the impacts of their trauma, and this should be as high a priority as possible.

An ethical approach, perhaps, is to see recovery not as the only or primary goal for funding and research, but as one major part of addressing sexual abuse in society, alongside support for those campaigning against CSA, and support for effective primary prevention and criminal justice. Taking that comprehensive view, we might argue for a legal advice office in all psychiatric hospitals (institutions crowded with the victims of serious crime), as well as for particular therapies to be available in those hospitals. We need effective multi-agency interventions which can provide co-ordinated measures to target the prevention and onset of CSA.

The male survivors interviewed for our research study (Nelson 2009) did not talk about 'healing', although they occasionally referred to 'recovery'. This was not because recovery from CSA trauma was unimportant to them. Rather, they tended to describe recovery in terms of positive changes in their lives, enabled by what they valued as good practice in care and support. These changes varied – sometimes considerably – from one person to another, depending on their own needs and on what mattered most to them. To give just three brief examples of this diversity:

||||||||||||||||||||||||||||||||||||||||||||||||||||||||||||||||||||||||||||||||||||||||||||||||||||||||||||||

CASE EXAMPLES 4.1: WHAT RECOVERY MEANT

- **Adam:**[1] Breaking free of the blanket of medication that blotted out his sensory awareness; being able to function in daily life; not losing periods of time and memory; being able to study for the qualifications he went on to gain; and achieving a happy marriage.
- **Alec:** Having a gay relationship where he was not victimised; not being afraid to leave his flat for the shops; keeping his flat tidy and manageable; and campaigning for justice for those who had been sent abroad to care institutions.
- **Dean:** Living without needing the constant numbing comfort of drugs; trusting other men and women again; managing to escape his home environment; and training for the work he sought to do.

||||||||||||||||||||||||||||||||||||||||||||||||||||||||||||||||||||||||||||||||||||||||||||||||||||||||||||||

However, what proved much more consistent and much less diverse among the male survivors we interviewed was their judgment of the types of professional support which enabled them to make at least a partial recovery from negative impacts of their abuse.

CHILDHOOD SEXUAL ABUSE AMONGST MEN: PREVALENCE, MENTAL HEALTH AND PROFESSIONAL FEARS

Research studies find that 11–17 per cent of males experience some incident(s) of CSA before the age of 16 years (Dube *et al.* 2005; Hopper 2008; Lisak, Hopper and Song 1996). However, under-reporting amongst men remains likely, due to masculine assumptions

---

1   In order to protect participants' anonymity, all names have been changed.

of responsibility and shame, and fear of being branded 'gay' (Goldman and Padayachi 2000; Kia-Keating *et al.* 2005). Some groups have much higher prevalence rates, including homeless men, non-sexual and sexual offenders, and users of psychiatric services (Holmes and Slap 1998; Hopper 2008; Lab and Moore 2005; Valente 2005).

Research also indicates that male survivors of CSA are at significantly greater risk than non-abused males of developing mental ill-health, including:

- post-traumatic stress symptoms
- personality disorders
- depression
- paranoid symptoms
- hallucinations
- dissociation
- self-harm
- actual or attempted suicide
- severe substance misuse
- loss of self-esteem.

> (Alaggia and Millington 2008; Dube *et al.* 2005; Holmes and Slap 1998; Read *et al.* 2003; Romano and De Luca 2001; Whitfield *et al.* 2005)

Despite a high prevalence of psychiatric patients with a CSA history, relatively few have this recognised through assessment. Many mental health professionals report feeling uncomfortable, incompetent or professionally unsupported about enquiring, reluctant to 'open a can of worms' (Day, Thurlow and Woolliscroft 2003; Holmes, Offen and Waller 1997; Nelson 2001, 2004; Nelson and Hampson 2008). Jennings (1994) summed up the major problem nearly 20 years ago, noting: 'There is evidence that a significant subset of psychiatric patients were severely sexually traumatised in childhood. Yet standard interview schedules consistently neglect to ask questions about such abuse, appropriate treatment is seldom available, and clients are often re-traumatised by current practices' (p.374).

Patients are even less likely to be asked about a CSA history if they are male, or if they have psychotic symptoms (Warne and McAndrew 2005). One study found that most psychiatric staff rarely enquired about sexual abuse in male patients, and used ineffective enquiry methods when they did ask; while two thirds had no training in working with CSA (Lab *et al.* 2000). Agar and Read (2002) found that even when abuse histories were known, only one in five psychiatric patients (male or female) had received abuse-related therapy. Yet the cause of mental ill-health does matter, both in terms of justice and in terms of finding appropriate therapies (Whitelaw 2009).

As Vardy and Price (1998) point out, increased awareness that CSA is linked to adult mental ill-health means mental health nurses and other professionals need to develop expertise with this client group, to observe the ethical principle of non-maleficence, or avoidance of harm. Cameron, Kapur and Campbell (2005) warn that the paucity of therapeutic contact with psychiatric nurses is antithetical to the aspirations of service users. Long and Smyth (1998) go so far as to describe it as 'uncaring and inhumane' for nurses not to be prepared to accept the sharing of painful, disturbing experiences. Cause for concern is that, in a study of male survivors' views on therapy (Draucker and Petrovic 1997), the majority had described negative experiences with therapists.

One avenue for improving understanding amongst mental health professionals is to consider survivors' own perspectives on their experiences and needs for support. Therefore research which seeks survivors' narratives is crucial; as Alaggia and Millington (2008) argue: 'We need to be reminded of the importance of the context of our clients' lives... Through a deepened understanding of the lived experience of sexually abused men, their narratives offer directions for therapy' (p.272).

THE STUDY

The key mental health themes which emerged from narratives by adult male survivors of CSA will now be presented. These themes formed part of the qualitative research study, 'Care and support needs of men who survived childhood sexual abuse' (Nelson 2009), a collaboration between the University of Edinburgh and the mental health charity Health in Mind.[2] The study also explored issues including child and adult disclosure, education, work, intimate relationships, sexuality, substance misuse and offending; and aimed to improve male survivors' well-being, through establishing their perspectives on their major care, support and intervention needs through the life-course.

Most participants were recruited through Scottish voluntary sector organisations: it was an ethical requirement of the research that they should have access to support. A subset of eight were convicted (largely non-sexual) offenders receiving support from a voluntary organisation. This did not imply narrow entry criteria; because there are still few statutory services for CSA survivors, especially for males, most tend to be referred to voluntary sector organisations. This means that a very

---

2   For more details about the work of this charity visit www.health-in-mind. org.uk.

broad spectrum of ages, social backgrounds and severity of conditions is available for recruitment to any research study.

As less is known about male than female survivors of CSA, and because we wanted to avoid any prior assumptions about the most significant experiences across men's lives, we used a life history approach. This enabled the survivors to pinpoint what *for them* were the most significant events, effects, needs and interventions at particular stages of their lives (Cole and Knowles 2001; Denzin and Lincoln 2003; Dhunpath 2000), an approach which has already proved valuable in other studies with sexual abuse survivors (Alaggia and Millington 2008; Harvey *et al.* 2001).

Participants were interviewed on two occasions. The first interview involved using a 'life grid' (a chart with age bands along one axis, and dimensions of life such as education, work and relationships along the other), an interview tool which has been found to assist recall and aid rapport (Berney and Blane 2003; Parry, Thomson and Fowks 1999; Wilson *et al.* 2007). Participants were asked open-ended questions designed to elicit biographical narratives, and the grid was annotated with details of the participants' narratives. Towards the end of the interview, interviewees were encouraged to use colouring pens on the grids to express their emotions about events, which often highlighted strong positive or negative feelings not necessarily conveyed by their words earlier in the interview.

The second interviews were conducted two to five weeks later and were tailored to each individual respondent, based on open coding from their first interview. These interviews further explored key themes which emerged from the life grid interview. The interviews, which lasted between 60 and 90 minutes, were audio-recorded and transcribed verbatim.

We used an iterative thematic approach, with subsequent topic guides and coding informed by earlier analyses. In these respects, our analysis followed some of the principles of grounded theory (Strauss and Corbin 1998). Initial transcripts were open coded by all authors to identify key themes, concepts and processes. We met to discuss the meanings of these initial themes and to agree a strategy for subsequent coding. We examined participants' life grids in conjunction with reading their interview transcripts in order to explore new or additional ways of understanding qualitative findings. Using a mixture of manual and computer-aided analysis supported by NVivo software, further analyses then focused on a more detailed coding of particular themes.

SUMMARY OF RESULTS

Table 4.1: Participants'[1] age bracket, type of abuse and abuser

Name	Age bracket	Type of abuse	Sexually abused by/abuser(s)
Adam	30–40	sexual, physical and emotional	• father • abuse rings (male and female)
Alec	50–60	sexual, physical and emotional	• monk at school
Dean	18–22	sexual, physical and emotional	• male family friend • female staff member at a children's home • abducted from street and raped by multiple gang members
Gordon	40–50	sexual, physical and emotional	• father • gang-raped in army as a young man
Hunter	18–22	Sexual and emotional	• older boy • foster carer
Jeff	30–40	sexual and emotional	• two older boys • a 13-year-old girl • two young priests
Liam	18–22	sexual and emotional	• brother
Padraig	40–50	sexual and emotional	• male neighbour
Pete	30–35	sexual and emotional	• youth club worker (male)
Roy	30–40	sexual and emotional	• male family friend • man on street
Scott	40–50	sexual and emotional	• mother
Stuart	40–50	sexual and emotional	• male youth leader who became a family friend

1 Participants listed in this table are those mentioned in the chapter.

MENTAL HEALTH SYMPTOMS EXPERIENCED

All 24 men had experienced mental health problems in adulthood. The seriousness of the symptoms listed below was noteworthy, since participants were not recruited specifically from mental health service users. Fewer than one-third could be described as regular service users; the rest were sporadic or occasional. All had seriously contemplated suicide; a majority had attempted it. This was the range of mental health symptoms found among the 24 respondents:

- suicidal thoughts
- depression, panic attacks and anxiety
- repetitive self-mutilation
- terrifying flashbacks, intrusive images
- 'dreamlike' memories of multiple perpetrators
- nightmares of being raped
- visual/auditory hallucinations of abuser
- severe substance addiction
- dissociation and depersonalisation
- eating disorders
- extreme anger and mood swings
- prolonged crying
- obsessive fear of death
- an urge to kill.

To give an example of visual and auditory hallucinations experienced: Pete hallucinated that his abuser's figure stood beside his psychiatric hospital bed, and heard him speak, 20 years after his abuse ended:

> *I was frozen stiff with fear and terror… I could see his figure, his shadow and everything.*

UNHELPFUL APPROACHES EXPERIENCED
The majority of respondents were confronted by a variety of unhelpful services and interventions aiming to address their symptoms.

GOOD PRACTICE POINTS

Unhelpful approaches to male CSA survivors:
- Not asking about a possible CSA history.
- Disbelieving an abuse history.
- Dismissing it as unimportant.

- Using cold and formulaic assessments.
- Employing only medical models of mental illness.
- Dealing with emotional pain by polypharmacy.[2]
- Re-traumatising patients with restraints.
- Not giving practical help with daily living.

---

2   Polypharmacy is the use of multiple medications by a patient, especially when *too many* forms of medication are used.

In the study, men in all age groups reported more negative than positive experiences of mental health services (discussed below).

Lack of recognition, disbelief, dismissal
The men's commonest complaint was that many psychiatrists, psychologists, psychiatric nurses and general practitioners never asked if CSA was an issue in their distress; or when CSA was raised, said they could not help, disbelieved them, looked uncomfortable with the subject, or discouraged discussion of it.

Pete described his experience of reading his notes in psychiatric hospital:

> It says in the medical records, 'P has reported that he was abused, apparently'…as if to say, he probably maybe wasn't.

Roy, suicidal and in the grip of several addictions, found no psychiatrist willing to discuss abuse issues:

> We spoke about St John's Wort, we spoke about my mother. Every issue but the central issue. The question was never even posed.

Jeff, abused in boarding school, went from psychiatrist to psychologist as a student, feeling increasingly demoralised:

> I wanted to talk about my past and my abuse but they weren't interested… 'I can't help you, I'll refer you to see my boss'… She [psychiatrist] saw me for ten minutes and said, 'No-one will take on your case; you're not mentally ill.' I just thought, not even the top person can help me!

When Jeff became a psychiatric nurse, he found that letting patients talk about their trauma was frowned upon:

I was told X had been quite manipulative and attention-seeking of my time, we should not have encouraged that, and I was really shocked.

Such experiences meant that these professionals failed to address the survivors' needs, and therefore to support their recovery.

Medical models of diagnosis and treatment, with polypharmacy

This related issue brought a range of complaints about receiving many different diagnoses and powerful medications. Effects described included 'chemical lobotomy', sedation, memory loss, weight gain, and low energy for study or work.

Alec, abused in care, summarised his medication history:

They speed you up and slow you down, and you feel tired or sweaty.

For Adam, victim of multiple sadistic assaults, heavy antipsychotic drugs and a polypharmacy of other medications, it:

Wiped me out...they actually stole four years of my life.

Following his father's violent assaults and a traumatic army gang rape, Gordon was repeatedly admitted to psychiatric hospital. Despite experiencing excellent care from individual staff, he recalled a bewildering range of diagnoses and medications, debilitating effects, failure to explore his trauma, and disbelief. He found opportunities for 'talking treatments' had actually decreased:

I was told being treated for schizophrenia, personality disorder... I was having flashbacks, seizures, ranting and raving... I would re-enact flashbacks to the rape and my childhood. I was [once] on 35 tablets a day...antidepressants, tranquillisers, painkillers, antipsychotics... [They] just suppressed all emotions. I was totally lethargic, slurred speech, drooling at the mouth.

Re-traumatising experiences of restraint

Pete's angry outbursts had evoked aggressive, frightening responses from mental health professionals. Removal of his trousers and underpants (for the injection of drugs) mirrored his anal assaults.

They said, 'If you don't take this I will have to enforce it on you.' He came at me, and eight nurses – they try and make you lie down on a bed and take your trousers down and de-humanise you... I was terrified.

Adam was injected in hospital in this manner:

I freaked out. It brought back pretty horrendous stuff.

'Cold', formulaic assessments

Most respondents had experienced mental health professionals filling in forms behind a desk. Younger respondents in the 18–22 age group in particular voiced dislike of continual note-taking, their suspicion and lack of information about who would read their notes next, and their sense that professionals were not genuinely interested in them. In the young prisoner Hunter's view:

> When they see someone taking notes they think they don't care, that they are just doing that for their job...

Lack of support with basic self-care

It appeared from this study that young males, especially, in their teens and early twenties, may have acute needs for support with basic living skills while mentally unwell in the community. Survivors described phases of completely failing to cope with daily living, needing basic practical help. For instance, Gordon took heavily to drink, self-isolated and could not organise his daily life. Stuart, abused by a male youth leader, recalled that when young he did not have his hair cut for three years, could not work, smoked cannabis, drank heavily and self-isolated.

HELPFUL APPROACHES EXPERIENCED

Male survivors' responses about treatments, attitudes and services which they found helpful reflected many of those of female survivors in the *Beyond Trauma* Scottish study (Nelson 2001, 2004).

GOOD PRACTICE POINTS

Helpful approaches to male CSA survivors:
- Small acts – recognition, listening, noticing, caring.
- Ability to ask about abuse history without fear.
- Informed understanding, belief and acceptance (for male survivors, understanding of male issues).
- Willingness to try eclectic range of treatments.
- Sympathetic general practitioners (GPs) as 'gatekeepers' to services.
- Warmth and safety of setting.
- Practical support with daily living (especially for males).
- Counselling, or other therapeutic approaches which focus on the needs that survivors themselves bring.

Small, helpful acts often made a strong positive impact. They most valued informed knowledge of CSA (including issues for males), empathy, skills and respectful consultation, rather than particular therapeutic approaches or qualifications. They also valued services to which they could return when needed.

'Small acts' often a catalyst

Professional fears that survivors may need complex interventions contrasts with many respondents' recall of apparently small acts by professionals, as catalysts to changing their lives. These could involve:

- acknowledging the abuse
- listening, noticing
- showing commitment
- booking a double (longer) appointment.

For example, no-one had asked Gordon about his abuse background until a hospital charge nurse he recalled by name noticed references to abuse in Gordon's own writings, and asked him about them. This eventually enabled Gordon to begin talking through his experiences in an atmosphere of safety.

Pete had long hated all authority: the psychiatric nurse whom he most appreciated 'merely' shouted at him. He was unused to professionals who were visibly caring and committed about him:

> This nurse, S, knew the court case [against the abuser] was coming up... I was being hyper...but he really got through to me. He was standing there with his arms – up and down – 'Pete, you've got to listen! We have got to get you in the best possible state for you to go through with this court case!' I says, 'S...not only do you just care, but you passionately care.'

Informed understanding, belief and acceptance

Jeff finally found a helpful psychologist and this proved a key moment in his life.

> [The psychologist]: 'I'm quite ashamed by the way my colleagues have treated you...and I'm here to help you.' And I remember starting to cry, that he was the first person in my life...he helped me realise that my dissociations or my panic attacks...were just part of the normal thing.

Professionals who understood the particular effects of CSA on males were especially valued.

Padraig, abused as a young child by a neighbour, said that his therapist:

Seemed knowledgeable about people's sexuality, the difference between men and women...how we portray sex, double standards...it absolutely made me feel that she would know the subtle stuff that goes on, and the subtle sort of pain you actually put yourself through.

Roy found his counsellor's eclecticism was informed by his own needs as a survivor, not by formulaic approaches. The responses were tailored to enable him to begin a process of recovery in some key areas of his life:

We've looked at self-worth, self-esteem issues... We've done EMDR [eye movement desensitisation and reprocessing[3]]... She's given me various books... C is fantastic, because she's got a variety of techniques she can use for each and every client.

Thoughtful general practitioners

General practitioners (GPs) appeared to play an important 'gate-keeping' role. Knowledgeable, sympathetic, listening GPs often initiated access to good services. For example, Stuart's GP took his disclosure seriously and referred him at once to the most helpful psychiatrist he had ever encountered. Adam's GP always booked him double appointments, discussed his issues and accessed a skilled therapist:

It was the first step in the NHS that I had any real support.

Warmth, safety and availability of setting

Thoughtful furnishings and initial responses gave an atmosphere of respect, calm, safety and human warmth.

Scott, abused as a small child by his mother, recalls his first interview with his voluntary sector support agency:

Positive, comfortable, friendly – the furniture, sofas, etc. – and even the initial interview, positive, understanding, professional, very calm. The calming aspect is a huge thing...because you are so uptight.

Like many survivors, Gordon appreciated that he could return to his sexual abuse support organisation when he needed it and was not tied to a strict number of sessions. It was also safe and reassuring:

The main factor is, the fact that...they've always kept in touch. It's genuine support, caring. Even if you phoned out of the blue, there's always a warm, sincere, empathic person on the end of the phone.

---

3   This is a form of psychotherapy which was developed by Francine Shapiro in the 1980s. See Shapiro (2001).

Practical support with self-care

Practical support was found valuable when survivors were too depressed or chaotic to care for themselves – so long as the worker also understood the effects of trauma. For instance, Alec found motivation from a support worker in his accommodation:

> *I don't have to educate her what* [abuse] *is all about, she understands from the point go, and I feel very relaxed in her company. She gets me motivated to get out of bed and tidy up the kitchen, wash the dishes and prepare the house a little, because I still shut myself in my head.*

Counselling: positive response from men

Most respondents had experienced counselling and found it helpful, especially the young convicted offenders (18–22 years); as males they did not consider it too 'touchy-feely'. Confidentiality brought feelings of safety, while being challenged respectfully about their assumptions was also valued.

Separately, convicted offenders all said strikingly similar things about the value of their independent counsellor. Referred by psychiatric and health staff, they were able to disclose very traumatic childhood events. All had managed to reduce their anxiety and aggression towards others. One key element was that without condoning their crimes, she treated them all with respect as individuals, and conveyed the belief that they themselves could change. She also enabled them to see the dynamics of power in their childhood and that they had lacked the power to prevent the abuse. A detailed description of the counselling process is given in the research report (see Nelson 2009, Chapter 22, 'Working Therapeutically with Prisoners').

Liam summarises the key points for him:

> *If I brought something up that I was finding really difficult, she'd leave it and come back to it. But she would ask me…what I was finding hard about it. She made me feel…that for once it wasn't actually my fault. Confidentiality was also really, really important… I'd always been more concerned about somebody talking about what I was disclosing.*

Counselling was not used, and valued, solely by less seriously ill people. For instance, a voluntary support organisation worked intensively with Pete throughout his court case, despite his auditory hallucinations and aggressive, frightened outbursts:

> *When the case was coming up to court, I was at death's door, I tried to commit suicide – in a terrible state, I heard a humming bird inside my head. I starved myself, etc. My house was a tip.* [My counsellor] *was just there to*

take the whole lot, and be there for me…it was reassuring that I was dealing with a professional.

Pete now lives in a therapeutic community.

CONCLUSIONS

All the male CSA survivors in this study had experienced mental ill-health; most had experienced severe, debilitating symptoms at points in their lives, despite only one-third being regular service users. A majority of the men had waited years and sometimes decades before they were actually asked about a possible history of sexual abuse. Although many studies have argued over time that health professionals have a responsibility to enquire sensitively, and have called for routine inquiry about CSA to take place, progress remains limited (Jacobson and Herald 1990; Jacobson and Richardson 1987; Lab *et al.* 2000; Read and Fraser 1998; Sorsoli *et al.* 2008; Valente 2005).

These survivors described a pattern of desired behaviour on the part of mental health professionals which might be called 'high-skill, low-tech'. Issues like safety, comfort, reassurance and environment were not trivial matters, but set a trusting atmosphere, within which difficult, distressing issues could be tackled with professionals skilled in working with abuse. Although voluntary sector organisations were prominent in providing such settings and values, they are adaptable to every sector. Adam, for instance, had some very negative experiences with statutory services, but his main *positive* experiences were from statutory staff – a GP, a social worker, a psychologist and a psychiatric nurse specialising in CSA trauma.

Many of these findings are paralleled in other studies – for example, Hopkins and colleagues' (2009) literature review of mental health patients found that they placed high value on places of safety and refuge. Havig's (2008) review of sensitive practice with CSA survivors emphasised facilitating disclosure and improving communication.

Thus too in Draucker and Petrovic (1997), therapist traits which survivors described as most helpful included being informed about male CSA issues, being connected to the client, and respecting his/her process. Dale (1999) foreshadowed Nelson's (2001) findings that the theoretical approach or qualification is less important than personal empathy and skills in the practitioner. Vardy and Price (1998), for whom Peplau's interpersonal theory of nursing gave a framework for working with male CSA survivors, stressed trust, acceptance, warmth, and recognition of nurses' own feelings and experiences. Peplau's interpersonal, or psychodynamic, theory of nursing focused on the therapeutic relationship that develops between nurse and client. In this humanistic approach, being able to understand one's own behaviour helps others identify their perceived difficulties. (Alligood and Tomey 2006; George 2002).

It is important to emphasise that these findings do not mean specialist training and specialised therapies are therefore unimportant in assisting recovery from sexual abuse trauma. Issues faced by some survivors of CSA will often require specialised techniques and more prolonged therapeutic interventions, from very experienced practitioners – for example, more severe forms of dissociation, psychotic episodes or non-epileptic seizures. Again, although the survivors in this study found that most professionals only treated symptoms rather than causes, this does not mean that ameliorating symptoms is unimportant. For example, some therapies can prove very helpful to CSA survivors for particular, distressing symptoms. One example is eye movement desensitisation and reprocessing (EMDR) (Edmond, Rubin and Wambach 1999; Edmond, Sloan and McCarty 2004), for post-traumatic stress symptoms such as flashbacks and nightmares. Rather, the message from these male survivors and from other studies is that:

GOOD PRACTICE POINTS

- An atmosphere of safety, trust and receptiveness to *any* form of therapy cannot even be established unless professionals working with them show the qualities of empathy, genuine warmth and respect which survivors value and have described here. Having specialised techniques (or any number of qualifications) at one's fingertips is not in itself sufficient.

- Willingness to consult with and listen to the expressed needs of individual survivors is also very important, so that any specialised help they actually need to change their lives can be identified and tailored, without prior professional assumptions about what those needs may be.

Jeff, himself now a mental health practitioner, looks forward to humanistic, holistic ways of working with CSA survivors:

So I have a real passion now...around recovery...a commitment in my heart to try and bring about some change in my lifetime for them. I think that passion also comes because I've actually looked at parallels between the psychiatric system and my school: in that there was silence, and it was not talked about.

Given that, through their narratives, our research respondents echoed the priorities of such a wide range of studies, a key question for current and future practice must be to examine why such clearly stated preferences still remain to be taken on board in many psychiatric settings. It is important for health professionals to address these issues. They need to bring about change: reducing, through humanistic training, professional and personal discomfort, fear and sense of inadequacy; through inquiring routinely about a CSA history; through improving inept inquiring styles; through moving from a narrow adherence to medical models of mental health to a full understanding and acceptance of trauma models; and through actually providing abuse-related therapy for mental health patients, whether male or female, who have a history of sexual abuse.

REFERENCES

Agar, K. and Read, J. (2002) 'What happens when people disclose sexual or physical abuse to staff at a community mental health centre?' *International Journal of Mental Health Nursing 11*, 2, 70–79.

Alaggia, R. and Millington, G. (2008) 'Male child sexual abuse: A phenomenology of betrayal.' *Clinical Social Work Journal 36*, 3, 265–275.

Alligood, M. and Tomey, A. (2006) *Nursing Theory – Utilization and Application* (3rd edition). Maryland Heights, MO: Mosby Elsevier.

Berney, L. and Blane, D. (2003) 'The lifegrid method of collecting retrospective information from people at older ages.' *Research Policy and Planning 21*, 2, 13–21.

Cameron, D., Kapur, R. and Campbell, P. (2005) 'Releasing the therapeutic potential of the psychiatric nurse: A human relations perspective of the nurse–patient relationship.' *Journal of Psychiatric and Mental Health Nursing 12*, 1, 64–74.

Cole, A. and Knowles, J. (2001) *Lives in Context: The Art of Life History Research.* Oxford: Altamira Press.

Dale, P. (1999) *Adults Abused as Children: Experiences of Counselling and Psychotherapy.* London: Sage.

Day, A., Thurlow, K. and Woolliscroft, J. (2003) 'Working with childhood sexual abuse: A survey of mental health professionals.' *Child Abuse and Neglect 27*, 2, 191–198.

Denzin, N. and Lincoln, Y. (2003) *Strategies of Qualitative Inquiry* (2nd edition). London: Sage.

Dhunpath, R. (2000) 'Life history methodology: "Narradigm" regained.' *International Journal of Qualitative Studies in Education 13*, 5, 543–551.

Draucker, C.B. and Petrovic, K. (1997) 'Therapy with male survivors of sexual abuse: The client perspective.' *Issues in Mental Health Nursing 18*, 2, 139–155.

Dube, S.R., Anda, R.F., Whitfield, C.L., Brown, D.W. *et al.* (2005) 'Long-term consequences of childhood sexual abuse by gender of victim.' *American Journal of Preventive Medicine 28*, 5, 430–438.

Edmond, T., Rubin, A. and Wambach, K.G. (1999) 'The effectiveness of EMDR with adult female survivors of childhood sexual abuse.' *Social Work Research 23*, 2, 103–116.

Edmond, T., Sloan, L. and McCarty, D. (2004) 'Sexual abuse survivors' perceptions of the effectiveness of EMDR and eclectic therapy.' *Research on Social Work Practice 14*, 4, 259–272.

George, J. (2002) *Nursing Theories* (5th edition). Upper Saddle River, NJ: Pretice Hall.

Goldman, J.D.G. and Padayachi, U.K. (2000) 'Some methodological problems in estimating incidence and prevalence in child sexual abuse research.' *The Journal of Sex Research 37*, 4, 305–314.

Harvey, M.R., Mischler, E.G., Koenen, K. and Harney, P.A. (2001) 'In the aftermath of sexual abuse: Making and remaking meaning in narratives of trauma and recovery.' *Narrative Inquiry 10*, 2, 291–311.

Havig, K. (2008) 'The health care experiences of adult survivors of child sexual abuse.' *Trauma, Violence, and Abuse 9*, 1, 19–33.

Holmes, G., Offen, L. and Waller, G. (1997) 'See no evil, hear no evil, speak no evil: Why do relatively few male victims of childhood sexual abuse receive help for abuse-related issues in adulthood?' *Clinical Psychology Review 17*, 1, 69–88.

Holmes, W.C. and Slap, G. (1998) 'Sexual abuse of boys: Definition, prevalence, correlates, sequelae, and management.' *Journal of the American Medical Association 280*, 21, 1855–1862.

Hopkins, J.E., Loeb, S.J. and Fick, D.M. (2009) 'Beyond satisfaction, what service users expect of inpatient mental health care: A literature review.' *Journal of Psychiatric and Mental Health Nursing 16*, 10, 927–937.

Hopper, J. (2008) *Sexual Abuse of Males: Prevalence, Possible Lasting Effects, and Resources.* Available at www.jimhopper.com. Accessed on 16 August 2012.

Jacobson, A. and Herald, C. (1990) 'The relevance of childhood sexual abuse to adult psychiatric inpatient care.' *Hospital and Community Psychiatry 41*, 2, 154–158.

Jacobson, A. and Richardson, B. (1987) 'Assault experiences of 100 psychiatric-inpatients – Evidence of the need for routine inquiry.' *American Journal of Psychiatry 144*, 7, 908–913.

Jennings, A. (1994) 'On being invisible in the mental health system.' *Journal of Mental Health Administration 21*, 4, 374–387.

Kia-Keating, M., Grossman, F.K., Sorsoli, L. and Epstein, M. (2005) 'Containing and resisting masculinity: Narratives of renegotiation among resilient male survivors of childhood sexual abuse.' *Psychology of Men and Masculinity 6*, 3, 169–185.

Lab, D.D. and Moore, E. (2005) 'Prevalence and denial of sexual abuse in a male psychiatric inpatient population.' *Journal of Traumatic Stress 18*, 4, 323–330.

Lab, D.D., Feigenbaum, J.D. and De Silva, P. (2000) 'Mental health professionals' attitudes and practices towards male childhood sexual abuse.' *Child Abuse and Neglect 24*, 3, 391–409.

Lisak, D., Hopper, J. and Song, P. (1996) 'Factors in the cycle of violence: Gender rigidity and emotional constriction.' *Journal of Traumatic Stress 9*, 4, 721–743.

Long, A. and Smyth, A. (1998) 'The role of mental health nursing in the prevention of child sexual abuse and the therapeutic care of survivors.' *Journal of Psychiatric and Mental Health Nursing 5*, 2, 129–136.

Nelson, S. (2001) *Beyond Trauma: Mental Health Care Needs of Women Survivors of Childhood Sexual Abuse.* Edinburgh: Edinburgh Association for Mental Health.

Nelson, S. (2004) 'Research with Psychiatric Patients: Knowing Their Own Minds?' In M. Smyth and E. Williamson (eds) *Researchers and Their 'Subjects': Ethics, Power, Knowledge and Consent.* Bristol: Policy Press.

Nelson, S. (2009) 'Care and support needs of men who survived childhood sexual abuse.' Report of a qualitative research project. Edinburgh: Centre for Research on Families and Relationships, University of Edinburgh.

Nelson, S. and Hampson, S. (2008) *Yes You Can! Working with Survivors of Childhood Sexual Abuse* (2nd edition). Edinburgh: Scottish Government.

Parry, O., Thomson, C. and Fowks, G. (1999) 'Life course data collection: Qualitative interviewing using the life grid.' *Sociological Research Online 4*, 2.

Read, J. and Fraser, A. (1998) 'Abuse histories of psychiatric inpatients: To ask or not to ask?' *Psychiatric Services 49*, 3, 355–359.

Read, J., Agar, K., Argyle, N. and Aderhold, V. (2003) 'Sexual and physical abuse during childhood and adulthood as predictors of hallucinations, delusions and thought disorder.' *Psychology and Psychotherapy: Theory, Research and Practice 76*, 1–22.

Romano, E. and De Luca, R.V. (2001) 'Male sexual abuse: A review of effects, abuse characteristics, and links with later psychological functioning.' *Aggression and Violent Behavior 6*, 1, 55–78.

Shapiro, F. (2001) *EMDR: Eye Movement Desensitization and Reprocessing: Basic Principles, Protocols and Procedures* (2nd edition). New York: Guilford Press.

Sorsoli, L., Kia-Keating, M. and Grossman, F.K. (2008) '"I keep that hush-hush": Male survivors of sexual abuse and the challenges of disclosure.' *Journal of Counseling Psychology 55*, 3, 333–345.

Strauss, A.L. and Corbin, J.M. (1998) *Basics of Qualitative Research: Techniques and Procedures for Developing Grounded Theory.* London: Sage.

Valente, S.M. (2005) 'Sexual abuse of boys.' *Journal of Child and Adolescent Psychiatric Nursing 18*, 1, 10.

Vardy, C. and Price, V. (1998) 'The utilization of Peplau's theory of nursing in working with a male survivor of sexual abuse.' *Journal of Psychiatric and Mental Health Nursing 5*, 2, 149–155.

Warne, T. and McAndrew, S. (2005) 'The shackles of abuse: Unprepared to work at the edges of reason.' *Journal of Psychiatric and Mental Health Nursing 12*, 6, 679–686.

Whitelaw, A. (2009) 'Why cause matters.' *Journal of Psychiatric and Mental Health Nursing 16*, 2, 206–210.

Whitfield, C.L., Dube, S.R., Felitti, V.J. and Anda, R.F. (2005) 'Adverse childhood experiences and hallucinations.' *Child Abuse and Neglect 29*, 7, 797–810.

Wilson, S., Cunningham-Burley, S., Bancroft, A., Backett-Milburn, K. and Masters, H. (2007) 'Young people, biographical narratives and the life grid: Young people's accounts of parental substance use.' *Qualitative Research 7*, 1, 135–151.

SUGGESTED READING

Apart from the papers and books referenced in this chapter, these suggestions give some valuable insights into the long-term effects of CSA on male survivors, and their own perceptions and experiences of living with CSA.

Etherington, K. (2000) *Narrative Approaches to Working with Adult Male Survivors of Childhood Sexual Abuse: The Client's, the Counsellor's, and the Researcher's Stories.* London: Jessica Kingsley Publishers.

Grossman, F., Sorsoli, L. and Kia-Keating, M. (2006) 'A gale force wind: Meaning making by male survivors of childhood sexual abuse.' *American Journal of Orthopsychiatry 76*, 4, 434–443.

Hunter, M. (1995) *Adult Survivors of Sexual Abuse: Treatment Innovations.* New York: Sage Publications.

Lisak, D. (1994) 'The psychological impact of sexual abuse: Content analysis of interviews with male survivors.' *Journal of Traumatic Stress 7*, 4, 525–548.

CHAPTER 5

RECOVERY THROUGH PSYCHODYNAMIC THERAPY
WORKING WITH MEN WHO HAVE EXPERIENCED SEXUAL VIOLATION

GEORGINA HOARE

This chapter is intended for professionals interested in expanding their understanding of working with men who have experienced sexual violation.[1] My hope is to encourage confidence in working with this often overlooked group by uncovering key themes and exploring some of the therapeutic challenges, using two case studies.[2] The setting of the clinical work is a leading UK charity in the field of male sexual violation in which I shall be referring to my experience as clinical services manager.

I will be focusing on psychodynamic theory and hope to illustrate through the clinical material my belief that, through awareness of unconscious communications and working with these, our clients are enabled to gain insight into their experiences which will ultimately guide their recovery and healing. My sense is that healing and recovery will mean very different things to different people. I believe healing for one client might be telling their partner, friends and family what happened to them and starting to feel less isolated in their experience. For another client, the process of either going through the criminal justice system or a report being made to another authority, therefore safeguarding children and adults, gives a sense of comfort in moving forward with their lives.

It is important for the reader to acknowledge universal impacts for any person affected by sexual violation, and while in this chapter I will give an overview of some of these, I shall primarily concentrate on those specific to the male client group.

---

1   The term *sexual violation* includes child sexual abuse, adult sexual assault and rape.
2   The case studies have been changed so that no clients are identifiable.

Issues specific to men

- Impact on sense of masculinity – the experience of being abused by a female can cause additional shame.
- Impact on sexuality/sexual identity – e.g. 'Did he make me gay?'
- Fear of being an abuser or being seen as an abuser (re societal stereotype).
- Physical arousal during sexual violation causes additional guilt and sense of complicity.
- Isolation – many men have never met another man who has had this experience, but they may also isolate themselves further.
- Men are more likely to exhibit acting out, such as violent or criminal behaviour, and therefore their vulnerability can be missed.

Many clients who self-refer for therapy commence full of confusion, including some of the above internalised beliefs. They may also wait many years before disclosing to anyone or getting any therapeutic support. Etherington comments: '"sexual victim" usually conjures up an image of a small, female, powerless creature trapped by a dominant male into a role of submission... Whereas it may be important to encourage a female to change "victim" to "survivor", it is equally important to encourage a man initially to accept his victimisation' (Etherington 2000, p.21).

There can be particular triggers leading clients to seek support:

Significant triggers for seeking therapy

- A significant ending or change (e.g. the break-up of a relationship; death or ill health of a parent or partner; or the end of a job/ education).
- Coming to terms with addictive behaviour (e.g. drug, alcohol, sexually compulsive behaviour).
- Something in the media/TV/radio or undergoing training (e.g. child protection or a topic which raises past memories).
- Considering becoming a parent, or their child is at the age they were when they were abused. This often relates to fear of being seen as a perpetrator.
- On-going confusion around sexuality or gender.
- Difficulties in sexual relationships/sexual dysfunction.

Typically many clients have difficulties with depression, anxiety, risk to themselves (e.g. self-harm, suicidal ideation or increased drug/ alcohol addiction), drug/alcohol history, interpersonal difficulties, psychosexual dysfunction and internalised homophobia. There are also more complex difficulties such as personality disorder, risk of violence towards others, bipolar disorder, schizophrenia, obsessive compulsive disorder (OCD) and post-traumatic stress disorder (PTSD).

This is a highly ambivalent group, and clients express anxiety about their readiness to be able to identify what happened to them and to explore the impact of their experiences. The word 'abuse' may not be what a child understood was happening to them; they may diminish it, or feel confused or complicit in what happened. Someone who experienced rape in a relationship, equally, may not use the word 'rape', as this word conjures up an image of violence by a stranger. Following the change in the Criminal Justice and Public Order Act 1994, the crime of rape was made equal for men and women. For years, legally, what happened to men was deemed a lesser offence, and my experience is that this change, alongside further changes which came in the Sexual Offences Act 2003, concretely validated many men's experiences.

Furthermore, my experience is that clients who engage well have a positive transference[3] to the organisation, which acts as the container[4] for many of their projections.[5] For example, there are some clients who have called the Helpline on and off over a period of years; the fact that the organisation exists and continues to exist for many years is proof that male sexual violation happens. Each year approximately 2000 men contact the organisation via its Helpline, website, email and office line. These overall figures are on the increase, in particular with clients initiating more support via online/email methods.

More than ever I believe that we are working with uncertainty and confusion; ambiguity can be at the heart of this therapeutic work and it is important for us to remember that clients are coming to find out what they do not know; there is both comfort and terror in the process that

---

3   *Transference* – represents a distortion or reproduction of emotions relating to repressed and unresolved (mostly unconscious) experiences left over from early relationships, especially parents, in childhood (Breuer and Freud 1991).

4   *Container* – Bion (1970) describes a dynamic relationship between the container and the contained, deriving from Klein's concept of projective identification, in which the projected element encounters a container or thinking function.

5   *Projection* – the location of feelings in others rather than oneself (often accompanied by splitting) (Hinshelwood 1994).

may unfold between you (Casement 1992). This sense of ambivalence and uncertainty is a key feature in my first case study of Ethan, below.

CASE STUDY 5.1: ETHAN

CASE STUDY OVERVIEW

Abuse experienced:
- Experienced rape by an older man as an adult.

Key themes addressed in therapy:
- Ambivalent attachment to therapist linked to abandonment by parents.
- History of risk to himself – alcoholism/drug addiction, suicidal ideation.
- Impact on feelings about his sexuality.

Ethan is a 38-year-old, white British man who presented with depression and experience of rape in his mid-twenties by Mickey, who was a friend of a friend. Ethan felt very unsure about engaging with therapy when we first met. He had also spent years going from one service to another. We agreed an initial contract of 12 weekly sessions of 50 minutes each, which we would then review together (with possible extension to maximum two years).

In the first couple of sessions Ethan spoke of being an only child, his parents divorcing when he was six years old, and living in foster care from his teens. He had memories of being very self-destructive around that time; for example: *'threatening to jump out of a window'*; *'I held a knife to my stomach and smashed things up'*. He told me this in a very matter-of-fact way, and I was aware of my counter-transference[6] and struck by how he was telling me of a very early trauma and memories of 'life and death' feelings and enactment.

Ethan ran away from his first foster family and then lived in bedsits throughout his teens and early twenties; he told me: *'It was messy, I was nowhere.'* I was aware that my counter-transference response was one of

---

6   *Counter-transference* – 'the analyst's reaction to the patient's transference, the material the patient brings in and the reactions of the patient to the analyst as a person'; a phenomenon that can include intense feelings which may feel inappropriate to the analytic situation (Heimann 1950, p.10).

concern, thinking about a lonely teenage boy who was not looked after or wanted by either parent.

Ethan did not do well in school, but after his first period of rehabilitation (rehab) for drug and alcohol addiction when he was 22 years old, he went back to college and now works in information technology (IT). He also indicated early on that he felt ambivalence about his sexuality. He first came out as gay when he was aged 17 years and met an older man in his forties in rehab. At the commencement of therapy he had not been in a relationship for some years.

How I work is to note my counter-transference and try and make sense of what might be unconscious communications from my clients. With Ethan the transference felt very alive from the first contact, and it was my impression that I was quickly put in the position of someone who was uncaring or neglectful in some way.

GOOD PRACTICE POINTS

- Be aware of both conscious and unconscious communications from clients.
- Think about the unconscious communications, how they manifest and how they make you feel (counter-transference).
- Ask yourself what your client is telling you through their communication in this moment.

Exploring the meaning of risk-taking behaviour

Ethan spoke about feeling suicidal in the past and acknowledged that the risk to himself was heightened by his weekly binge-drinking and daily cannabis smoking. My thinking about his addiction was that it was a way of blocking out everything, a refusal to think, feel and make connections. The drugs and alcohol were objects that he could control; they are always there and never disappoint. I think that Ethan's bulimic pattern of alcohol/drug abuse indicated a huge ambivalence in taking in or allowing dependence on a good object.[7] Therefore it was my view that he had a dependence on a bad object (something bad in his mind). How this typically presented in our work together was that he indicated a huge ambivalence in allowing himself to make use of me as someone

7   Klein describes the process of splitting in the paranoid schizoid position, in which good and bad objects are split off, alongside part object relating (Hinshelwood 1994).

who could be consistently helpful and supportive in his mind (a good object).

I was able to make use of my awareness about this by making reference to these different, conflicting parts of him within our sessions. He was quite responsive to this and told me how he felt aware that there was a part of him that wanted to stop drinking and taking drugs, but also a part of him that was sabotaging this. As a result of our discussions he started to attend a drop-in meeting at a drug and alcohol centre within a lesbian, gay, bisexual and transgender (LGBT) service, and also had more regular contact with his general practitioner.

When Ethan started to get this additional support, a split manifested in which I noticed David (his keyworker at the drop-in) was idealised, and I was made to feel second-best in comparison. I would regularly hear how helpful David was, how David understood him and how disappointed Ethan was when the sessions with David had to end. David was also a gay man, and I wondered about Ethan's interest in him. I was most aware of my counter-transference response of annoyance, but also wondered about the addition of a third person or father figure. In a later session I had the opportunity to make an observation about this and commented that perhaps Ethan had a wish that two people could think about him together. Ethan was quite thoughtful after this comment and I noticed real sadness in his silence afterwards. It left me thinking about his early life in which he had not experienced two adults who could think about him together. It is my view that what he was enacting with me was an experience in which one parent was played off against the other.

GOOD PRACTICE POINTS

- Helping a client become aware of split-off parts of themselves which we think about together is a key tool in psychodynamic work.
- This way of working can increase a client's capacity to make sense of their experiences and integrate the learning from their therapy.

Impact on sexuality and sexual relationships

I was mindful of the fact that when Ethan spoke of his experience of sexual relationships and sexual violence, he was telling me, a female therapist. What I noticed was that he indicated that he had thoughts about what he imagined my sexuality to be and that he was very aware of our difference in gender and the impact this had on him. Over several sessions we were able to explore his fears. He expressed a belief that a gay male therapist would not be able to hold a professional boundary with him, would be unable to stop himself wanting to have sex with him. It was as if, in Ethan's mind, being gay meant that there are no boundaries around sexual relationships, that no-one is able to say 'no'. We were also able to think about this concretely in relation to his fantasies about David, a gay man.

In a later session I commented: 'I think you fear that I too may not be able to hold the professional boundaries.' I was aware of a sense of relief that this fear had been voiced and could now be spoken about. This interpretation seemed to help Ethan and he was able to talk about the shame he felt about his body betraying him during the rape by Mickey, because he became erect and ejaculated. We were then able to explore further his mixed feelings; that some part of him identified as having been raped, whilst another part of him felt that he had colluded with something. It was clear to me that he needed to feel that it was safe for him to start to explore these mixed feelings without fear of judgment.

It was my impression throughout that Ethan's struggle could be indicative of the paranoid schizoid position;[8] the work between us was about trying to help him become aware of these splits.

GOOD PRACTICE POINT

Being aware of a client's fantasies about us (their therapist) and being able to explore them together can give us insight into key concerns.

When Ethan talked about his past sexual relationships there was little sense of love or desire; he always described his sexual experiences in a part object way and referred to violent role-play in sex. I was aware of his lack of desire when he spoke about sex, as if this had got split off in some way. It also became apparent that he had had repeated experiences as an adult in which he had sex when he had not wanted to (although, interestingly, he did not define these experiences as rape).

8   Klein describes the paranoid schizoid position as including the unconscious processes of splitting (including idealisation/denigration), projection and projective identification, and defending against envy and omnipotent control (Hinshelwood 1994).

It was almost as if he had learnt that this was what being a gay man was; the sense of being able to consent had got lost.

I commented on a pattern he had noticed of not being very physically attracted to his partners: 'perhaps it feels dangerous to have a relationship with someone you are sexually attracted to'. Ethan was thoughtful, but agreed that he did not know what that might be like, that it felt scary to consider this. The more we explored this together, the clearer it became that, for Ethan, sexual desire seemed dangerous because it had become closely linked to violence, which he had eroticised in his sexual role-play with previous partners. I felt it important to hold in my mind the possibility that he might also fear that something powerful and sadistic might happen between us.

I thought about the significance of Ethan continuing to have a friendship with Mickey; that it was as if Ethan was telling himself he had chosen this, that it was not a sexually abusive relationship, in order to manage his defences and the pain of the realisation of what had happened to him.

In thinking about our work together I am aware that at times I had difficulty recalling information, and on several occasions noticed finding it hard to stay focused for the first half of the session; I felt as though I mirrored Ethan's fragmentation. It was as if it was hard for me to hold onto a state of mind in which I could retain my separateness and find a space to think helpfully. At these times it was not possible to allow meaning to exist; there was an obliteration or attack on thinking, or capacity to think or make links (Bion 1959). I found it helpful to stay in touch with my internal supervisor[9] when I became aware that this had started to happen, and I was mindful of thinking about what Ethan might be trying to block out through the projective process (Casement 1992). I wondered, too, if this experience might relate to the transference as a potentially neglectful mother; someone who could not hold him in mind, or whom he could not trust with his difficult feelings.

Prior to session 11 there had been no planned or unplanned breaks. Near the end of the session we were talking about how Ethan found it difficult to manage the break between the sessions. I commented that perhaps by attending regularly he was getting in touch with the needy part of him. He told me: *'There are 167 hours until the next session.'* It was as if the end of the session was experienced concretely as a rejection, and I think that Ethan let me know that he felt vulnerable; the spaces between the sessions were particularly hard for him to bear; he had

---

9   *Internal supervisor* indicates the therapist's capacity to have a third position, a state of mind in which they can both experience the unconscious communications but also be able to consider a possible interpretation through trial identification before commenting (Casement 1992).

to take over the mothering, therefore telling me about his need for a strong container.

However, there was one very unfortunate situation in which another client walked into the room near the end of our session. This client appeared quite confused and stated that they were sure that this was their usual therapy room. I was aware that I moved into a more active role to manage this, before Ethan and I could continue with the remainder of his session. Ethan joked about this sarcastically afterwards, whilst also making it clear that he experienced it as unprofessional and uncontaining. It was only afterwards that I was able to get in touch with my anger that this had happened.

After this Ethan contacted me the following week to let me know that he was ill, then left a voicemail telling me that he did not wish to continue, stating: *'It was foolish to begin in the first place and I wish I hadn't. At the end of the day I would rather get stoned – I just can't find anything worth giving it up for.'* I felt saddened by this communication; that it was a very triumphant and angry end. I felt in my counter-transference that I was seen as powerless, and I was also aware of feeling angry with the part of him that had engaged well in the therapy, but that seemed unable to connect to come back and think about the meaning of what had happened.

I communicated with Ethan acknowledging that it had been an unfortunate experience, and although he wished to end his therapy I suggested that he attend to try and have a different kind of ending to the one he was anticipating; however, he did not wish to return at that time. I think that Ethan had allowed a certain amount of healing to take place by sharing some of his thoughts and experiences, but it had started to feel painful for him gaining some insight, and he was not ready at that point to continue the journey of his recovery together.

Exactly a year later he got back in contact and told me that he would like to return for further therapy. We met in the same room, and at first he seemed anxious about this and made a joke about whether we would be interrupted again. He told me that when he had ended therapy before he had also stopped all contact with his mother, which seemed significant, given my prior thought about the maternal transference. During this initial meeting we agreed a contract of 12 weekly sessions of 50 minutes each, which could be extended after review.

It was clear that something had become freed up by the break in therapy and Ethan indicated that he had gone away and internalised some of the issues we had started to explore. I too noticed that I had been able to reflect on what had happened and the impact this had had on me. For example, I thought about how Ethan came to therapy not expecting a good-enough object and used me in some way as a dispenser of therapy, rather than someone that he could depend on, miss and need. I also wondered about him protecting me from his destructiveness.

In this second period of therapy Ethan started to be more able to explore his experience of rape and his concerns about his sexual experiences. He told me that Mickey was someone who had been around for years, ever since his parents' divorce. He revealed an environment in which he was young and vulnerable and over time felt he had become complicit in something with Mickey; a secret between them that finally led to the rape. Ethan seemed to feel relieved to tell me all of this, as if he had gone away and thought about his childhood and was starting to piece things together too. We were able to think about the muddle in his mind about his sense of responsibility and confusion about what happened to him.

We were also able to explore how he was becoming aware of how he had tried to split off the various difficulties he had had for years, with his solution of taking one problem to one person/organisation (e.g. drug addiction), and another problem to another place. We talked about the importance of him being able to get help in thinking about the whole of him with one person, and how hard it was for him to trust someone to do this.

I believe that something healing happened both during and after his first period of therapy. Ethan showed that he was able to internalise something from his experience with me and come back to try and continue to explore this together. At the time the intrusion into his session was experienced quite concretely, but Ethan's capacity to be able to move into what one might consider more depressive position functioning,[10] and think about what got stirred up within him, enabled us to continue to work together to make sense of this.

I would like to now move on to my second case study, Reece. I have deliberately chosen this very different case example because, alongside the overall isolation of male sexual violation in general, abuse by a female abuser is often overlooked or diminished.

CASE STUDY 5.2: REECE

CASE STUDY OVERVIEW

Abuse experienced:

---

10   In the transition to and within the depressive position there is more ambivalence in which a client is able to hold onto an increasingly realistic view of the part-objects (Hinshelwood 1994).

- Sexual abuse by a female cousin (four years older) from the age of eight for several years.

Key themes in therapy:

- Impact of disclosure to wife and feelings about being a parent.
- Focus on how to disclose to his family and friends.
- Difficulty in understanding and managing the therapeutic boundaries.
- The challenge of working through erotic transference with a female therapist.

Reece is 48 years old and married with three children, all aged below 15 years. He is an only child who grew up in Canada and has had a successful career as a history teacher. He made contact soon after telling his wife about the abuse he experienced as a child. We worked together for a total of six months.

This disclosure some years into his marriage came as a result of his fear that his wife was being unfaithful to him, as he had seen the name of an ex-lover of hers in an email. It became apparent quite quickly in the therapy that this theme of unfaithfulness was linked in his mind to the abuse he had experienced. Additionally he indicated that the age gap between his own son and daughter (four years) was similar to the age gap between him and his cousin. This connection in his mind raised a great deal of anxiety for him about his own experiences, alongside fear about his parenting and of being seen by others as a potential perpetrator.

Working with erotic transference
From the start of therapy Reece made it clear that he found it very difficult to manage the boundaries; for example, he did not wear a watch, would not arrive on time, then would appear shocked when it was time to end after 50 minutes, and start a conversation at the door. He was clearly very intelligent, and I often felt bombarded by the fact that he spoke non-stop, and also by his regular references to academic literature that I felt I was expected to know, but often did not. So I noticed feeling rather stupid and often denigrated to the position of a not-knowing therapist.

There was a real sense of confusion in Reece's mind around 'who was the perpetrator?' and 'who was the victim?' and he had read a great deal to try and understand this. The primary sexual contact with his cousin involved him performing oral sex on her. On a number of occasions he described in great detail how his female cousin would tell him what to do so that she could reach orgasm. It was clear that he described an experience of feeling dominated by a powerful woman and I wondered how much of this dynamic he was bringing to our encounter.

I was conscious of having a very strong counter-transference response. For example, I suddenly became aware of how small the room felt and noticed myself pushing myself into the back of the chair as if I wanted to get away from him; something felt very dangerous. I also became aware of an anxiety in the language I used in the sessions with him, as if something very intrusive had been projected into me and I could not hold onto the capacity to think clearly.

I found it particularly helpful to think of Bion's idea of there being 'two frightened people in the room', which was very much my experience (Bion 1990). I observed that in these moments it was as if I was being experienced as a potential abuser, and our conversations could be felt quite concretely by him as another kind of 'oral sex'. For example, I noted that in the therapeutic frame (such as time and fee) were rules that at times he would concretely indicate as something rather familiar, therefore tantalising, seductive and sexually arousing; rules to push against. I was pushed into the role of female abuser in the transference, someone who had to be seduced, but also hated as someone cruel and abusive. What was confusing for Reece was that I was a different kind of 'cousin', an unknown kind; someone who was not an abuser, but it felt as if he always had to find ways to test this out.

I had this strong sense that he went away feeling that he had had 'good sex', got what he had come for, and he would regularly report how helpful the therapy sessions were. I, in comparison, was aware of a strong counter-transference response of rage and irritation and feeling as if we were speaking a different language. I also felt that I received a strong message that any mixed or more confusing feelings were at first very firmly dismissed.

Working through an impasse

After our first planned break, ten sessions in, I returned to find that Reece had contacted the organisation and asked to see someone else in my absence. I experienced this as a real attack, but was also relieved that the organisation had held the boundary that this was not possible.

It was clear that this break of two weeks had been experienced as very traumatic, and when Reece returned he spoke almost non-stop, telling me how difficult the break had been and that he had been unable to manage. He cited several dramatic situations related to his family and relationships that had been a challenge. I felt there was a strong message that 'I can't cope without you', but also that he pushed me to treat him as special; he wanted an extra therapy session. I wondered what it meant to him to get a woman to 'do his bidding', and I wondered about a split in his mind in which I was idealised as a saviour with all the answers, but could just as well be denigrated as an abusive, abandoning woman.

I became aware during this period of therapy that there was a huge resistance. I observed feeling bombarded with information he seemed to require me to remember in specific detail (usually dates/times/names), which he would later refer to and check whether I had remembered. I also noticed a counter-transference reaction of finding it hard to stay awake. Interestingly, it was during this period that Reece started to talk about his father for the first time, and his anger towards him for having left when Reece was five years old. There seemed to be two strong, opposing messages that I was receiving – that it was important for him that I heard and remembered important details in his life, and that it was an affront if I forgot. Conversely, I was 'supposed to know…but not explore', a strong message of ambivalence.

Reece spoke quite manically at times about an incident in which he had read a text from a male friend to his wife which ended in 'xx', and then later seen this man's eyes on his wife in an admiring way. It was clear that Reece experienced this as something his wife had wanted and enjoyed, and treated it as if she were unfaithful to him. By my commenting on and observing his feelings and finally making a more direct interpretation, Reece was able to uncover the connection with his past. What came out of this was a memory that the sexual abuse with his cousin had come to an end when she had got a boyfriend. Reece remembered feeling rejected in this moment, as if she had been unfaithful to him.

It took some time for us to be able to get to this link together because Reece seemed quite obsessional about the story with his wife, and I felt as if I was being told I 'just wasn't getting it' for some time. I also thought about the idea of there being transference to me as a woman who was seen as unfaithful to him every time I ended the therapy session or saw another client; I was then unavailable to him. I experienced him as a very needy baby, insatiable.

Through thinking about these difficult dynamics and making use of my counter-transference, over time there was some movement from the sense of impasse and I noticed that Reece started to have empathy for his cousin for the first time, alongside his longstanding anger. He was able to start to think, at first intellectually, about how the break-up of both their families had led to an environment in which both children needed to feel close, to feel cared for, and that this had led to something sexual happening between them.

Reece started to keep a journal in order to help him feel contained outside of the therapy sessions and he also expressed a wish to be able to share some of these thoughts with close family. At times he brought his journal to his therapy and it was interesting to note that it contained a great deal of anger, although this anger was at first kept out of the therapy.

A significant piece of writing was to his father, expressing the rage and pain of a young boy who grew up feeling his father did not want him, but preferred other half-siblings. I noted that some accounts in his journal were of things that had not happened in his therapy and I was aware of a feeling of being manipulated to collude with something false. However, I think he needed me to see this false act; that he was duplicitous. It was as if he had turned the recounted story into what really happened, and I wondered if reality was too much for him, so that he needed to change the reality to make it more bearable. It is interesting that I took the decision not to challenge this (which is not typically my way of working), but my instinct was that this would produce a different dialogue at that point in the therapy and that his use of the journal had been very cathartic for him, although it had not all been accurate.

Our work eventually enabled Reece to contact his cousin and say how he felt about what had happened. She responded and indicated that she too was seeking help, and conveyed a wish for them to be able to stay in contact. Additionally he disclosed about the abuse to his father, although he had been very fearful of this some months before, expecting a cold and uncaring response. We thought together about how he might start this difficult conversation, and he reported that his father had cried when he had told him about what had happened. This response was one he had never imagined possible, and helped him enormously in feeling heard and understood.

It was around six weeks later that Reece started to talk about ending the therapy; there was a real sense that he had got what he had come for at this point. He spoke repeatedly about the sense of relief that his secret was out in the open, and a sense of hope for the future as a husband and father.

I have a strong sense that Reece had not really known what to make of therapy and his eyes were opened to a very complex and sometimes uncomfortable experience. Reece started to reach out and gain support from others and conveyed a sense that, whilst at the start of therapy he had had no-one to talk to about this, there were now a number of people he felt he could trust to share his feelings. He indicated that he was now more robust and resilient; and despite engaging at the start in a familiar pattern of seductive behaviour, he was able to end in a different way. There was a shift in his relationship with me which allowed him to feel more contained and able to move on in his recovery with others alongside him.

CONCLUSION

The trauma of sexual violation can often result in a breakdown of containment, and I believe that the preceding case studies illustrate how working psychodynamically allows for effective containment of many of the anxieties and complexities this client group presents (Garland 1998). For example, with Reece we explored together how managing boundaries and erotic transference was crucial to understanding his experience. With Ethan, enactment of the abusive cycle within the transference of the therapeutic relationship was also played out in his sexual life around his issues with power and authority. In both cases there were issues around ambivalence and isolation, as well as fears of being seen as, or becoming, perpetrators.

As an ending note, whilst the focus of this chapter has not allowed time to explore the organisation in more detail, it is my view that exploring the unconscious at work is vital. The impact of working with issues such as the cycle of abuse (between victim/perpetrator) and power and authority is such that these issues can all be acted out within the staff team or organisation (Obholzer and Roberts 1994). I believe that it is important, both for the individual practitioners and for the organisation, to foster a culture of reflective practice in which these issues can be thought about together, in order to enhance the overall containment of the organisation, its staff and clients.

REFERENCES

Bion, W.R. (1959) 'Attacks on linking.' *International Journal of Psycho-Analysis 40*, 5–6, 308.

Bion, W.R. (1970) *Attention and Interpretation*. London: Karnac Books.

Bion, W.R. (1990) *Brazilian Lectures. Parts 1 and 2*. London: Karnac Books.

Breuer, J. and Freud, S. (1991) *Studies on Hysteria*. London: Penguin.

Casement, P. (1992) *Learning from the Patient*. New York: Guilford Press.

Criminal Justice and Public Order Act 1994. London: HMSO.

Etherington, K. (2000) 'When the Victim is Male: Working with Men who were Sexually Abused in Childhood.' In H. Kemshall and J. Pritchard (eds) *Good Practice in Working with Victims of Violence*. London: Jessica Kingsley Publishers.

Garland, C. (1998) *Understanding Trauma: A Psychoanalytic Approach*. London: Karnac Books.

Heimann, P. (1989) 'Counter-transference.' In P. Heimann and M. Tonnesman (eds) *About Children and Children-no-Longer: Collected Papers 1942–1980*. London: Routledge.

Hinshelwood, R.D. (1994) *Clinical Klein*. London: Free Association Books.

Obholzer, A. and Roberts, V.Z. (eds) (1994) *The Unconscious at Work: Individual and Organisational Stress in the Human Services*. London: Routledge.

Sexual Offences Act 2003. London: HMSO.

SUGGESTED READING

Etherington, K. (2000) *Narrative Approaches to Working with Adult Male Survivors of Child Sexual Abuse*. London: Jessica Kingsley Publishers.

Gartner, R.B. (1999) *Betrayed as Boys: Psychodynamic Treatment of Sexually Abused Men*. New York: Guilford Press.

Grubman-Black, S. (1990) *Broken Boys/Mending Men*. New Jersey: Blackburn Press.

Lew, M. (2004) *Victims No Longer: The Classic Guide for Men Recovering from Sexual Child Abuse*. New York: HarperCollins.

McCluskey, U. and Hooper, C. (2000) *Psychodynamic Perspectives on Abuse*. London: Jessica Kingsley Publishers.

Mezey, G. and King, M. (2000) *Male Victims of Sexual Assault* (2nd edition). New York: Oxford University Press.

USEFUL ORGANISATIONS

SurvivorsUK – supports adult men over 18 who have experienced sexual violence at any time in their lives, by providing a national helpline and low-cost counselling and group therapy.
Ground Floor
34 Great James St
London
WC1N 3HB
Telephone: 020 7404 6234
Website: www.survivorsuk.org

The Survivors Trust – the umbrella organisation for more than 130 organisations working with male and female survivors of sexual abuse across the UK.
Unit 2
Eastlands Court Business Centre
St Peter's Road
Rugby
Warwickshire
CV21 3QP
Telephone: 01788 550554
Website: www.thesurvivorstrust.org

NAPAC (The National Association for People Abused in Childhood)
PO Box 63632
London
SW9 1BF
Telephone: 0800 085 3330
Website: www.napac.org.uk

DABS – information source for people who have been abused.
Directory and Book Services (DABS)
69 Woodberry Way
Walton on the Naze
Essex
CO14 8EW
Telephone: 01255 851115
Website: www.dabs.uk.com

Boarding School Survivors – information and support for survivors from the boarding school system.
Website: www.boardingschoolsurvivors.co.uk

MOSAC – supporting non-abusing parents and carers of abused children.
141 Greenwich High Road
London
SE10 8JA
Telephone: 020 8293 9990
Website: www.mosac.org.uk

Stopitnow! – aims to prevent child sexual abuse and also supports adults who have worrying thoughts about abusing children.
Helpline: 0808 1000 900
Website: www.stopitnow.org.uk

CHAPTER 6

Surviving Sex Trafficking
Recovery and Healing

KRISTA HOFFMAN

Body autonomy is a fundamental right of all people. Sex trafficking violates this right by restricting or eliminating the self-determination of a person surviving in sex trafficking, including the right to determine who touches, accesses, and receives sexual gratification from their bodies. In order to understand how to effectively assist people who have survived this crime through recovery and healing, it is important to understand the dynamics of sex trafficking, coping strategies often employed by survivors, and the impact of this form of trauma on survivors' outlook on the self, others, and the human experience.

The experience of survivors of sex trafficking is unique. Their victimization is not solely in the sexual acts committed against them but also in the lack of control, the numerous acts of betrayal, the isolation in a lifestyle of perpetual sexual abuse, and the selling of their persons as a commodity to be used over and over again. Advocates for survivors[1] can assist them with recovery after victimization in coming through the stages of initial identification as a victim of sex trafficking, medical procedures, being mislabeled as a criminal, counseling, and healing. This assistance empowers a survivor of sex trafficking in reclaiming control over their own body autonomy and self-determination.

After the initial recovery, survivors of sex trafficking may need assistance in the longer process of healing from the trauma that was inflicted upon them. Many people who have survived sex trafficking may meet the diagnosis of complex trauma or "disorder of extreme stress not otherwise specified" (DESNOS) (Evans-Weaver 2012) which refers to a condition resulting from multiple exposures to one or more traumas (Courtois 2008). This is not to be confused with

---

1   The role of advocates will be discussed in depth in the chapter. For information about legal advocates, direct service advocates, and outreach advocates also see www.pcar.org.

post-traumatic stress disorder (PTSD), which is a result of exposure to a single trauma (Foa, Keane, and Friedman 2000). An understanding and experience of survivors who have experienced complex trauma is beneficial in working with sex trafficking victims during the healing process. Sex-based therapies such as sexual scripting have been used to assist those who have survived sex trafficking in their healing process (Evans-Weaver 2012). The important thing to remember and project to survivors is that healing is possible after sex trafficking.

HUMAN TRAFFICKING

Human trafficking is when a person is recruited, transported, transferred, harbored, or received by another to be used ultimately for labor or services (US Department of State 2011). The term "trafficking" seems to imply movement from one destination to another. However, for a situation to be trafficking, movement is not necessary. For example, if a 14-year-old child is sold by their parent to a landlord for him to sexually abuse in exchange for a month's rent being waived, this is trafficking. The child was never transported anywhere, but was sold sexually for something of value (rent money), and this is what makes it trafficking.

Human trafficking is a diverse issue that can be found in almost every country (United Nations Office on Drugs and Crime (UNODC) 2009). It is the second largest criminal enterprise in the world, second only to drug trafficking (US Department of State 2011). It is a crime under international law and many national and regional legal systems (INTERPOL 2012). In most countries, for it to be considered an illegal act of human trafficking, there needs to be an element of force, fraud, or coercion (UNODC 2009). In cases involving minors there typically does not need to be an element of force, fraud, or coercion for most countries to consider it human trafficking. Currently, not all countries have anti-human trafficking laws. Regardless of the situation of human trafficking being legally defined as a crime in a particular country, the acts a person is subjected to through human trafficking are traumatic. The nature of human trafficking reduces humans to the condition of a commodity, with limited or no autonomy, to be used by others for a profit or servitude.

SEX TRAFFICKING

Sex trafficking is when a person is recruited, transported, transferred, harbored, or received by others, ultimately to be sold and used as a sexual commodity (UNODC 2009). Where and how people are sold as a commodity in sex trafficking is largely dependent upon the social, legal, and economic dynamics within any given community (Lyles, Cohen, and Brown 2009). When a person is sold to someone who uses them for their own sexual gratification, historically this action has been called prostitution. The term "prostitution" is incorrect when describing a situation in which a person is sold to another to be used sexually, when the person being sold is physically forced, mentally forced, coerced, deceived, a minor under the age of 18, or being used sexually to pay off a debt. If consent is not given freely, and without implied or actual force or coercion, it is not prostitution; it is sex trafficking.

The demand for sex trafficking is driven by those who wish to purchase another sexually. In any given population there are certain adults who, due to poverty, limited employment options, preference, or addictions to controlled substances, become involved in prostitution to make money to sustain themselves in life. This number of adults meets the demand for purchased sex in their areas. However, when the demand increases, exploitive individuals identify the area as having a market for more people to be sold sexually. Therefore, whereas previously there had been prostitution, now traffickers become involved and identify people in the area to be trafficked, or bring them in from other locations. A major way demand increases is with an influx of groups of transient males, particularly those without family ties in the area (Estes and Weiner 2009). These populations can include any group dynamic that is predominately male, including:

- military populations
- truck drivers
- tourists traveling with the interest or intent to purchase sexual acts
- male migrant workers
- traveling businessmen
- territorial and organized gangs, and terrorist groups.

Venues for sex trafficking

These can include:
- brothels
- massage parlors
- truck stops
- agricultural migrant camps

- military camps
- internet sites
- on the streets
- hotels/motels
- homes—being sold by spouse, parents, other family members, or caregivers in exchange for drugs, money, rent, and other items of monetary value.

VICTIMS

Victims of sex trafficking can be children and adults, females and males. People who commit sex trafficking target those who are perceived as having vulnerabilities, and a lack of physical security (Estes and Weiner 2009; Smith, Healy Vardaman, and Snow 2009; UNODC 2009). Because of this targeting, poverty increases the vulnerability of certain populations including the homeless, immigrants, refugees, people displaced due to natural and manmade disasters, children looking for educational opportunities, children and adults fleeing abusive homes, and those looking for work outside of their communities to sustain their families.

VICTIM RESPONSE

The emotional and physical traumas of human trafficking are felt differently by each individual (Herman 1992). Victims do not cease living while they are victims. They continue to cope and survive. Coping and survival take many forms; depending on the individual, the person may, for example:

- turn inward and shut down emotionally
- turn to self-medicating physical and emotional pain by using drugs and/or alcohol
- lash outward at people and the world that allows such abuse to occur
- try to remain optimistic and make the best of the situation
- accept their fate as part of a cultural or religious upbringing
- come to feel they can only rely on themselves
- be overwhelmed with hopelessness that they will ever be free of suffering.

(Adapted from van der Kolk 1989)

These reactions need to be understood by those who are working with victims. By understanding and not judging why victims may turn to these forms of coping, advocates and therapists can better assist survivors of sex trafficking in discovering healthier tools and techniques to establish control and equilibrium.

RECOVERY
Advocates

GOOD PRACTICE POINT

Advocates are an essential component in assisting survivors of sex trafficking through the recovery process. The role of the advocate is two-fold:

1. education of communities
2. empowerment for survivors.

To assist victims of sex trafficking in recovery, advocates take on various roles, depending on the situation specific to each survivor. They can:

- work as community educators
- raise awareness in their communities
- be a voice for survivors' rights and respect while negotiating the criminal justice and medical systems
- provide counseling.

The various roles of advocates are a reflection of the services survivors find helpful during recovery.

Advocates need to meet victims where they are at emotionally. The recovery process is about empowerment by helping a survivor to reclaim control and make decisions on what s/he wants for their life. It is about providing them with healthy tools and techniques to cope with the initial aftermath of trauma and possible triggers—such as smell, sound, or touch—that may remind them of past victimizations. When survivors are empowered, they have a voice, and their voices help in informing systems on how to better identify, assist, and counsel survivors of sex trafficking.

Community awareness

An advocate can provide awareness programs to better inform communities on how to identify possible cases of sex trafficking, and what to do after the identification has been made. Despite the historical background and ever-growing prevalence of human trafficking, many communities are still ignorant of the realities of the crime. If people in a position to recognize sex trafficking are not educated on the dynamics and conditions, they miss the opportunity to identify people profiting as traffickers, people surviving victimization in sex trafficking, and people who sexually abuse these survivors. When communities are better educated they are more empathetic and supportive of survivors. This empathy and support can be extremely helpful for survivors in finding empowerment during the recovery process.

Negotiating the criminal justice system

An advocate's support and guidance during a survivor's interactions with the criminal justice system are very important in the recovery process. Many victims of human trafficking will first be discovered by law enforcement through investigations of prostitution. Most survivors will not identify themselves to law enforcement. Some of the reasons for this are:

- threats of violence or intimidation by traffickers
- shame over what they have done, or has been done to them, while surviving
- fear that law enforcement will further victimize them
- lack of awareness that what is being done to them is illegal and that there is help available.

Advocates are instrumental in stepping in and assisting in identification, service delivery, and ensuring that survivors are treated with respect.

In cases where survivors are criminally charged for prostitution, they are in reality being charged for the sexual abuse that is being done to them. This is extremely problematic. These charges re-victimize a person who is being chronically abused, mislabel them with the stigma of criminality, and reinforce control tactics used by traffickers who claim law enforcement will never believe a survivor if they reach out for help. All these effects further traumatize survivors emotionally, isolate them from much-needed assistance, and allow sex traffickers who sell survivors, and people who purchase survivors for sexual abuse, to escape accountability.

Advocates are trained to identify those who are surviving in sex trafficking, and how to advocate on a survivor's behalf to criminal justice professionals. This will include law enforcement officers, prosecutors, and judges, so that survivors are treated with the dignity and respect all crime victims deserve. Once survivors are correctly identified, criminal charges may be brought against the offenders. The criminal justice system can be very confusing and intimidating. Therefore, advocates are trained on the process so they can explain terms, legal motions, and the various steps in the process. When advocates can predict and prepare survivors on what the process will be like in moving forward with the criminal justice system, it decreases their confusion and feelings of being overwhelmed. Additionally, advocates can let survivors know they are entitled to access legal representation, have a right to voice complaints and concerns, and are allowed to determine for themselves to what degree they will be involved in the criminal justice system.

GOOD PRACTICE POINT

An important part of recovery is for survivors to be empowered and in control of their own destiny. An understanding of the criminal justice process and the role they may choose to play in it can be very empowering.

Medical systems

For many survivors of sex trafficking, empowerment can also be felt in gaining access to medical care. Medical care is often denied to victims of sex trafficking, or limited to being provided only when conditions affect the survivor's ability to earn money. Survivors may suffer multiple sexually transmitted infections, broken bones, and head trauma, and never be allowed access to medical care. This is very dehumanizing and physically agonizing to someone in need of care. They may internalize the neglect as their own fault, their lot in life, or believe that they are not worthy of care. If they are encountered by advocates, law enforcement, or medical staff, it is important they are provided with medical care, options, and safety. It is crucial to ensure survivors receive the treatment they need and are treated with respect. Advocates need to collaborate with emergency rooms and free health clinics, and to educate them on indications of sex trafficking so medical personnel can better identify them if they do happen to come in for care. Additionally, advocates should advocate for medical personnel to call them directly if a survivor presents at their facility.

GOOD PRACTICE POINT

Medical care is a crucial step in the recovery process. People who have survived sex trafficking and find themselves at a point where they are able to determine for themselves that they want medical care and what that care looks like are on the path of recovery.

Medical advocates can assist people who have survived sex trafficking in:

- finding accessible health care
- learning what treatment options are available
- gaining treatments for existing conditions, including possible sexually transmitted infections
- obtaining the option of preventative care, including contraceptives
- having evidence of sexual abuse collected during a forensic rape exam.

Counseling

Advocates will listen without judgment and enable the survivor to work through the anger, fear, guilt, sadness, and confusion so often felt after sexual abuse. They are trained in:

- victim behavior
- effective communication
- counseling techniques
- crisis intervention.

In some jurisdictions communications between advocates and survivors are considered privileged communications. In these jurisdictions advocates cannot be called upon by any court or law enforcement entity to share information a survivor has confided to them. Privileged communications can help survivors feel confident in confiding to advocates because they know what they confide will remain private. Therefore, survivors can talk and work through embarrassing and conflicting emotions that otherwise they would be hesitant in revealing to another person. It is very important in the recovery process for survivors to be able to express themselves without fear of judgment or exposure.

Crisis intervention

The forms of counseling advocates can employ are determined by the needs of the survivor. Advocates are trained in crisis intervention and can assist survivors in crisis via a hotline or in-person meetings. Survivors will have moments of doubt, shame, terror, overwhelming grief and loss, and hopelessness. They need to know a non-judgmental counselor is only a phone call away at all times. All this forms part of the recovery process.

GOOD PRACTICE POINTS

- Hotlines should be available 24 hours a day and 7 days a week whenever possible.
- Access to immediate emotional support is crucial during the recovery process and in helping victims to get from one day to the next.

Counseling sessions

Frequent counseling sessions with advocates are also important during the recovery process. Set appointments give survivors a time and place in the near future that they can work towards meeting. During these counseling sessions advocates work with survivors in determining what stressors in their environment are most likely to trigger negative emotional and physical responses as a result of the trauma they experienced. Once triggers have been identified, healthy strategies can be developed that the survivor can employ to help decrease the effects of the triggered response (Herman 1992).

Positive coping strategies

These strategies are necessary for helping survivors to manage in the short-term the responses they experience as a result of the trauma of sex trafficking. Assistive strategies during the recovery process include visualization, in which a person visualizes a non-threatening and comforting image every time they experience a negative, traumatic response. With time and practice, their mind will immediately conjure this comforting image to counter negative responses. The same effect can be achieved with a mantra or by encouraging and affirmative words repeated by the individual every time they begin to experience a negative response (Van Dernoot Lipsky 2007). To coincide with visualization or verbal affirmations, survivors of sex trafficking can focus on the pace of their breathing and practice exhaling negativity and pain out through their mouth, fingertips, and toes, and inhaling positivity, hope, and empowerment.

The recovery process is a time of intensity and struggle. People who have survived sex trafficking may bounce between reaching out and embracing help and turning away from it (Evans-Weaver 2012). The survivor may have experienced a great sense of betrayal, which leads to a loss of trust not only in others but also in themselves and their ability to make decisions (Herman 1992). In response people may tend to internalize the victimization and hold themselves responsible, while simultaneously viewing all people as distrustful and self-serving (Evans-Weaver 2012). Survivors may lash out verbally, turn silent, miss scheduled appointments, or turn away from working with advocates all together. They should not be penalized for these inconsistencies by being denied access to support and advocacy.

GOOD PRACTICE POINT

It is imperative that survivors are able to build trust with their advocates, and this can only be accomplished if advocates prove through patience, and unconditional support, that they are the survivor's personal advocate.

HEALING

The recovery process allows a survivor to move away from the victimization and into a position where they can start focusing on themselves and their healing. It is important to remember that healing is a journey, not a destination, and that it is different for everyone. Some survivors may surprise people by how quickly they come to a place of empowerment and a place where they feel sex trafficking happened to them but does not define them. It may confuse others if the healing is at a pace that for onlookers seems too quick. However, that is the onlookers' issue, not the survivors'. Survivors should never be made to feel they have healed too quickly, or are not reacting at a level that is socially accepted as appropriate for a person who has been traumatized.

On the other side, some survivors may work on healing for the rest of their lives. This may seem to onlookers as if the survivor is beyond healing and damaged for life. "Damaged for life" is a horrible term to use in description of a survivor of sex trafficking. It is a term that says more about the person who is endorsing its negativity and feelings of helplessness, than it does about the survivor. It is important to remember that healing is a journey. If someone embraces this journey for a lifetime, then that journey is theirs and needs to be respected. There is always the capacity for healing after sex trafficking.

Therapists
Some people who have survived sex trafficking may be able to work with an advocate during both the recovery and healing journey. Others may need counseling by a trained, licensed therapist who can assist them more deeply with cognitive behavior therapy or sex-based therapies along their journey. Where the survivor was emotionally and cognitively before victimization plays a part in how they internalized the victimization, and in how they will attempt to reconstruct the trauma cognitively into something they understand and can manage (Evans-Weaver 2012). Advocates and therapists who work with survivors are trained in helping them to identify where they are at emotionally, and how their healing reconstruction can best be realized. This is an intricate process and can be confusing, scary, and overwhelming. When referring survivors to a therapist it is important that the therapist has experience of working with survivors of sexual abuse and/or domestic abuse, and can understand the dynamics and control tactics in sex trafficking.

GOOD PRACTICE POINTS

During the healing process a therapist must assist survivors of sex trafficking in healing from:

- the trauma they experienced
- reactions they have in response to the trauma they experienced
- negative coping strategies they may have employed during their struggle for survival.

Chronic trauma symptoms
The long-term effects of trauma that survivors might need assistance in reconstructing into healthier responses are different, depending on the individual. Dr. Erika Evans-Weaver is a therapist and founder of Lessons in Freedom and Empowerment (LIFE) in Philadelphia, Pennsylvania. In her practice she has found the following trauma symptoms exhibited by survivors of sex trafficking:

- difficulty controlling expressions of anger
- self-destructiveness
- chronic sense of guilt
- self-blame
- intense shame
- negative sense of self
- sense of worthlessness
- amnesia or dissociative episodes
- depersonalization.

The healing journey
The symptoms and manifestations of trauma set out above may read like a list of despair and hopelessness. However, it is important to remember that survivors who exhibit these symptoms are not lost. Advocates and therapists help survivors in recognizing these symptoms and understanding how they manifest, and why, taking a whirlwind of emotions, behaviors, and expression that for many seem inexplicable, and giving them a context. The context is logical and can show survivors that they are not responding inappropriately. In reality they are responding in ways that are neurobiologically determined and grounded in the very basic human instinct for survival.

GOOD PRACTICE POINTS

- Providing a survivor with an understanding of the symptoms of trauma can be empowering.
- This understanding helps survivors in reconstructing how they view the crimes committed against them, the offenders, and their own responses and decisions during their survival of sex trafficking.

With an understanding of their own reactions to the trauma they experience and their survival, survivors may begin to develop a more positive view of their healing. During the healing journey survivors will work through:

- reconstructing a life view based on optimism
- finding and trusting support people
- self-identity

- reconstructing intimacy
- sexuality
- individual expressions of family reunification or acceptance.

These are not steps to healing, they are *elements* of healing. Healing is a journey with difficult turns and beautiful realizations negotiated along the way. What a survivor finds easier or more difficult to work through while healing depends on:

- their personality
- genetic make-up
- where they were at emotionally and cognitively before sex trafficking
- their length of time in sex trafficking
- their treatment by society, the criminal justice and medical systems, and individuals after escaping from sex trafficking.

Optimism

It is understandable that survivors often come to believe in a broad, global sense that all people are venal and self-serving, and that people's motivations in life are to get what they can by whatever means necessary (Evans-Weaver 2012). As part of the structure of all people, "any means necessary" is understood to include using, manipulating, and physically abusing others. This is not a realistic world view and it is not conducive to healing. Some people are untrustworthy and self-serving but others are considerate, empathetic, and supportive. If survivors are to feel healing is worthwhile, they need to fully conceptualize that the world is made of individuals—some of whom are sometimes kind and generous, and others who may be cruel and self-serving. Individuals are sometimes victimized, but that victimization does not need to define their existence. Individuals have the power to determine for themselves the choices they make after victimizations (be they legal, medical, personal, or financial), and this choice is an expression of control over personal destiny. The beautiful thing about self-determination and belief in your ability to control your own destiny is that the world does not feel so oppressive and the notion of optimism is not so far-fetched.

Support people

It can be intimidating to trust new people after trust in an individual, humanity, or, in a sense, of justice has been betrayed by sex trafficking. However, in coordination with embracing optimism, it is important for survivors to develop trust in people they can rely on for support.

It is a huge step when survivors are able to trust individuals, such as an advocate or therapist, based on those individuals' own merits and expressions of support and trustworthiness. The process of trust can begin to develop during advocacy and be embraced fully as an individual heals. However, support people are not only advocates and therapists. It is important for survivors to have other supportive people in their lives as well. It may be a family member, friend, or group of other survivors. When survivors are able to establish a support network of non-abusive and positive people who can be trusted, there are wonderful benefits to healing. The benefits of having support people are the following:

- It reinforces a new reality where people can be trustworthy. This reinforces an evolving optimistic outlook.

- It shows the survivor that they are capable of finding support people who are trustworthy. They have the ability to recognize trustworthy people and develop relationships that are not based on manipulation or abuse.

- It reinforces to the survivor that people care about them and want to be supportive. This can help the survivor in embracing a more positive self-view and feelings of self-worth.

Self-identity

Survivors of sex trafficking may feel they have lost their self-identity during sex trafficking. Many will say during their recovery and healing that a part of them died while being victimized. They may feel that who they were before sex trafficking has been lost forever, and that what was done to them during sex trafficking now defines who they are. How survivors struggle with identity depends on the individual. Additionally there are nuances of the dynamics within the trafficking situation that impact on how survivors view themselves in relation to the sex trafficking.

- They may internalize the traffickers' expressions toward them of being less than human, unlovable, disposable, as the truth.

- Some traffickers use love to control and manipulate the people they sell via sex trafficking. They may create a story to the survivor where they are together to achieve a better life, in which the trafficker is a father figure, or a protector, and the survivor will be lost and loveless without the trafficker. This emotional manipulation is very traumatizing. It can make a survivor cling to their abuser as a safety net during the victimization. After the victimization the survivor may long for the trafficker, who has manipulated them into believing their identity is tied to the trafficker.

- If family members were the traffickers, then the survivor may question who they are in relation to familial connections and their place in the world.

In any of these dynamics a survivor may adapt to feel separated from themselves, their bodies, and their minds as a way of coping. This separation can be quite problematic. It is important for survivors to reconstruct their sense of self on their own terms.

Reconstructing the sense of self

Advocates and therapists can assist survivors with reconstruction by:

Using storytelling about:
- their life prior to sex trafficking
- how they want their life to be in the present
- how they want their life to be in the future.

All the above can be verbal, written, or creative expression, e.g. art, dance, acting.

Empowering survivors to:
- recognize how they uniquely survived sex trafficking as an individual and the power and strength that survival demonstrates
- identify what aspects of their pre-victimization self they want to reconnect with post-victimization
- realize that the verbal techniques used to control them were the failings of the traffickers and not a reflection of the worth of the survivor
- nurture hobbies, interests, and skills in which they take pride (dance, reading, gardening, math problems like sudoku, volunteering, etc.).

Healing requires a connection to self and others (Simon and Gagnon 1986). Therefore, in order for a person who has survived sex trafficking to heal, they need to be able to work through perceptions of a lost identity and reconstruct who they are on their own terms. With a connection to self, survivors are also at a place where they can better acquire a connection with others.

Intimacy

Intimacy is not about sexual intercourse. It is feeling emotionally connected to another human being and having the connection returned (Carlton 2010). It involves liking or loving another person and being able to connect on an emotional level. It does require being at ease with vulnerability and emotional openness, and confidence in being accepted as who you are as a person. These are ingredients for experiencing closeness with another human being. Intimacy can be difficult for people who have never been traumatized through sex trafficking; and for someone who has survived sex trafficking the expressions of emotional openness, vulnerability, and self-worth can be more than difficult—they can be traumatizing. As a result, survivors may feel hopeless about finding anyone to understand them or their suffering.

Ways in which advocates and therapists can support survivors in reconstructing intimacy can be by assisting them to identify what aspects of intimacy they are comfortable in embracing at each phase, and to identify in advance with what type of people they will be willing to explore intimacy—characteristics, personality, behavior, physical appearance. As survivors come to trust themselves and others more fully, they become more willing to explore intimacy with others.

Sexuality

Sexuality impacts on our lives at the physical, psychological, intellectual, and spiritual well-being levels. It is not just an expression of sexual acts; it is an expression of the individual as a person. The idea that survivors of sex trafficking often want to express their sexuality, including engaging in consensual sexual acts, can be difficult for some people to understand. I think this is in part due to the historic idea of women who were raped being damaged goods. In our contemporary views we have largely left the "damaged goods" idea behind, but now often embrace the idea that if a person is truly a victim, they will not want to be sexual for a very long time. For some survivors consensual sex acts can feel empowering. It can feel like they are reclaiming control. For others being sexual may be something they enjoy or a way they express physical intimacy. Therefore, disruptions in sexuality can impact self-perception and the ability to form intimacy and healthy relationships (Carlton 2010).

Reconstructing healthy sexuality can be very important to a survivor and an essential step in their journey of healing. Reconstructing a sexual script is an effective tool to assist survivors in healing. It helps survivors of sex trafficking in managing their ideas or beliefs regarding sexual experiences (Evans-Weaver 2012). It can be written, typed, reflected upon in detail, or verbally expressed. It is different for everyone and is an expression of a person's goals, values, and short-term and long-term plans for their own personal sexuality.

Elements that can be included in a survivor's sexual script

- **Sensuality:** What makes them feel sensual; what they are comfortable in feeling regarding sensuality; what they would like to do to explore/experience sensuality (clothing, bathing rituals, music, etc.).
- **Sexual intimacy:** With what type of person they will become sexually intimate; personality traits of people they will become sexually intimate with; what physical traits people must possess for them to be sexually intimate with them; what acts they will not perform during sexual intimacy; what acts they do want to perform during sexual intimacy; what language they do want expressed during sexual intimacy.
- **Sexual identity:** How they view their sexual identity; whether they are heterosexual, gay, lesbian, bisexual.
- **Gender identity:** Whether they view themselves as female, male, or as having no gender.
- **Reproduction:** Whether they want access to birth control options; how they plan on using birth control; how they will initiate conversations about birth control with partners.
- **Sexual health:** How they envisage their current and future sexual health; whether they will have yearly medical examinations; whether they will use condoms during sexual intercourse; how they will initiate conversations with partners regarding sexual health.
- **Sexualization:** What they feel comfortable with regarding how they are perceived sexually; how they want to project themselves sexually; what boundaries they want maintained and respected by others.

(Adapted from Evans-Weaver 2012)

When advocates and therapists assist survivors of sex trafficking in creating their reconstructed sexual scripts, they empower them with a valuable tool in long-term expression and management of healthy, safe, and beneficial beliefs regarding their current and future sexual experiences, and in their personal sexual behaviors. Therefore, sexual scripting has been helpful to some in assisting people who have survived sex trafficking during the healing process.

Family reunification or acceptance

In many cases of sex trafficking, parents or other family members are involved to some degree. Examples of these dynamics include the following:

- A person is sold or traded by their family sexually for money, rent, drugs, or to another trafficker for further sale.
- A person is sold by their family to another for marriage.
- A spouse forces their partner to engage in sex acts for money, drugs, rent, or to repay a debt.

The dynamics involved in the situation play a large part in a survivor's healing. The survivor may feel that they:

- shamed their family
- let their family down
- were betrayed by their family
- fear further victimization from their family.

These feelings may also co-occur with confusion around the love and loss they feel in relation to their family. At some point in their healing a survivor may want to reconstruct their relationship with their family. This does not have to be with the family directly. It can be an internal reconstruction with the survivor's own perceptions and acceptance of their family and their relation to that unit.

Some survivors may choose an outlet for expressing the reconstruction. They may develop an oral or written story, begin an on-going journal, or even a family script that defines what behaviors, responses, and interactions they are comfortable with from their family, and will allow in their life. If they choose to meet with their family members (even those who may be imprisoned due to the crime), it is recommended to have a support person with them; and to have counseling both before and after meeting. It may seem counterintuitive for survivors to want to reconnect with family members who aided in the sex trafficking. However, it is important to remember that during healing survivors are to be supported and empowered to respect their own role in making decisions, based on what they feel is needed to assist them in their personal journey.

CONCLUSION

Advocates are instrumental in empowering survivors during the recovery process through education and advocacy on criminal justice, medical, and counseling issues. Advocacy leads to educated communities and professionals who may encounter survivors and traffickers. Advocates reduce re-victimization of survivors through the criminal justice process, ensure health care is accessible, and provide safety and non-judgment to survivors in crisis when they need to reflect upon or process what they have experienced in sex trafficking. Recovery is vital to the wellness of survivors and in empowering them to move closer to healing.

Healing after recovery is a journey that looks different for all survivors. Advocates or therapists who are trained on the dynamics of sex trafficking and experienced in counseling adults or children who have survived sexual abuse and domestic abuse are important for healing. Through healing, survivors reconstruct a life view based on optimism, finding and trusting support people, self-identity, reconstructing intimacy, sexuality, and individual expressions of family reunification or acceptance.

In the poem "The Dream Keeper" Langston Hughes expresses a desire to wrap the dreams of dreamers "away from the too-tough fingers of the world" (Hughes 2007, p.4). Beautiful and comforting as this imagery may be, we know it is impossible to keep people away from the "too-tough fingers of the world." However, those who have survived sex trafficking, the people who care about them, and the professionals who work on their behalf can find comfort in the reality that recovery and healing are possible. When advocates and therapists assist survivors along the path of recovery and healing, then survivors become more aware of tools for finding empowerment. When survivors are empowered they know they can exist positively beyond what was done to them during sex trafficking. They know they have a voice that they have a right to use. They know their dreams are not meant to be wrapped away—they are meant to be seized and realized.

REFERENCES

Carlton, L. (2010) "Intimacy and Sexuality." In S. Wilgren, C. Scott, and A. Rinaldi (eds) *Health and Wellness for Life*. Champaign, IL: Human Kinetics, Inc.

Courtois, C. (2008) "Complex trauma, complex reactions: Assessment and treatment." *Psychological Trauma: Theory, Research, Practice and Policy S 1*, 86–100.

Estes, R. and Weiner, N.A. (2009) *The Commercial Sexual Exploitation of Children in the US, Mexico, and Canada*. Philadelphia: University of Pennsylvania. Available at www.sp2. upenn.edu/restes/CSEC_Files/Complete_CSEC_020220.pdf. Accessed on 12 October 2012.

Evans-Weaver, E. (2012) "Counseling practices for victims of sex trafficking." Presented at the training of the Pennsylvania Coalition Against Rape, Allentown, PA.

Foa, E., Keane, T., and Friedman, M. (eds) (2000) *Effective Treatments for PTSD*. New York: Guilford Press.

Herman, J. (1992) *Trauma and Recovery: The Aftermath of Violence from Domestic Abuse to Political Terror*. New York: Basic Books.

Hughes, L. (2007) *The Dream Keeper and Other Poems. 75th Anniversary Edition.* New York: Knopf Books for Young Readers.

INTERPOL (2012) "INTERPOL. Trafficking in Humans: Fact Sheet." Available at www.interpol.int/Crime-areas/Trafficking-in-human-beings/Trafficking-in-human-beings. Accessed on 17 August 2012.

Lyles, A., Cohen, L., and Brown, M. (2009) *Transforming Communities to Prevent Child Sexual Abuse and Exploitation: A Primary Prevention Approach.* Oakland, CA: Prevention Institute.

Simon, W. and Gagnon, J.H. (1986) "Sexual scripts: Permanence and change." *Archives of Sexual Behavior 15*, 97–120.

Smith, L., Healy Vardaman, S. and Snow, M. (2009) *The National Report on Domestic Minor Sex Trafficking: America's Prostituted Children.* Washington, DC: Shared Hope International.

The United Nations Office on Drugs and Crime (UNODC) (2009) *Global Report on Trafficking in Persons.* New York: UNODC. Available at www.unodc.org/documents/Global_Report_on_TIP.pdf. Accessed on 17 August 2012.

US Department of State (2011) *Trafficking in Persons Report 2011. Annual Report.* Washington, DC: US Department of State.

Van der Kolk, B. A. (1989) "The compulsion to repeat the trauma, re-enactment, revictimization, and masochism." *Psychiatric Clinics of North America 12*, 2, 1–6.

Van Dernoot Lipsky, L. (2007) *Trauma Stewardship: An Everyday Guide to Caring for Self While Caring for Others.* Fort Lauderdale, FL: Las Olas Press.

SUGGESTED READING

Amnesty International USA (2005) "Fact Sheet on Sexual Violence: A Human Rights Violation." New York: Amnesty International USA.

Dailey, D. (1981) "Sexual Expression and Ageing." In F. Berghorn and D. Schafer (eds) *The Dynamics of Ageing: Original Essays on the Processes and Experiences of Growing Old.* Boulder, CO: Westview Press.

Dawgert, S. and Hoffman, K. (2011) *Pennsylvania Sexual Violence Legal Advocate's Handbook.* Enola, PA: Pennsylvania Coalition Against Rape.

Kates, A. (1999) *Cop Shock: Surviving Posttraumatic Stress Disorder.* Tucson: Holbrook Street Press.

Mahay, J., Laumann, E.O. and Michaels, S. (2001) "Race, Gender, and Class in Sexual Scripts." In E.O. Laumann and R.T. Michael (eds) *Sex, Love, and Health in America: Private Choices and Public Policies.* Chicago: University of Chicago Press.

Sedlak, A.J., Finkelhor, D., Hammer, H. and Schultz, D.J. (2002) *Missing, Abducted, Runaway and Thrown Away Children in America* (Report 2). Washington, DC: US Department of Justice, Office of Justice Programs, Office of Juvenile Justice and Delinquency Prevention.

Sexual Health (2012) *The World Health Organization.* Health topics: Sexual Health. Available at www.who.int/topics/sexual_health/en/. Accessed on 17 August 2012.

Tedeschi, R. and Calhoun, L. (2004) "A Clinical Approach to Posttraumatic Growth." In P.A. Linely and S. Joseph (eds) *Positive Psychology in Practice.* Hoboken, NJ: Wiley.

USEFUL ORGANIZATION

Pennsylvania Coalition Against Rape (PCAR)
125 North Enola Drive
Enola
PA 17025
Telephone: 717 728 9740
Website: www.pcar.org

CHAPTER 7

'TO BE WHO WE REALLY ARE'
RECOVERY AND HEALING AFTER DOMESTIC ABUSE

HILARY ABRAHAMS

INTRODUCTION

Every experience of domestic violence and abuse is different because
every individual is different. Only by genuinely listening to the voices of
those who experience abuse can we learn what the impact on them has
been and what help they need to rebuild their lives. As a researcher I have
been listening, for the past 12 years, to women[1] who have left abusive
relationships and, in particular, working with a group of 12 women
from the time they left, during their early years of independent living
and up to eight years later. My perceptions of recovery and healing
stem directly from their words and actions and from talking to refuge
and outreach workers across England.

Taken in this context, *recovery* involves finding physical and
emotional safety and gaining the knowledge and confidence to live
independently in the wider society. Some women may be able to reach
this position on their own, or with support from family and friends;
most will require support from a variety of sources, depending on their
individual needs. Nor should recovery be regarded entirely as short-
term; women may move forward and back during what can be regarded
as a process of recovery, rather than a 'one-off' occurrence. Indeed,
many women will leave and return to an abusive relationship a number
of times before they are finally ready to move on, having accepted that
the relationship is never going to change.

Healing, however, is something which cannot begin until the
process of recovery is well under way, and is likely to take far longer
to be recognised by women as having occurred. It involves a changed

---

1   Although some men are abused by women and violence can occur in
    same-sex relationships, domestic violence is most commonly perpetrated
    by men against women. A discussion of the impact of domestic violence
    and abuse on children is beyond the scope of this chapter.

perception of themselves, their identities and their role in society, which I have also described as 'realignment' (Abrahams 2007). Women have told me that this is not an easy process. Liz[2] explained what it meant to her:

> To be who we really are…it's not easy and it's a long, hard road to go by.

As a worker from a specialist Asian refuge pointed out, this may be a much longer and more difficult process for women whose families had exercised control over them throughout their lives. In this case, women had to be deeply involved in the search to find out who they were in the first place. As Liz's comment shows, taking this step is not easy, and some women may prefer not to undergo what may be painful, even though (or perhaps because) it may create radical and permanent change in their lives.

To understand the complex nature of recovery and healing, we need to look first at what domestic abuse (indeed, I would argue, most forms of abuse) does to the human spirit. Placing this in the context of Maslow's 'hierarchy of human needs' (Maslow 1987) offers a theoretical perspective which can then provide a way of understanding both the destructive effects of abuse and the essential elements involved in recovery and, ultimately, healing.

WHY IS THE PROCESS OF RECOVERY AND HEALING SO HARD?

Domestic abuse can take many forms. The shared Association of Chief Police Officers (ACPO), Crown Prosecution Service (CPS) and government definition of domestic violence is:

> Any incident of threatening behaviour, violence or abuse (including psychological, physical, sexual, financial or emotional) between adults, aged 18 or over, who are or have been intimate partners or family members, regardless of gender or sexuality.

> (Association of Chief Police Officers and National Policing Improvement Agency 2008, p.7)

In fact, physical and emotional aspects of domestic abuse are inextricably entwined, since the first act of physical violence will create feelings of anticipatory fear and anxiety, and once abuse has taken place, women can never predict when, or where, a further incident will occur or what will happen. When anything you do is likely to be wrong – even if it

---

2　All the names used in this chapter have been anonymised to protect the identities of the women involved.

was right an hour beforehand – there can be no sense of physical or emotional safety in life. Women become unable to trust the events or people around them, thus isolating themselves from possible sources of support, while family and friends feel uncomfortable and begin to stay away, leaving their abuser as their only source of communication and information. Since this is inevitably critical and controlling, women feel unable to trust their own thoughts and feelings and to lose any belief that they are worthy to exist. A number of women in the group had attempted suicide in this belief.

Although many had suffered persistent and extreme acts of physical and sexual violence, some of which had resulted in permanent damage to their health, the women were adamant that it was the *psychological* and *emotional* abuse that had caused the most damage to them. The mind games, manipulation and control that they had endured had eroded their sense of personal integrity – of being a person in their own right, with their own ideas and ideals. This was all the more corrosive because it left no visible scars and those around them seemed unable to understand how damaged they were. Hayley explained to me:

> *You know, you look alright, you look like you're alright and you're really a strong person, but inside of yourself, you might not be. You know?*

In trying to understand the impact of abuse, I find it helpful to look at Maslow's 'hierarchy of human needs' (see Figure 7.1). He argued that people have higher natures and needs and that, once their basic physiological requirements are met (the need for food, water, clothing and shelter), they will actively seek to achieve some degree of safety and freedom from fear. They then seek to feel that they belong, that they have a place in the community and that they are accepted and acceptable. This, in turn, begins to develop feelings of self-esteem and self-respect and leads to a point where people feel able to develop their own potential as full human beings in whatever way they feel is right for them (self-actualisation). What can hold individuals back from this progression are the social and economic disadvantages they face and the memory of past failures, which may block or damage their attempts to meet these higher needs.

Self-actualisation
Reaching full potential, develop own capabilities

Esteem
Self-confidence, worth, self-respect, esteem of others

Belongingness
Belonging, being accepted, giving and receiving love, connection to others

Safety
Freedom from fear, security, protection, safety

Physiological
Food, water, clothing, shelter

Figure 7.1: Adaptation of Maslow's Hierarchy of Human Needs (1987; first published 1954)

Domestic violence and abuse destroy this structure, first by removing any sense of safety – the base on which the other needs depend – then by gradual isolation from any sort of community support, and the loss of any feelings of personal worth. Perhaps the saddest loss was that of any higher aspirations that women may have had. Amalie said:

> *He took my hopes and my dreams and my reach for the stars.*

The end result was a feeling of total annihilation. Jeannie conveyed this succinctly:

> *I felt like nothing and then having someone telling you constantly you're nothing...no-one's ever going to want you, you're nothing, you've got nothing. You know just destroying you.*

Given these effects, it takes an immense amount of courage and determination to leave the relationship.[3] The trigger for making the break may be a sudden surge of anger, the final realisation that nothing is going to change or, commonly, a threat to the children. And leaving brings an additional factor into the lives of women – grief. It may

---

3   Leaving is not necessarily the best option, since two women a week are murdered by partners or former partners and research has shown that the most dangerous time is when a woman decides to leave and makes this known to the abuser, or immediately after leaving the relationship.

seem strange to consider grief as an outcome of leaving an abusive relationship. Surely women should be glad to be away from the situation that had taken so much from them? But when leaving, they are incurring physical and emotional losses: homes they may have put time and effort into maintaining, cherished possessions, perhaps older children and pets that have to be left behind, and an environment which they knew, however dangerous it might have become. And are leaving a relationship which may have shaped their lives over many years and where, as a consequence, feelings are likely to be confused, ambiguous and painful. Women need time to grieve for all that has become lost to them, and these losses need to be understood and appreciated.[4] Using Maslow's theory can help us to understand how domestic abuse and violence demolish the structure of a life, leaving an empty space inside and a legacy of loss and grief, perhaps also a sense of shame and guilt at what has happened. It is from that sense of being and having nothing that recovery and healing must begin.

THE ROLE OF REFUGES

For many women, refuges are the places where this regeneration can start; they offer safety, a sense of community and the sort of support that can begin to grow self-worth and confidence. Peer support, ranging from practical information and advice to much deeper emotional exchanges, was welcomed by all of the women whom I met, as were the knowledge and experience of the workers. Where counselling and group work were available, a number of women were starting to reach beyond recovery and into a deeper sense of themselves and their identity (healing).

At some point, however, women needed to move back into the community and to continue the process of recovery and healing. The factors that they saw as key to making this transition were clear – a safe place to live, support while they settled in and for some time afterwards, and being able to make links to their new communities. As with the refuge, this pattern of needs accords with those identified by Maslow, and meeting them can begin to restore the structure demolished by abuse.

THE IMPORTANCE OF HOME

'Home' is a word that has deep emotional significance for women. Perhaps because, for centuries, we have been socialised into our role

---

4   Worden (1991) provides a useful guide to the tasks and process of bereavement.

as homemakers and carers, it has become a central focus of the lives of most women (Abrahams 2010; Malos and Hague 1997). Losing their homes, then, tears up the roots of their lives. Because of this, obtaining safe, suitable and permanent accommodation has been seen as the key to a new life from the earliest days of research into the needs of women leaving abusive relationships (Binney, Harkell and Nixon 1981), echoing Maslow's vision of safety and a secure base as the essential foundation for growth. Being placed in bed-and-breakfast accommodation, or a hostel (especially one shared with men), means that life remains unpredictable and uncertain, and it is hard for women to begin to tackle the other problems in their lives. As Jeannie's story shows, this situation can adversely affect mental health and further delay the process of recovery and healing.

CASE STUDY 7.1: JEANNIE

Jeannie fled an abusive relationship with her two young sons (aged 13 and 4 years). Over the next 18 months, due to continued harassment, and conflict within the extended family, they lived in three refuges across the country, with all the disruption to their lives that this entailed. Jeannie was then offered a private let via the council, but failed to understand either the conditions attached, or the long-term implications for her benefits. After 12 months she became unable to pay the rent and was eventually taken to court and became homeless again. She and her children were placed in bed-and-breakfast accommodation in yet another location, where she was routinely visited and monitored by council workers. The unpredictability and uncertainty of her life was causing stress and anxiety, and she saw no point in investing time and energy in her surroundings or looking for training or work within the community. Her sole wish was for her and her sons to be finally settled in a place of their own.

Not only was finding a permanent home crucial to recovery, it was also important that the new property was in reasonable condition, since substandard accommodation reinforced the claims of their abusers – that they were rubbish and second-class citizens. Decent accommodation, on the other hand, conveyed the message that they were considered to be worth helping and were of value to the community. And creating a new home for themselves and their children was, in itself, a healing process, giving a sense of pride in what they could do. Lindy was exultant:

I decorated it...I hung the lamps, I changed the plugs and...it's mine! It's not a man's. It's mine!

PRACTICAL AND EMOTIONAL SUPPORT

Moving to a new environment, even just to the other side of a large city, is strange and unsettling. Women welcomed the local knowledge that could guide them to appropriate areas to live in, to buy basic household goods and furniture and to find their way around the neighbourhood. Many had never been allowed any management of their affairs and needed to learn (or relearn) the necessary skills, with the help of someone who understood the effect that domestic abuse had had on them. All of this could be quite overwhelming and it was, therefore, equally important to provide the emotional support to build up confidence and competence in taking decisions and acting independently. This was particularly noticeable when women needed to contact local agencies and service providers. The lack of confidence and self-esteem resulting from the abuse meant that women wanted assistance in contacting other agencies and presenting their cases to start with. Often they were fearful of making contact; many had been told by their abusers that they were mad, or bad mothers, that they would be 'put away', or have their children taken away, or that no-one would listen to them. Because of these feelings, signposting (e.g. providing a list of contact numbers for women to ring by themselves) just did not work, since women delayed making contact or failed to make it at all. They felt that outcomes were much better when they made the initial approach in company with a support worker, and they then felt comfortable in handling things for themselves.

As Molly found, a single worker can also act as an advocate, to enable help to be more effectively targeted.

CASE STUDY 7.2: MOLLY

Molly had experienced violence both within her family and in her personal and intimate relationships over many years. She and her children were deeply involved with a range of voluntary and statutory agencies, each dealing with a different aspect of their lives. Often their roles would overlap and Molly felt harassed and confused by apparently contradictory demands. 'Everybody was on my back...everybody was against me...

slagging me off.' With the support of the refuge resettlement worker, she was able to explain how she felt to the agencies concerned, and they were able to talk with her about how they saw their role in helping her and her family. Priorities were agreed with them, so that everyone was working together and, as a result, Molly felt less frightened. She began to function more effectively and gained confidence which, in turn, reduced the need for greater agency involvement and enabled the growth of a positive spiral.

This shows the importance of working on 'soft' outcomes (building confidence and self-worth) for ensuring the successful achievement of 'hard' outcomes (maintaining a tenancy, finding education, training or employment). However, support was not always about encouragement – women accepted that, at times, they also needed to be challenged to go beyond their comfort zone.

Women commented on how much they needed emotional support during the early stages of their move to independent living. They could, at times, feel immensely lonely, isolated and in a strange and possibly hostile environment, and might then consider returning to their abuser and a life they knew and had coped with before.

Coping strategies

During an abusive relationship, many women find ways of relieving the stresses they are experiencing and, sometimes, of shielding themselves emotionally. The use or misuse of prescription or illegal substances and/or alcohol was a way out of what could be intolerable pain. Leanne said, 'If I was smashed out of my face, it didn't hurt so much.' Self-harming actions, from minor (like picking and pulling the body) to potentially fatal, were also widely in evidence. These strategies were unlikely to disappear overnight and might well be particularly prominent just after leaving, when life was in chaos, but could also resurface in situations perceived as stressful or threatening. This should not be seen purely as attention-seeking behaviour, but understood as a return to defence mechanisms that had helped women in the past, and where support can enable more appropriate reactions to emerge.

Practical and emotional support can be seen as the key element in a successful transition to independent living, but also as a safeguard against the need for expensive crisis interventions in the future.

For most women, support was likely to be needed more intensively in the first six months and could then be expected to taper off gradually. It needs to be accepted, however, that some women have been so badly damaged by abuse that they will always require some degree of support if they are to lead independent lives.

GOOD PRACTICE POINTS

In offering support the following should be considered:
- Safety – any breach of confidentiality could have fatal consequences
- Just one person whose prime concern is with the woman and her children
- Having someone who understands the effects of domestic violence and will not give up on the woman
- Being treated with respect and being believed
- Being shown choices and options but able to stay in control (controlling behaviour can replicate the abusive behaviour)
- Being helped to stand on her own feet and make her own decisions
- Taking a flexible approach as to how support is given
- Consistent and predictable support (in contrast to the abuse).

COMMUNITY AND FRIENDSHIP

The final element of a successful transition to recovery and independent living was to build their own support network. In Maslow's terms, by this time women had got the basic means of physical survival, established a secure base in the shape of a home and accessed reliable support. They now needed to establish, or re-establish, links to people and places where they felt accepted and where, in some sense, they felt they belonged. For many of us, families are places where this support comes from. However, this was not always the case for women who had experienced domestic abuse. Sometimes they had protected their families from full knowledge of the abuse they were suffering, or contact had been broken by the abuser. If women were able to re-establish these relationships, this could provide a valuable source of emotional support, but not all families were able, or willing, to provide this, for a variety of reasons. Women might also be unwilling to further put their families in danger, or feel that communicating might prove a means for their whereabouts to become more widely known. Peer support from women who had also experienced domestic abuse had been invaluable during the time they had been in the refuge. Women shared a common experience – there was no need to explain or justify their actions; they were understood and accepted as they were. For the most part, these individual contacts did not last after leaving the refuge, although a very few had formed strong friendships which they maintained by texting, phone calls and the occasional meeting. Drop-in centres, however, where women could meet up and chat, with access to a refuge support worker, were a welcome addition to their personal support networks.

The most important task, though, was to reach out to the people immediately around them, to feel that they belonged and were accepted in the community where they lived. This was not easy; either implicitly or explicitly, their abusers had restricted access to social life and had deterred others from making contact with them, so that social skills had become rusty. Although this step was essential if they were to conquer their feelings of loneliness and isolation, women were still wary of trusting others, unsure of how much to disclose about themselves, and concerned about their own safety and that of their children. This was especially true for South Asian women, who might desire contact with their own faith communities, but feared reprisals and so-called honour killings for having escaped. For many women, challenge, as well as encouragement, from a support worker could provide the impetus for action. Liz remembered the direct and no-nonsense advice she received:

Take the leap. You get out there. They're only people.

She reported that taking the plunge had worked:

And the people are lovely. They've took me in with open arms.

REACHING BEYOND RECOVERY

The women I met who had moved to safe, permanent accommodation, received quality support and made friends within their community had succeeded in rebuilding their lives after their experiences of domestic violence and abuse. Life was not necessarily easy – at times they still felt anxious and fearful and it could be hard to trust others. In general, though, they felt positive about their lives and able to look to the future, whereas, before, they had been unable to think beyond the next day or even, for some, the next hour.

But at some point in the years that I knew them, all expressed the need to feel a change within themselves at a much deeper level. Rather than talking of healing, they spoke of:

Being a stronger person

Being who I want to be

Finding your own destiny.

This desire to be free to develop and change can be seen as a realignment of their approach to life and as seeking the self-actualisation that Maslow saw as the ultimate need of individuals. Many, like Sylvia, wanted to deal with the pain and move on:

> *I want just to move forward, because it's pointless, all this pain and anguish – you can't live like that, it just destroys you.*

Some women were experiencing intense feelings of anger and hatred – emotions that had been repressed during the abuse for fear of making matters worse, and which were now demanding to be heard. At times sadness and depression over the past could also suddenly affect them. Acknowledging and dealing with these feelings is seen as an important part of healing by many professionals working in the fields of therapy and counselling (Herman 2001; Sanderson 2008).

The point at which these deeper desires surfaced varied for each woman. When they were ready to move on they knew what they needed in terms of personal support; when to move from one type of support to another; when supportive networks were the best option; and when group work or personal counselling was needed. Equally they knew when these were not appropriate.

Someone to talk to

For some, the support they had received in the refuge, both from workers and from other residents, had been enough to start this process. Keira said:

> *And things that I never thought I'd ever talk about again...I actually did talk about and I found that very therapeutic. But once I'd gone past that, I was ready to move on.*

Others had found similar sources of support from their families and people within the community and were now ready to draw a line under the past. Briony felt:

> *There's no point living in the past, you've got to get on with it now. That's just what we're doing.*

Counselling

Another option which women felt should be widely available for them and their children was access to a range of counselling services.

Whether this was successful or not depended on finding the right model and style for the needs of the woman concerned, since no-one therapeutic approach will work best for everyone. Leanne's counsellor had felt she needed to look at the past, whereas she felt her need was for support to manage the future:

> Talking about it…it just brings it all back. I'd rather just put it in the past and forget about it.

Sally, however, talked of a deep need to unravel and understand the past, whereas her counsellor had tried to help her with the future:

> It was my past I wanted to talk about, not my future… I wanted to get it in the open so it's not all blocked up in my mind all of the time.

For these women, the models available were not right for them at this point in their lives. Where the therapeutic relationship and model fitted, however, the outcome could be spectacular. Liz was emphatic:

> I've got to admit, if anything out of life…them sessions with her were the best ever what has put my mind straight. I come out a more confident, stronger-willed person that I were before.

One woman took a slightly different approach to this area of knowledge, signing up for a counselling training course, which had been tough, but ultimately rewarding.

Group work and support groups
Self-help and appropriate counselling were ways in which women were able to develop their inner strength, but research (Hester and Westmarland 2005) has found that support groups and structured group work programmes are also valuable in helping to change women's perceptions of themselves, enabling them to see themselves as individuals in control of their lives and as worthy of respect from those around them. The range of support available includes the Freedom Programme, Changing Patterns and many other locally developed groups.[5] Evaluation of a number of these groups has been carried out, with women reporting that they had gained inner strength and confidence in their ability to manage on their own,[6] and that they now

---

5   The Freedom Programme is available in many locations across the UK (Craven 2000). Changing Patterns has been developed from an American model and has been run extensively in Devon.

6   A number of evaluations have been carried out, including on the Freedom Programme, by Barns with Abrahams (2008) and Cordis Bright Consulting Ltd (2006). McTiernan and Taragon (2004) have evaluated pattern changing.

demanded mutual respect in any future relationships, including with those at work or in the home. Although the majority of the women I talked with had clearly been able to develop insight and understanding without additional support of this nature, others are very likely to benefit from this additional impetus. Making courses of this nature readily available would be of benefit in increasing self-awareness and understanding, enabling women to make balanced judgments before starting or returning to a relationship.

A new way of being
Discovering who they were and what they stood for was frequently the catalyst for more change, as women examined the implications of their new understanding for themselves, their families and friends, and for the future. Some who had known them at an earlier period of their lives had found it hard to accept the change, while others had rejoiced with them. One significant change was the way in which the majority of the women were now able to utilise their past experiences in a positive way, reaching out to help others, either in their work, in a voluntary capacity, or by working directly with individuals in their own communities. For a small number, their personal growth had resulted in a deeper level of connection in the formation of new intimate relationships. They had been able to overcome their earlier memories of love and trust betrayed, and felt able to give and receive love again. There was no doubt though, that the new relationship would be on a very different footing from the past, as Lindy explained to me.

CASE STUDY 7.3: LINDY

Lindy came to a safe house deeply traumatised by the emotional abuse she had suffered at the hands of her partner, unable to trust herself, or those around her and needing a high level of support. Physical and emotional safety gave her a space to begin to reflect on what had happened and to restore her confidence and belief in herself. It was very difficult for her to feel that she could ever risk lowering her defences and have a loving and caring partner, so that, when she became friendly with a man who was totally different from her previous partners, she needed encouragement from her support worker to take the relationship further. Even though he proved to be 'everything I've ever wanted' it was hard for her to fully trust the strength of the relationship and recognise that she could be happy. It was clear, though, that she had developed an inner strength and a sense of her own worth and that this new relationship was based on love, not dependency. She had told him, 'Just remember I don't *need* you, I *want* to be with you.'

CONCLUSION

Moving from a situation of domestic violence and abuse, grieving for all they had lost, making the transition to independent living and moving forward to develop a deeper sense of their own worth was not something that could be achieved overnight. Even after eight years, traces of the impact of domestic abuse could still be seen in the lives of the women who talked to me; in the way they reacted to unexpected events and the reluctance to fully trust others. At the end of our final meeting, we worked together on looking back over all the years since they took the decision finally to leave, enabling them to see how they had changed and how their lives had changed. The negative images of themselves as worthless rubbish, inculcated by their abusers, had gone; they were now individuals with their own identity, own values and sense of personal worth. As such, they were clear about how they expected to be treated, and able to set boundaries for themselves and others.

The growth of these changes in attitude and outlook was not sudden – they had developed over a long period and often women were surprised to look back and realise quite how different they had become. Nor had the process been an easy one; indeed, in some ways, being strong and independent made life more difficult and exhausting as they wrestled with new problems and learnt new skills. Becoming pro-active and assertive after years of subjugation was, in itself, a hard task, and was even more of a struggle when new attitudes and relationships had to be developed and maintained with friends, family and former partners.

Women recognised that this was now a continuing process and that, as they moved forward, there were going to be new challenges to face and new possibilities to explore. There were still going to be problems in their lives; there were still days when past pain and loss resurfaced. Nevertheless, they knew, at last, where they were headed and could blossom into who they really were.

CASE STUDY 7.4: SYLVIA

In Sylvia's words:

It hasn't been easy and I wouldn't say that every day is a success – that would be a lie. There are days... But they're less and less, and more cope-able. So I suppose it's just...an on-going project is how I look at it, every day is different... Be it years apart, it's still that journey when you saw me when I was like very insecure, couldn't talk to anybody, was rubbish, to the person more like what I was before all this happened. Not all the way there and if I'll ever get all the way there who knows, but I will always strive to get there.

I said to my mum, I said, 'I sometimes feel like a spring flower.' She goes 'Why?' I goes "Cos the bulb sits in the earth so long closed in on itself and then suddenly Mr Sun comes out, Mr Showers comes down, and out he bursts with all his glory, you know, and says "Hello world, here I am."' You know. And I says 'It is that real feeling of rebirth...and at 46 it's a bit old to be reborn!'

REFERENCES

Abrahams, H. (2007) *Supporting Women after Domestic Violence: Loss, Trauma and Recovery*. London: Jessica Kingsley Publishers.

Abrahams, H. (2010) *Rebuilding Lives after Domestic Violence: Understanding Long-term Outcomes*. London: Jessica Kingsley Publishers.

Association of Chief Police Officers and National Policing Improvement Agency (2008) *Guidance on Investigating Domestic Abuse*. London: ACPO and NPIA.

Barns, R. with Abrahams, H. (2008) *Pilot Evaluation of Survive Services*. Bristol: University of Bristol in association with Survive, Kingswood.

Binney, V., Harkell, G. and Nixon, J. (1981) *Leaving Violent Men*. Bristol: Women's Aid Federation of England.

Craven, P. (2000) *The Freedom Programme*. Available at www.freedomprogramme.co.uk. Accessed on 17 July 2012.

Cordis Bright Consulting Ltd (2006) 'Evaluation of the Freedom Programme Medway.' Unpublished report for the Children's Fund, Medway.

Herman, J. (2001) *Trauma and Recovery* (2nd edition). London: Pandora.

Hester, M. and Westmarland, N. (2005) *Tackling Domestic Violence: Effective Interventions and Approaches*. Home Office Research Study No. 290. London: Home Office.

Malos, E. and Hague, G. (1997) 'Women, housing, homelessness and domestic violence.' *Women's Studies International Forum 2*, 3, 397–409.

Maslow, A. (1987) *Motivation and Personality* (3rd edition; first published 1954). London: Harper and Row.

McTiernan, A. and Taragon, S. (2004) *Evaluation of Pattern Changing Courses*. Exeter: Devon's ADVA Partnership. Available at www.devon.gov.uk/pattern_changing.pdf. Accessed on 17 October 2012.

Sanderson, C. (2008) *Counselling Survivors of Domestic Abuse*. London: Jessica Kingsley Publishers.

Worden, J.W. (1991) *Grief Counselling and Grief Therapy: A Handbook for Mental Health Practitioners*. London: Routledge.

SUGGESTED READING

Hester, M., Pearson, C. and Harwin, N. with Abrahams, H. (2007) *Making an Impact.* (2nd edition). London: Jessica Kingsley Publishers.

Kirkwood, C. (1993) *Leaving Abusive Partners.* London: Sage.

USEFUL ORGANISATIONS

Below is a very small selection of groups and organisations within the UK and Republic of Ireland offering support and information to women who experience domestic violence and abuse. Similar organisations now exist in many countries across the world.

It is important to be cautious when accessing any of the websites from a computer that an abuser has access to. Many of the sites contain information on actions that can be taken to minimise the chance that access might be discovered.

National 24-hour Domestic Violence Helpline
Run in partnership between Women's Aid and Refuge – Freephone service for support, advice, information and access to a range of other services, including safe houses and outreach. Callers can be signposted to many other sources of help to meet individual requirements.
Telephone: 0808 2000 247 (minicom available)
Websites: Refuge – www.refuge.org.uk
Women's Aid (Federation of England) – www.womensaid.org.uk

Advice, information and support to those experiencing domestic violence and abuse, together with links to local groups and other sources of support on a wide range of associated topics. Women's Aid Federation of England has sister organisations in Northern Ireland, the Republic of Ireland, Scotland and Wales, which are listed below.

Black Association of Women Step Out (BAWSO)
Offers specialist advice and support to black and minority ethnic women who have experienced, or are experiencing, domestic violence and abuse.
Telephone: 24-hour helpline 0800 731 8147
Website: www.bawso.org.uk

Broken Rainbow
Service for lesbian, gay men, bi- or trans-gendered people experiencing abuse. Advice and information for all fathers, with chat line and links to other sources of support.
Telephone: 0845 260 4460
Website: www.broken-rainbow.org.uk

Hidden Hurt
A domestic abuse website, run by a survivor, with information and support.
Website: www.hiddenhurt.co.uk

Irish Women's Aid (Republic of Ireland)
Telephone: 1800 341 900
Website: www.womensaid.ie

Jewish Women's Aid
Telephone: 0800 59 12 03
Website: www.jwa.org.uk

Northern Ireland Women's Aid Federation
Telephone: 24-hour helpline 0800 917 1414
Website: www.niwaf.org

Scottish Women's Aid
Telephone: 24-hour helpline 0800 027 1234
Website: www.scottishwomensaid.org.uk

Southall Black Sisters
Specialist advice and support for Asian and Afro-Caribbean women suffering violence and abuse.
Telephone: 020 8571 9595
Website: www.southallblacksisters.org.uk

Victim Support
Service for the victims of crime, and those acting as witnesses in court.
Telephone: 0845 30 30 900 (see also telephone directory for local services)
Website: www.victimsupport.org.uk

Welsh Women's Aid
Telephone: 24-hour helpline 0808 8010 800
Website: www.welshwomensaid.org

CHAPTER 8

HELPING RECOVERY AND HEALING
A SUPPORTED HOUSING PROJECT APPROACH

JACQUI SMITH

INTRODUCTION

In this chapter I shall discuss the work we do as a supported housing project in Sheffield to help in the recovery and healing process with young women survivors of sexual abuse. It is hoped that other professionals involved in supporting these clients will find some practical and useful ideas to help in their work with this vulnerable group.

This chapter aims to promote a better understanding of the effects of abuse on people and the reasons behind the often chaotic and challenging behaviour they can present. I will discuss the various methods of support we offer and the benefits we find, and hope that this will encourage others to adopt a more caring and consistent approach that puts the client at the centre of their work.

BACKGROUND

Development of the Young Women's Housing Project (YWHP)

In the early 1980s the local housing department found that amongst the young women who presented to them, sexual abuse was the primary reason for becoming homeless. The council decided to fund a post for someone to co-ordinate support for these young women (via a team of volunteers) and provided a two-bedroom flat for accommodation. Thus the YWHP was formed and became a charity in 1986. We have since grown and can now accommodate 13 women and their children; and in addition ten women can be supported on the outreach service at any one time. The project continues to provide accommodation and specialist support for homeless young women aged 16–25 years (and their children), who have been affected by sexual abuse, sexual exploitation or sexual/domestic violence. It is a unique specialist provider within Sheffield and one of a very small number of such specialist services within the UK.

Objectives

A key part of our work is the initial provision of a safe, secure place to live, then giving clients the opportunity to work through and resolve issues from the past in a positive, supportive environment. The safe house has a confidential address and is monitored by CCTV; clients have a monitor in their rooms so they can see who is coming and going. There are panic alarms around the building, security fobs for access, and no visitors are allowed. The staff offices are in the building and are covered during office hours (08.30 to 17.00 on weekdays). A night-worker works evenings to offer further support to clients. Clients have an on-call number to ring if they have an emergency. The night can be a very stressful and anxious time, so it is important for clients to know there is someone around if they need any support during this difficult time.

The clients

Since opening our doors in 1984 we have supported approximately 1000 young women and 600 children.[1] The clients have included women who:

- are leaving care
- are homeless
- are leaving hospital with enduring mental health problems
- self-harm
- are at risk of suicide
- have substance abuse problems
- are victims of domestic violence
- are at high risk of sexual exploitation and further abuse.

Referrals

From 1 April 2011 to 31 March 2012 there were 85 referrals to the YWHP (from figures compiled for the Annual Report 2012). We do encourage self-referrals, but referrals mainly come from:

- the local housing authority homeless section
- social services
- general practitioners
- midwives
- health visitors

---

1   Statistics compiled from various data files, internal reports and annual reports compiled between 1984 and 2012.

- the probation service
- schools and colleges.

Key facts from referral statistics 2011–2012[1]

In 2011–2012 the referral statistics showed that:
- 31 per cent of the referrals were regarding 16- to 17-year-old women
- 20 per cent were care leavers
- 50 per cent were White British; 7 per cent were Black British; 3 per cent were Asian British; 5 per cent were dual heritage (White/Black African); 2 per cent were White/Asian; 3 per cent other; 30 per cent unknown/declined to say.

As well as being homeless the young women had the following issues to deal with:
- 34 per cent had experienced sexual abuse
- 11 per cent had been raped
- 44 per cent had experienced domestic violence
- 20 per cent had experienced sexual exploitation and further abuse
- 6 per cent had been trafficked
- 41 per cent had depression
- 33 per cent had self-harmed
- 18 per cent had attempted suicide
- 20 per cent had other mental health issues (e.g. anxiety, panic attacks, low mood, obsessive compulsive disorder (OCD), or unspecified)
- 20 per cent had substance misuse issues
- 10 per cent had a physical disability
- 28 per cent had involvement with social services
- 17 per cent had been involved in the criminal justice system.

(Compiled from YWHP Annual Report 2012)

---

1   These statistics do not include information about the children of clients.

Whilst the majority of women have multiple issues, this can be difficult to assess when they are first referred. It can take many months of getting to know a client before some issues are disclosed (e.g. eating disorders, self-harming), or the extent of abuse they have suffered, because of the secrecy, shame and guilt that surrounds these issues.

Other agencies

A client may also be involved with several other agencies and their workers at any one time because of their needs and different aspects of their lives that are affected by the abuse. These can include social workers, housing workers, doctors, mental health workers, midwives, health visitors, sexual health workers, nurseries/early years workers, schools, colleges, universities, the police and the criminal justice system, safeguarding and sexual exploitation prevention services. We find that some organisations still have very little understanding of the long-term damage that abuse can do to an individual and how this can impact on all areas of their lives. This lack of understanding can lead to comments or actions that can actively damage the healing process for some clients:

> *If you had behaved yourself at home, you wouldn't be here [told repeatedly to a client when she was in a children's home].*

> *You* just *have depression.*

> *Ignore her – she's just attention-seeking.*

Staff

The staff in the YWHP come from various backgrounds; some are trained social workers, but the majority are women who have many years' experience in the supported housing sector, working with clients with complex needs. There are workers with specialist training in sexual health, drug and alcohol misuse, parenting, sexual exploitation and mental health issues; all of whom are highly trained in safeguarding work because of the vulnerable clients and children with whom we work. Regular line management and support of workers is vital to ensure their well-being and that high standards of good practice are being met. This should allow time for reflection on any difficult or distressing cases. Reflection helps identify when and where a worker's own anxieties or distress about certain issues may be impacting on their work.

RECOVERY AND HEALING: THE YWHP PERSPECTIVE

I shall now consider how recovery and healing is promoted as part of the day-to-day practice in the YWHP, where we talk about recovery and healing being different stages in the same process. There is a continuum between recovery and healing. Healing often starts when someone is finally in a safe place and able to focus on something more than just surviving. Recovery can be seen as much more practically based – maintaining a home, buying food, organising money and bills, registering with a GP, keeping safe and well. Healing can be the process of starting again (that is, mentally, physically, socially, emotionally and educationally), which can involve:

- re-learning how to function in the world
- handling social situations and conversations
- feeling safe in groups and in public spaces
- going to new places.

In order to heal, the client also needs to:

- regain some kind of control over their life
- feel worthwhile
- increase their self-esteem and confidence
- be able to think about the future
- be able to hope and dream again.

RECOVERY: WAYS OF WORKING

Once clients have been accepted by the project they are allocated a keyworker who will work with them to identify their needs and goals, and then draw up a support plan. This is reviewed every three months. The client and the keyworker meet weekly, though in the initial stages this can be more frequent if necessary. A client's needs and wishes are central to their support plan. If clients have ownership of their plan and the direction it takes, they are much more likely to engage with it and achieve the objectives within it.

Support plan

The support plan covers various areas under the following five headings:

- **Achieving economic well-being:** education, employment, volunteering, training, money management.
- **Enjoy and achieve:** social networks, positive relationships, living in your own home, moving on.
- **Be healthy:** physical health, emotional well-being, mental well-being, sexual health.
- **Staying safe:** personal safety, parental responsibility, child/adult protection.
- **Making a positive contribution:** meaningful use of time, hobbies, participation in community, religion, cultural issues, family relationships.

As well as keywork sessions we also offer one-to-one short intervention sessions and group activities on key areas that often hold difficulties for our client group:

- developing and maintaining healthy relationships
- managing anger and aggression
- confidence, self-esteem building and assertiveness
- coping with depression and anxiety
- sexual health
- parenting
- risky behaviour/self-harming behaviour.

This work is designed to complement keywork sessions – that is, to help clients recognise problems they may have in these areas and develop coping skills they can use in day-to-day situations. Clients will already have ways of coping, and we help them to identify the strengths they already have and encourage building on these. This work helps promote resilience in clients and will therefore aid the healing process. We also run several other projects that our clients can get involved in: Nurture by Nature Project; Parents as First Teachers (PAFT); and Can You Hear Me? (a service-user-led training project).

PRACTICAL ISSUES IN THE RECOVERY PERIOD

It is now necessary to give attention to the many practical issues which need to be dealt with during the recovery process.

Providing a welcoming and comfortable place to live

Many of our clients have had to leave their family home due to abuse; they may have lived for years in appalling conditions. Being homeless is very stressful. So it is important that the accommodation we provide is furnished and maintained to a high standard, and creates an environment of 'home'. This gives a comfortable and stable base for clients to begin the recovery process, and makes them feel valued.

Ensuring privacy and personal space

Privacy is very important to many of our clients who may have had very little control over their personal space when they were younger. All clients in the safe house have their own lockable bedroom, and a communal area and bathroom separate from the facilities for workers based in the house. We do not enter rooms without notice unless we have serious health and safety concerns. This gives clients somewhere they can escape to if they need time alone and gives them back some control over who can be near them at any time.

Providing basic items

Clients sometimes arrive with nothing, and it may be necessary to provide toiletries such as shower gel, shampoo, sanitary towels, a toothbrush, toothpaste, a towel or even access to spare clothes. This helps them to settle into their new environment. A small gift of toiletries can also help encourage self-care if a client struggles with this.

Ensuring clients have some food

When someone first moves in they may have no money and be waiting for benefits to be paid. The project provides basic food items (tea, coffee, milk), toilet roll and cleaning products, and may take the client to the local supermarket to buy some other basic items until her money comes through. Workers will also access food parcels from local voluntary agencies for clients who are struggling long-term with little or no income.

Providing information about the local area

If a client is escaping an abusive situation she may need to move to an area she is not familiar with to escape the perpetrator. It is important to take the client around the local neighbourhood to familiarise her with the local shops, amenities and public transport. This knowledge can help her feel safe in a new area, more confident to go out and about alone, and give her more control of her day-to-day life.

Addressing personal safety issues

It is important to discuss personal safety with a client, including areas it is safe to go to, using a personal alarm, the importance of keeping a mobile phone charged and available at all times and the importance of informing someone of her whereabouts. Many clients underestimate risky situations as a result of the long-term abuse they have been through and can find it hard to recognise potential danger signs. We cannot stop risky behaviour, but through the recovery process we can help clients recognise potential problems and the impact they can have, and help minimise the risks.

Ensuring that clients are receiving the correct benefits

Without this input clients can be left with no money for their basic needs and could lose their tenancy if rent is not paid. Without an income they are also more likely to take out loans they cannot afford and end up with serious debt problems. They are also more vulnerable to sexual exploitation and further abuse in exchange for food, cigarettes, money, mobile phones, etc.

Devising a budgeting plan

To help a client manage her money and bills it may be necessary to take her to the supermarket to help her do her weekly shopping to a budget, until she is confident enough to do this alone.

Helping with phone calls and form filling

Some clients have literacy problems or lack the confidence or concentration to deal with difficult forms or telephone calls. They are often dealing with organisations that can be intimidating and have difficult systems to navigate. Workers will support the client to do this until she is able to manage alone. It is an important skill to learn so that the client can become independent and fully confident to deal with her own problems in the future.

Registering for utilities

Some clients have never lived on their own previously or managed their own home, and will require more support with this initially. They need to learn this procedure for when they have their own property to manage in the future.

Setting up payment plans for bills

This helps clients budget and manage their bills. It is difficult for some clients to remember to do this in the middle of a crisis or because of mental health issues. Paying bills is not always seen as a priority. Workers encourage clients to keep up to date with payment plans so they are not left in debt or without essential amenities.

Holding cooking sessions

These help clients learn how to cook some simple, cheap but nutritious dishes. Staff also cook a weekly breakfast for clients, which encourages social interaction between clients and workers.

Keeping aware of issues around food

Often clients have eating disorders and have a difficult relationship with food. This needs to be handled sensitively, ensuring they have some food available but not forcing them to shop, cook or eat.

Registering with a local general practitioner (GP) and dentist

Many of the clients have on-going health problems or do not look after their health. Workers help clients to do this, and may also take a client to initial appointments until she feels confident to do this alone. Building a relationship with the GP can also help workers to monitor and support a client's physical and mental health needs.

Signposting clients to other specialist services (e.g. drugs/ alcohol agencies, mental health services)

A support worker will liaise with workers in specialist services and advocate for the client, to ensure she is receiving the level of support/ service needed. They may attend some initial appointments with the client if she finds these meetings difficult. If a client is experiencing depression she may find it hard to motivate herself to attend without support. A past negative experience in a similar setting may also add to this difficulty.

Accessing translating services

It is necessary to access these services when English is not the first language of a client. It can be very isolating for clients who cannot join in with conversations or simply say how they feel. Workers will also find local groups or college courses that women can join to help them learn English, link up with people who share their culture and develop social networks.

Helping access local resources

Often clients are isolated from their family and community, so it is important to help them access community groups, toddler groups, libraries, advice services and local health services. Encouraging clients to fill their time and get involved in activities and group opportunities can decrease their isolation, increase their social skills and help them make new friends. As they move through the recovery stage they will be more able to participate in the outside world. The ability to help others and increase involvement in the local community is a sign that clients are moving into the healing process.

Helping to access college or training courses

Negative experiences at school can affect a client's confidence in attending college or training, and being in groups can be particularly distressing for them. Low educational attainment, literacy problems, lack of qualifications or undiagnosed learning difficulties will severely limit their opportunities in the job market and their capacity to earn money and move out of the poverty trap. Our work focuses on finding something that they are interested in and encouraging them to take small steps to go to college or undertake volunteering work. Workers make links with course tutors and trainers to ensure our clients are receiving the extra support they need to maintain attendance. Confidence and qualifications can move a client into the job market and into earning her own money. Achieving economic well-being is key to clients gaining control over their own lives and being able to move on and heal.

Ensuring clients have their basic needs met – a roof over their heads, food, warmth, clothes, regular income and people to support them – enables them to settle into their new environment, helps them feel safe and reduces extra anxiety and pressure on them. It enables the young woman to deal with her current situation and start the recovery process. Workers need to be aware that past traumas will often unexpectedly encroach upon someone's day-to-day life and the client will need continuing support with this, but the work undertaken is no longer about averting a crisis. The client will slowly be developing the skills to deal with difficult situations herself, and as she feels more settled her priorities will start to change. She will begin thinking about long-term goals and move into the healing stage.

IMPORTANT KEY ELEMENTS OF THE WORK UNDERTAKEN
Treating clients as individuals
Each support plan is unique, just like the client, and what works with one person will not necessarily work with another. Initially the emphasis of the plan is on recovery, and it is continually reviewed in order to facilitate the long-term healing process.

GOOD PRACTICE POINT

The support plan should not overwhelm the client but should be a useful tool to help set realistic goals for the next few months.

Sometimes there may be a difference of opinion in what the client and the worker consider to be the immediate priorities. While the client is best placed to decide the direction she wishes to go in and what she believes can be achieved, she may overlook or underestimate the importance of some areas. Consequently, she may need input from the worker to guide her. Experience of abuse can result in a young woman being unable to recognise feelings and signs of danger and keep herself safe. We encourage clients to value themselves, to learn to recognise and manage difficult situations. A risk assessment is also carried out to identify and manage any areas where the client may be at risk of harm to herself or others, and this is reviewed regularly.

GOOD PRACTICE POINT

People who have experienced trauma can be affected in many different ways, and workers need to be flexible in their approach.

Recognising strengths, encouraging resilience

Resilience is the ability to cope and bounce back from all types of challenges. Resilience can be increased if young people have high self-esteem, can self-reflect, have positive role models in their lives and have coping strategies for negative situations. These strategies include:

- having support networks to turn to – family, friends, local resources
- having the ability to problem solve
- seeking help when needed
- having confidence to take control of the situation.

Our work aims to empower clients to be able to act when faced with difficult situations, rather than feeling helpless and paralysed. The more they deal successfully with difficulties, the more confident they will become, and this builds further resilience and aids the healing process.

GOOD PRACTICE POINT

Do not focus on the negatives of a client's situation but find the strengths and assets they are already using and help them to build on these.

Keeping professional boundaries

Professional boundaries set limits on what is and what is not acceptable behaviour in the workplace, to protect both client and worker. Clear boundaries mean a client knows what to expect from staff, and encourage professionalism and consistency among workers. Many clients may have difficulties with boundaries because of early abusive experiences where boundaries were often crossed by those whom they trusted to care for them; they can find inconsistency very confusing and distressing.

GOOD PRACTICE POINT

Workers must be aware that clients can develop strong or close feelings for their worker, and this has to be managed responsibly so as not to abuse the power imbalance in the relationship.

Workers should act in a way that promotes and safeguards the well-being and interests of these vulnerable clients at all times. Being honest with a client is vital to build a relationship of trust; therefore it is important to state clearly both what you can and cannot do as a worker and not to make promises that cannot be kept.

Working confidentially
Clients report that it is very important to feel confident that any information passed on will be treated respectfully and confidentially. We are very clear with our clients before they move into the accommodation that confidentiality is within the staff team in order that we can all provide the support needed. They are also informed that we will have to break confidentiality without their consent where there is evidence or reasonable cause to believe that a child is suffering, or at risk of suffering, significant harm; or to prevent a serious crime (Section 11 of the Children Act 2004).

HEALING: WAYS OF WORKING
Discussing abuse with clients
While the keywork session is an important arena for addressing issues with a client, we do not force clients to divulge their experiences of abuse. This can be very distressing and uncomfortable for clients, and we accept that clients may not want to address their past experiences while they are with us. Workers should maintain an awareness of how abuse can affect a client, as this can help inform us about the behaviour a client may be displaying or a particular area they are finding difficult to deal with. People who have experienced repeated trauma in childhood may not have had the chance to develop the skills necessary to cope as an adult. The behaviour they are presenting now can be the result of a coping mechanism they developed as a child in response to their abuse. Clients do not always make the link between how they are acting now and what has happened to them in the past. The worker's role is to help them understand why they react in a certain way in some

situations and what triggers this behaviour. They will also point out the coping strategies the client already has and work to strengthen these or develop new ones if necessary.

> *When I needed to talk to a worker, I found having a coffee a help, as it made it easier to talk. I also found just going out of the house made it easier to talk. I think you should never force someone to talk, because this puts pressure on the service user, and when talking it should be on the service user's terms, not the worker's.*

> (Client A, 2012)

Disclosure can occur at any time, and for some clients it may be the first time they have told anyone about their experiences. It is important that the reaction they receive is not a negative one. Reliving past trauma can be very distressing and the client must consider whether she is able to cope with it at the present time.

GOOD PRACTICE POINTS

- Ensure the client has privacy and your full attention.
- Listen carefully without interruptions.
- Do not question or dig for details; just ask enough for clarification.
- Do not be afraid of silence. Sometimes the client just needs to 'be'.

It is important to let the client go at her own pace; sometimes a client will talk about the same event over several keywork sessions, trying to make sense of it. It is important to allow her to do this as part of the healing process. The worker must stay calm, not rush into action or feel that they have to provide answers.

GOOD PRACTICE POINTS

- Keep professional boundaries and be careful about touching clients; a reassuring hug can be very traumatic for some clients.
- Inform the client that you will have to make notes about what has been discussed and you will have to act on any concerns (i.e. report to your manager, the police, social services or safeguarding authorities if relevant).

Workers can also offer informal support, either in person or by telephone, when someone wants to talk. These sessions can vary in length from a few minutes to an hour. Topics discussed may be a traumatic event that has recently happened, an event from the past that is causing distress now, difficulties at college, with family members, relationships, worries about being pregnant, friendships, money problems, someone feeling very low, considering self-harming, or trouble between clients. Sometimes clients just want to chat about their day or an upcoming event they are looking forward to. Workers should be encouraged to have passing chats with clients as often as possible. Making contact and saying 'hello' helps build relationships and trust between staff and clients; and makes it more likely that clients will speak to someone when they are in real distress. It also keeps workers aware of what is happening in a client's life and the support she needs.

> Those little passing chats I had with workers were so important to me, sometimes they were the only adult interaction I had in days.

(Client B, 2012)

During the recovery stage clients are making links with workers and building these relationships. It may take months for them to be able to sit down with someone who is not their keyworker and talk through a difficulty they are having. They will do this more frequently in the healing stage.

> One of the night staff used to let me talk to them in the morning instead of at night; this helped me a lot because I find talking at night harder than in the morning. I really appreciated that.

(Client C, 2012)

When I first started hearing voices, I felt the staff didn't know how to help me and how to act around me. I think they should have just asked me more about how it affects me and what I think they can do to help me.

(Client A, 2012)

Working with self-harming behaviour

We recognise that self-harm can be used as a coping strategy by clients who are deeply distressed, and that there are infinite ways that self-harming can take place. Often these clients are excluded from other housing providers. We work with clients who are able to manage their self-harming in such a way that the degree of risk to themselves (or others) is low-level, and we will support them to do this. We recognise that to try and prevent self-harming can actually be more harmful in the long run.

We can provide practical assistance, emotional support, information, crisis support, education, and therapeutic activities. We cannot provide medical care, intensive therapeutic support, accompaniment to hospital for treatment of injury, or clinical counselling. We encourage clients to be open and honest about their self-harming so that we can look together at triggers, particular situations/events that tend to lead to self-harming, and strategies to help reduce the incidence of its happening or minimise the self-harm that occurs.

A client may react to traumatic experiences by isolating herself and cutting off her feelings. She may appear to have little interest in anything around her and generally seem to feel numb. She may have repressed painful emotions and thoughts to such an extent that she self-harms in order to feel something. It is useful to explore this with the client and encourage her to start to recognise feelings, thoughts and bodily sensations, to name them and practise being aware of them in various situations.

Some clients may seem to be the opposite – that is, they are so overwhelmed by painful emotions and thoughts that they almost have too many feelings to cope with. They may have a tendency to be manic and chaotic and may self-harm in order to manage their feelings. These clients need support to bring them back to the present and help them find ways to calm themselves and focus on the task in hand. Clients will draw up a self-harm management plan with their support worker to manage any risk, and all being well, over time incidences will reduce.

GOOD PRACTICE POINT

Self-harming should be done in a private place away from other clients, and the client is responsible for cleaning and dressing any wounds herself, and for cleaning up the environment.

When I self-harmed, what helped me was knowing I had someone to talk to if I needed to.

(Client D, 2012)

Don't judge us when we do self-harm, don't ask questions why we self-harm and don't look at our scars.

(Client A, 2012)

We encourage clients to talk to someone when they feel like hurting themselves – sometimes the right support at the right time can help the individual avoid, delay or reduce the extent of the self-harm. It is important that clients get the chance to talk about their feelings and actions and feel supported and heard, rather than judged. First aid kits are provided around the safe house, but clients can also have their own as part of the management of their self-harming:

I do think first aid kits should be provided initially and then it is the client's responsibility to stock up the kit.

(Client A, 2012)

These are some ideas that have helped our clients when they are distressed (but these do not work for everyone):

- listening to soothing music
- writing poetry
- going for a walk
- doing exercises
- talking to someone
- taking a long bath
- reading a favourite book
- cleaning the house
- de-cluttering their wardrobe
- watching something funny on TV

- breathing/relaxation exercises
- meeting a friend.

Continuity of support

Maintaining continuity of support is very important to the healing process. Change can be difficult for some clients to deal with, especially if they feel that trust has been built up between them and the worker. We aim to keep any changes to a minimum because we have seen the distress it can cause to a client. Many of our clients have experienced being let down, or feelings of abandonment by those they trusted, and we do not want to repeat this in our work. By providing stability and consistency, workers are trying to replicate the attachment process that has been damaged in childhood by abuse and neglect. We work as a close team so that clients are usually familiar with all members of staff and may have seen other staff in group settings or in joint working.

We encourage joint working among the team where appropriate to deliver specialist one-to-one work, group work and activities. This means that if staff are on holiday or off work due to illness or leave the project, someone else the client knows can take over support with as little disruption as possible. The best outcomes have been with clients we have had a chance to work with over a longer time, who have been able to work on building healthy relationships with others, and who see over time that workers will not abandon them or let them down when things are not going well. Ex-clients know that they are welcome to ring up for a chat, some advice, or to let us know what they are up to at any time. They often get in touch years later to share good news with us.

CONCLUSION

Sexual abuse not only damages someone's childhood, it can also severely limit a young person's future opportunities. Our ethos is to provide a safe place to live where clients can feel supported and cared for in order to recover and heal from past experiences of abuse. The practical tenancy support provided is underpinned by specialist knowledge on the issues involved in sexual abuse and how they affect young women and their children.

The recovery process can start once the client has her basic needs met and a stable, secure base from which to work. By using a mixture of one-to-one methods and group work we can support the client to take control of her own life; to increase her self-confidence and self-esteem; and to form healthy relationships and build supportive social networks that will bring about long-term self-sufficiency. This work builds on clients' existing strengths, helping them gain an insight into their feelings and emotions, and therefore their actions, and to develop strategies for real and longlasting change in their lives.

Our multi-agency approach ensures we can obtain the appropriate specialist support for our clients' many diverse needs. Consistency and strong professional boundaries are vital in this work, as is listening to and learning from our clients and being flexible and willing to change our approach when necessary to guarantee the best outcomes for them. All this work takes time and can lead to greater independence for clients and a reduction in their dependency on statutory and voluntary agencies. Without this investment of time a client is unlikely to move much beyond the recovery stage and may continue to require the input of external services for many years to come. It is vital we give these young people a future that includes choices, hope and the opportunity to thrive, and improves the long-term quality of their and their children's lives.

REFERENCES

The Children Act 2004. London: The Stationery Office.
Young Women's Housing Project (2012) *Annual Report 2011–2012*. Sheffield: YWHP.

SUGGESTED READING

Allnock, D. and Hynes, P. (2012) *Therapeutic Services for Sexually Abused Children and Young People: Scoping the Evidence Base*. London: NSPCC.

USEFUL ORGANISATION

Young Women's Housing Project
PO Box 303
Pond Street
Sheffield
S1 1YD
Telephone: 0114 268 0580
Website: www.ywhp.org.uk

CHAPTER 9

LOUDER THAN WORDS
ART THERAPY WITH INDIVIDUALS WITH INTELLECTUAL DISABILITIES WHO HAVE BEEN ABUSED

AMANDA GEE

INTRODUCTION

As an art therapy student I took a part-time job at Vita Community Living Services in Toronto, Ontario, Canada, working with individuals with intellectual disabilities. While working at a day program I noticed that at Vita the only therapy available internally to the individuals receiving service from the organization was behaviour therapy. While behaviour therapy plays an important role, there was something missing. I could see how offering art therapy within the organization could have a huge benefit for some of the individuals I was supporting: those who were dealing with grief and loss, had experienced traumatic events, or who had difficulties with expressing their emotions in appropriate ways. I felt that art therapy could help these individuals to work through their thoughts and feelings in ways which verbal therapy and behaviour therapy could not. So I submitted a proposal to start an art therapy program and it was accepted. I am privileged to work at a community living organization that believes in providing a variety of healing therapies for individuals with intellectual disabilities.[1] What follows is based on my experiences working as an art therapist for this organization.

In my experiences as an art therapist working with individuals with intellectual disabilities who have been abused, I have learned that recovery and healing go together but are still very different things.

---

1   An intellectual disability is "a disability that significantly affects one's ability to learn and use information. It is a disability that is present during childhood and continues throughout one's life" (Community Living Ontario 2012). In Ontario this definition is not just strictly based on the IQ of the individual but also on the individual's need for support in activities of daily living.

From these experiences I have learned that *recovery* is what happens right after the abuse has taken place. Recovery is the immediate aftermath; it starts in the disclosing of the abuse, in the investigation, in the people coming around the individual to provide strength and support. Recovery is getting through the shock of the immediate event, it is in the bandaging of the wounds, and it is in the holding of hands.

Healing is more of a long-term (sometimes a very long-term) process. There is no timeline, and for each individual who has been abused it will be different. It can take months, it can take years, and sometimes healing never happens. Healing for some, takes time, support, and just knowing that they are safe and being believed. However, for others healing sometimes takes professional support, someone such as a therapist or a counsellor to help them to process their thoughts and feelings.

In my role as an art therapist I am often called in right from the beginning (recovery stage) to support an individual with intellectual disabilities:

- through the immediate aftermath
- through disclosing and reporting
- to begin the journey of healing from their experiences through art therapy.

At other times I am contacted to help support when someone has been abused and healing is just not happening; the individual requires some extra-specialized support to start down that path.

ART THERAPY

GOOD PRACTICE POINTS

- Art therapy can only be practiced by professionally trained art therapists.
- Art therapists should also be members in good standing with the Art Therapy Association in their area.
- Registered art therapists can be found through national and local art therapy associations.

Art therapy is therapy that uses simple art materials and processes in a therapeutic setting to facilitate the individual's self-expression.

Art therapy, like other therapies, involves an individual and a trained therapist working together for the common goal of the well-being of the individual. It is based on psychological theory and follows many of the principles of traditional psychotherapy (Malchiodi 2007; Rubin 1984).

GOOD PRACTICE POINT

The art making process is an important part of the therapy, which is not entirely about the finished product; the process of creating the art can often be more important than the finished piece.

Some feelings and experiences are difficult to express using words. In art therapy the art becomes the language; it expresses an individual's inner world and helps to create a dialog between the client and the therapist that may not be possible in words (Malchiodi 2007).

Often when someone hears "art" they think "Well, I'm not an artist"; however, art therapy is not just for artists, or for people "who can draw." Everyone is creative; we all have creativity inside of us; and humans have always used the arts to express themselves. Everyone is capable of making art, especially in a safe and non-judgmental environment where they are free to explore without fear of "not being good enough."

Art making, and the act of being creative, can in itself be healing. People often use art to heal in times of crisis or illness; this may be on their own or within a therapeutic relationship such as art therapy (McNiff 2004). Art making is also inherently therapeutic. Making the art and expressing the difficult thoughts and feelings into the art is cathartic. It provides a release and "gets those feelings out." Once the thoughts and feelings have been put into images or visual form, it is also often easier to talk about the art and what is being expressed than to talk about the feelings themselves.

Art therapy

Art therapy is practiced with an extensive range of people in a wide range of settings. It can be:

Effective with:

- adults as well as children
- individuals with mental illness
- individuals with intellectual disabilities.

Beneficial to individuals experiencing:

- grief
- relationship problems
- chronic illness
- abuse.

Practiced in:

- hospitals
- schools
- community centers
- private practices.

For:

- individuals
- couples
- groups.

ART THERAPY WITH INDIVIDUALS WITH INTELLECTUAL DISABILITIES

It was once thought that individuals with intellectual disabilities could not benefit from any form of therapy—except for behaviour therapy. It was felt that psychotherapy would not, or could not, benefit individuals with intellectual disabilities. This opinion seems to stem from the belief that if someone could not "talk" about their thoughts, feelings, and experiences, the therapy would not be effective (Rees 1998; Upton 2009). However, individuals with intellectual disabilities have the same mental health and healing needs as everyone else.

As Cindy Caprio-Orsini (1996) wrote, "art therapy is an important part of the healing process for this population and sometimes the only way to heal from trauma due to limited range of communication" (p.51). Art provides a way to express difficult feelings that may not otherwise be expressed. Traumatic feelings are difficult to put into words for anyone, and if an individual has difficulty communicating verbally already, it becomes that much more difficult. If these difficult and traumatic feelings are kept inside they can manifest in other ways, such as depression, anger, anxiety, aggression, or other challenging behaviours (Caprio-Orsini 1996). Left unexpressed, feelings can become behaviours. Thus maladaptive behaviours become the "voice" of the trauma, and behaviour therapy can serve as a means of silencing the "voice," thereby compounding the tragedy of victimization.

IIIIIIIIIIIIIIIIIIIIIIIIIIIIIIIIIIIIIIIIIIIIIIIIIIIIIIIIIIIIIIIIIIIIIIIIIIIIIIIIIIIIIIIIIIIIIIIIIIIIIIIIIIIIIIII

CASE EXAMPLE 9.1

Scott,[2] aged 35 years, was referred to art therapy when his anger became too much to handle. Scott had been sexually and physically abused as a child and was never given an opportunity to work through the feelings he had from the trauma. Scott's staff discovered art therapy when trying to find a suitable therapy for him, and since he loved to draw they thought it might help. Scott was quite apprehensive in the beginning sessions, unsure of what to draw. When encouraged to explore his thoughts and feelings in the art he began to express his anger in the art. Week after week he poured his anger onto paper, and outside the sessions his anger began to decrease.

IIIIIIIIIIIIIIIIIIIIIIIIIIIIIIIIIIIIIIIIIIIIIIIIIIIIIIIIIIIIIIIIIIIIIIIIIIIIIIIIIIIIIIIIIIIIIIIIIIIIIIIIIIIIIIII

Art therapy can help individuals with intellectual disabilities to express themselves in ways that words cannot; it can help:

- by providing an avenue for communication and self-expression
- the individual to process difficult emotional and psychological issues.

Since art therapy does not rely entirely on language or verbal skills, for an individual with significant communication and language impairment it allows for enhanced communication of feelings and thoughts in a safe and supportive environment.

---

2   All names and identifying details have been changed to protect the privacy of the individuals.

ADAPTING ART THERAPY FOR
INDIVIDUALS WITH DISABILITIES

There are many things that a therapist must consider in providing art therapy for an individual with intellectual disabilities. The art therapist should have some experience and understanding in the area of disability, and of the systems in place. On the part of the therapist there needs to be a level of comfort in working with individuals with intellectual disabilities, and the willingness to be flexible according to the individual's needs and their own understanding of that individual's history. Art therapists, like any other therapists who decide to provide a service to people with intellectual disabilities, need to confront any prejudices and misconceptions they may have about who people with disabilities are and about the right to treatment for all.

It is important to remember that each person must be considered individually—what works for one person may not work for the next. The therapist has to be very creative and flexible in relation to "what will work" for each individual client. The therapist must also be very creative in how they adapt the process, the space, and the materials (Caprio-Orsini 1996). It is also important to note that art therapy will not be an effective therapeutic modality for everyone. The main thing is to make the therapy as accessible and therapeutic as possible to allow recovery, healing, and personal growth to take place.

||||||||||||||||||||||||||||||||||||||||||||||||||||||||||||||||||||||||||||||||||||||||||||||||||||||||||||

CASE EXAMPLE 9.2

Mary, aged 24 years, was referred to art therapy after her support staff began to notice that she was experiencing anxiety, and was having angry outbursts and panic attacks after she was sexually abused by a family member. Mary needed help but she also had limited verbal communication skills due to her profound disability. At the beginning of her therapy Mary could only manage 20-minute sessions, which built up to 40 minutes over the course of a year. Mary also needed to leave the room frequently to walk a little when she became frustrated or upset.

Mary enjoyed the art materials, and especially enjoyed working with the "feeling faces" that were provided. Mary would focus on the mad and sad faces in the beginning—she cut them out and stuck them on everything, and as she did this she would express verbally that she was "mad." By the end of her year in art therapy Mary began to focus more and more on the happy and laughing "feeling faces." She continued to stick the faces on things, but would also take them with her when she left the session.

The flexibility provided in the sessions regarding time and her need to leave the room allowed for the therapy to move forward in a way that worked for Mary.

IIIIIIIIIIIIIIIIIIIIIIIIIIIIIIIIIIIIIIIIIIIIIIIIIIIIIIIIIIIIIIIIIIIIIIIIIIIIIIIIIIIIIIIIIIIIIIIIIIIIII

REFERRALS

At Vita Community Living Services, referrals come in directly to the art therapist. These referrals are filled out on a general referral form by support staff, families, other clinical professionals, or the individuals themselves. As each referral comes in it is reviewed for suitability. If any clarification is needed the person who completed the form is contacted. If the referral is deemed appropriate for art therapy it is put onto the waitlist until an appropriate spot becomes available. This waitlist is prioritized so that if someone is in immediate need of therapy they are moved to the top of the list and fit in as soon as possible. For example, if someone has been abused or has experienced another traumatic event, they are prioritized. If there is an immediate need for a crisis intervention plan, the referral would go to a behaviour therapist on the team first, to address the safety concerns while arrangements were made to start the therapy.

INDIVIDUAL VERSUS GROUP THERAPY

In the immediate recovery period after the abuse, individual art therapy might be the best choice to enable the art therapist to focus on that one individual. However, in the long-term, if there is an appropriate art therapy group that the individual could join, a group therapy setting can be quite helpful in the healing process. In a group, individuals who have had similar experiences can provide support to each other in a very dynamic way (Liebmann 2012). Ultimately this depends on the needs of the individual and whether they will thrive in a group setting. The size of a group should really depend on the needs and abilities of the individuals, the agency, and the therapist (and if there is one, co-therapist); other considerations will be the comfort level of the individuals, the comfort level of the therapist, and the space available. Personally I think having four to eight people in a group works well.

INTAKE PROCESS

The intake process is hugely important for the success of the therapy. In addition to the usual intake information, it is during this process that the therapist can find out how the individual communicates, whether the individual communicates traditionally, and what certain words and gestures mean. Knowing how someone communicates is immensely important to developing a therapeutic relationship with them, and ultimately in being able to help them recover and heal.

GOOD PRACTICE POINTS

- Develop an intake form that can be used each time an individual begins therapy so that things are not missed.
- Include reason for referral, medical information, assistive devices, as well as anything else that you feel would be helpful.
- The intake form should also have a section on communication: How does the individual communicate "yes" and "no"? How do they communicate if they like something, or dislike something? How do they communicate "hurt" and "upset"? How do they communicate "happy," "sad," "mad," and "scared"? Does the individual use any assistive communication strategies such as a communication board?
- Include the individual in the intake process, but also speak to staff and/or family to gather as much information as you can.

The therapist should use this time to find out who will be supporting the individual to attend the sessions. Things to consider are:

- Who will be bringing them?
- Will the support person stay at the site or will they leave and come back to pick the client up?
- Would it be useful for the support person to stay to support in case the individual does not want to stay in a session?

While these things may seem trivial, they are vital to the therapeutic process. Individuals with disabilities rely on others; this is one factor in their vulnerability to abuse, and also in their vulnerability in other areas of their life.

THE THERAPEUTIC RELATIONSHIP

The therapeutic relationship is crucial to the therapy being effective. This is the relationship that allows the therapy to happen. The therapeutic relationship is about two individuals working towards the same goal—that is, the well-being of the individual in therapy; and it is based on trust. To begin the journey towards healing, this trusting relationship must exist (Ogiers and Oz 2006).

Establishing a therapeutic relationship with an individual with an intellectual disability may take a long time, for several reasons. There can be communication barriers, a slower "getting to know you" process, and, as mentioned above, the issue of trust. Often the therapist can be seen as linked with or allied with the staff. The individual with an intellectual disability sees the therapist as staff, and therefore allied with staff, rather than with them. This is a major hurdle to overcome in order to move forward in the therapy. The therapist has to earn the client's trust. One of the most important ways of doing this is through maintaining confidentiality.

||||||||||||||||||||||||||||||||||||||||||||||||||||||||||||||||||||||||||||||||||||||||||||||||||||||

CASE EXAMPLE 9.3

Mark, aged 62 years, began art therapy after being physically hurt by a member of staff. He would come to his art therapy sessions every week and would make art but would barely acknowledge his art therapist. When Mark did start to interact with his art therapist he was very careful about his words and seemed very nervous about expressing his thoughts and feelings to the therapist. Mark would ask if she was going to tell his staff, and the therapist reassured him that she would maintain his confidentiality. After several months in art therapy Mark announced that he trusted her to not tell, and began to tell the story of his life through his art and his words.

||||||||||||||||||||||||||||||||||||||||||||||||||||||||||||||||||||||||||||||||||||||||||||||||||||||

Maintaining confidentiality is not only important for a therapist, it is required by the profession. What makes confidentiality difficult when working with individuals with intellectual disabilities is their support staff and/or families. The support people often want to know: "What's happening in therapy? What are they talking about?" The therapist needs to be able to say "that is confidential" when necessary, and to know how to communicate that things are progressing without breaking that trust. It is important to keep the lines of communication open without breaching confidentiality.

During the first meeting or session with the individual the therapist should explain confidentiality and what it means. There are some things that legally cannot be kept confidential, such as if an individual with an intellectual disability is being hurt. In Ontario, if there is a clear allegation of abuse, the therapist is required either to support the individual to call the police, or to make the call themselves with the individual. It should be made clear to the individual from the beginning that there are some exceptions to the confidentiality rule.

The therapist must be patient, as the therapeutic relationship may take a while to develop to the point where it feels like the therapy is moving forward. When working with someone who has been abused there is also the level of fear and distrust, as they have been betrayed, often by the people who are supposed to protect them (Ogiers and Oz 2006).

GOOD PRACTICE POINTS

- Maintain confidentiality when you can.
- Inform the client from the very beginning that there are exceptions to what you can keep confidential—such as abuse.
- Know the laws in your area about reporting abuse of individuals with intellectual disabilities.
- Remember confidentiality when talking to support people.

Trust is also earned over time by the therapist being careful regarding the issue of "power." The power dynamic exists in almost every interaction that people with disabilities have with care providers or with therapists. Individuals with disabilities are used to being "told" how they feel, or how they should or should not feel. They are used to subverting their will to keep staff happy and to avoid punishing consequences that can come from truthfully speaking their minds. Therapist need to ensure that they communicate to the individual that they are safe in sessions and will not contradict or punish their feelings. The "right" to feelings is a major right, and individuals with disabilities sometimes do not have experience of being able to express any emotion other than "happy."

GOOD PRACTICE POINT

The therapist's job from the beginning is to demonstrate through behavior, not words, a vitally important message: "You are safe here, both with me and from me."

TREATMENT GOALS

It is important to establish treatment goals with the individual. These goals should be made *with* the individual and not for them by staff or parents. They should reflect the reason for referral but also should include goals related to the art therapy in the beginning, such as:

- developing a trusting relationship with the therapist
- learning to identify simple feelings using images
- exploring different art materials and learning how to use them
- learning to use the art making process to express thoughts and feelings.

Goals should change as the therapy progresses, to reflect where the client is in their treatment and the progress they have made. Goals should also reflect what the client wants to achieve in art therapy.

ENVIRONMENT

The therapeutic environment has to be a safe and creative space, but it also needs to be carefully considered to be optimally therapeutic for each individual who comes for treatment.

||||||||||||||||||||||||||||||||||||||||||||||||||||||||||||||||||||||||||||||||||||||||||||||||||||||||||||||

CASE EXAMPLE 9.4

Sarah, aged 43 years, was referred to art therapy after being sexually abused by a peer at her day program. Staff recognized that she was having a difficult time processing her thoughts and feelings about what had happened, and so they submitted a referral. From the first moment that Sarah came into the art therapy room she was very focused on the wall clock, which ticked loudly. She would stare at it and become agitated when the therapist attempted to interact with her. Sarah loved to make art but she would not explore any of the art materials.

Prior to her next session I removed the clock from the room. When Sarah came in she asked about the clock, but when told that it was gone she was able to focus on the art making and begin her journey towards healing. Sarah eagerly came and participated in the art therapy sessions once the clock had disappeared.

||||||||||||||||||||||||||||||||||||||||||||||||||||||||||||||||||||||||||||||||||||||||||||||||||||||||||||||

The therapeutic environment or therapy room is very important. The space must be:

- private
- calm
- accessible
- therapeutic.

If an art therapy room is not available, any private space (with the obvious exception of the individual's bedroom) will work, as long as there is space to create art. It is important that no-one will be walking in on the session and the space is not too loud or too chaotic. If necessary the space should be tailored for each individual.

GOOD PRACTICE POINTS

- Consider the space carefully, based on each individual.
- Consider supplies, seating, lighting, and other elements, in the room, based on the needs of the individual and the information collected in the intake process.

SESSIONS

Typically sessions take place once a week at a specific time; however, in times of crisis the number of sessions a week can be altered. Sessions typically run for 30 minutes to one hour. This depends on the needs of the individual. In my practice I typically start at 45 minutes for each session and then assess as the sessions continue. Often session length can build over time as the individual develops trust in the therapist and comfort in the therapeutic environment. For example, one individual may have 30-minute sessions once a week for the duration of the therapy; another individual could start at 20 minutes and could build up over time to 45-minute sessions over the course of their therapy.

It is important not to go into the first session with expectations of how it will go. It is often best to start with an introduction session where the individual is introduced to the therapist and the art therapy room. This session is where any necessary paperwork can be filled out and it is a chance to talk about "what happens" in sessions. This is also the time when any consent forms and contracts can be filled out, and duration for the therapy can be discussed.

Often a support person will be present in the first session, so that they are also introduced to the process. If the individual is comfortable with exploring some art materials that first session, the support person can leave the space to allow the therapy to begin.

MATERIALS

As an art therapist it is important to have a wide variety of materials available.

Materials for use in art therapy

- paper
- markers
- wax crayons
- pencil crayons
- pastels
- paint
- paint brushes

- clay
- pipe cleaners
- fabric scraps
- pom poms
- glue
- scissors
- glitter

Any art material really is suitable, though I stay away from complicated materials such as oil paint. It is important that the therapist is comfortable with all of the supplies that s/he has in the room, so that if an individual wants to use them but does not know how, the therapist can provide direction. It is essential that the art therapist has materials available that can enable the individual to experience success.

When considering materials for a session with an individual with an intellectual disability, there are some important things to keep in mind—and remember that every session is different because every person is unique. Consider how many supplies you have available; there should be enough to explore but not too many, so that they are not distracting. It is also important to be aware of which materials are non-toxic and to make sure that you have plenty on hand. If you are working with an individual who puts their hands in their mouth, you need to make sure that they will not get sick. Another thing to be aware of is gross motor functioning: make sure that you have a variety of brushes with thick and thin handles, chunky pastels, and thicker markers, to ensure that everyone can use the materials. Clay can be challenging as it is messy and inedible; if you feel that an individual could benefit from the tactile experience of working with clay, you can easily make play dough, and the homemade dough is non-toxic. Finger paints can also easily be made at home.

Having a variety of image sources available is also useful, in case an individual would rather work with collage materials instead of drawing. Having a variety of different magazines and old calendars on hand makes this easy. Sometimes an individual is struggling to express something in a drawing, and being able to rip out images instead of drawing them can make the process easier.

It is also useful to have a selection of "feeling faces" available for the individual to use. These can be purchased or drawn, and some can be found on the internet. Individuals with intellectual disabilities often have a difficult time naming or identifying their feelings (Upton 2009), and being able to identify basic feelings in oneself is very important to healing. Having different faces available to use in the art opens a dialog about what different feelings look like and feel like.

GOOD PRACTICE POINTS

- It is important to have a good supply of non-toxic materials. Consider who your client is: will they put their hands in their mouth? Most markers and crayons are non-toxic, and you can also purchase non-toxic pastels and paint.
- Non-toxic supplies can also be made easily in the kitchen. You can find recipes for play dough and finger paints on the Internet.
- It is important to consider the fine motor skills of the individual you will be working with. Make sure that you have a variety of brushes—thick/thin handles, long/short handles, round handles. Other materials need to be considered as well—markers, pastels, and crayons are all available in a variety of sizes and thicknesses.
- Travelling material kit: it is good to have a small set of supplies and paper that you can take to a different site if an individual cannot come to your art therapy room for some reason. In this kit it is good to have markers, pencil crayons, paper, scissors, a glue stick, as well as any other supplies that may come in handy. I often have beads with me, as I find these can be cathartic if the individual is not interested in the other art supplies that day.

DIRECTIVES

To use directives or not is always a consideration. A directive is when the therapist provides a direction or suggestion regarding what the individual should draw or make in session. In my work I find that it is best to start by encouraging the client to work spontaneously. In the first session it can be useful to suggest that they decorate a folder to keep their work in—this is a good way to get the individual involved in the art materials in a non-threatening way. A piece of poster board folded in two makes a simple folder so that the art is kept safely together.

If an individual is having a difficult time figuring out "what to make" or "what to draw," it can be useful to offer up a directive, such as "draw a house" or "draw a person/yourself," or to do a scribble drawing. There are many books and resources available full of possible directives, or you could develop your own.

DOCUMENTATION AND COMMUNICATION WITH OTHER PROFESSIONALS

As in all therapies, it is important for the therapist to maintain regular documentation regarding the sessions. It is also important for the art therapist to keep the artwork created in session safe if the individual chooses to leave it in the art therapy room or with the art therapist. Often individuals want to take their art home to share with staff or families. Safety needs to be considered when artwork is being taken home, especially if that artwork is expressing feelings regarding the abuse that the individual experienced. If the artwork is not "safe" to be shared with others, reassure the individual that the artwork will be kept safe, and explain why it is "unsafe" for the artwork to go home. All of the artwork left with the therapist should be kept locked in a safe place.

When working with individuals with intellectual disabilities the art therapist will most likely be part of a team of professionals who work with that individual. There could be many other people supporting the individual, including a psychologist, a behavioural therapist, day program staff, residential staff, supervisors, and contract workers. It is important to have open communication with the whole team without breaching confidentiality. It is also important to reassure the individual about that confidentially on a regular basis.

TERMINATION

Termination is inevitable in therapy. Sometimes termination happens not because the treatment goals have been achieved but because there was a limited number of sessions allowed, transportation becomes impossible, or money runs out. Ideally, therapy can continue until the goals have been reached and the individual can participate in the decision regarding when the therapy will end.

Since therapy involves a strong working relationship, termination can be a significant loss. It is best practice to involve the individual in the termination planning process; this will help them to feel as though they are also in control of what is happening. Once termination has been decided upon, it is helpful to have an open dialog with the individual about ending and how that will happen. The individual can be encouraged to help pick an end date and to plan what that last session will look like. If appropriate the therapist can give the individual a goodbye gift of art supplies to encourage them to continue expressing themselves creatively (Rubin 1984).

GOOD PRACTICE POINTS

- When struggling to decide if it is time to terminate the therapy, check in with the individual, look at the treatment goals, and talk to the individual's support staff or family to see how the individual has been outside of session.
- If the therapy is no longer demonstrating a therapeutic benefit, it is time to terminate the therapy.

CONCLUSION

Art therapy continues to be an amazing therapeutic modality for supporting individuals with intellectual disabilities who have been abused to recover, grow, learn about themselves, and ultimately heal. It allows for a level of communication and self-expression that is often not possible in words.

The art therapist must be creative, flexible, and adaptive to the individual needs of each client. The environment, the materials, and the process must also be adapted for each individual to allow for freedom of expression and success in the creative process.

Art making is inherently healing. Through the art making process, and with the support of an art therapist, individuals with intellectual disabilities who have been abused can express and process the difficult thoughts and feelings associated with the abuse, and can begin the journey towards healing. For individuals with intellectual disabilities the artwork that they create in art therapy can speak louder than words.

REFERENCES

Caprio-Orsini, C. (1996) *A Thousand Words: Healing through Art for People with Developmental Disabilities*. Eastman, Quebec: Diverse City Press.

Community Living Ontario (2012) *What is an Intellectual Disability?* Available at www.communitylivingontario.ca/about-us/what-intellectual-disability. Accessed on August 17, 2012.

Liebmann, M. (2012) "Developing Themes for Art Therapy Groups." In C.A. Malchiodi (ed.) *Handbook of Art Therapy* (2nd edition). New York: The Guilford Press.

Malchiodi, C.A. (2007) *The Art Therapy Sourcebook*. New York: McGraw-Hill.

McNiff, S. (2004) *Art Heals: How Creativity Cures the Soul*. Boston, MA: Shambhala.

Ogiers, S. and Oz, S. (2006) *Overcoming Childhood Sexual Trauma: A Guide to Breaking Through the Wall of Fear for Practitioners and Survivors*. Binghamton, NY: Haworth Press.

Rees, M. (ed.) (1998) *Drawing on Difference: Art Therapy with People who have Learning Difficulties*. New York: Routledge.

Rubin, J.A. (1984) *The Art of Art Therapy*. New York: Brunner/Mazel.

Upton, J. (2009) "When Words are Not Enough: Creative Therapeutic Approaches." In T. Cottis (ed.) *Intellectual Disability, Trauma and Psychotherapy*. New York: Routledge.

SUGGESTED READING

Cottis, T. (ed.) (2009) *Intellectual Disability, Trauma and Psychotherapy*. New York: Routledge.

Hingsburger, D. (2006) *Black Ink: Practical Advice and Clear Guidelines for Dealing with Reports of Sexual Abuse from People with Intellectual Disabilities*. Barrie, Ontario: Diverse City Press.

Hingsburger, D. (2010) *Home Safe*. Barrie, Ontario: Diverse City Press.

Makin, S.R. (2000) *Therapeutic Art Directives and Resources*. London: Jessica Kingsley Publishers.

Malchiodi, C.A. (ed.) (2012) *Handbook of Art Therapy* (2nd edition). New York: The Guilford Press.

USEFUL ORGANIZATIONS

Vita Community Living Services and Mens Sana Families for Mental Health
4301 Weston Road
Toronto
ON
M9L 2Y3
Canada
Telephone: (416) 749-6234
Website: www.vitacls.org

The Canadian Art Therapy Association
www.catainfo.ca

The British Association of Art Therapists
www.baat.org

The American Art Therapy Association
www.arttherapy.org

CHAPTER 10

RECOVERY AND HEALING IN SURVIVORS OF THE HOLOCAUST

JUDITH HASSAN

INTRODUCTION

This chapter focuses on the aftermath of severe trauma experienced by those who survived the Nazi Holocaust and details the therapeutic responses needed to aid recovery and healing.

- It begins by looking at the factors that impeded recovery for survivors after liberation in 1945.
- It indicates how survivors attempted to aid their own recovery, and highlights the incomplete nature of that process in terms of emotional healing.
- It points out how survivors' unhealed emotional wounds re-open as they get older, and stresses that it is never too late to work towards some sense of peace and healing, even if there can be no complete cure for the survivors' suffering.
- It details the adaptations professionals need to make in their professional practice to reach out and engage with re-traumatised survivors.
- It describes the therapeutic model that developed in partnership with the survivors, and how the model contributes to further recovery and healing.
- The chapter concludes by looking at the last part of the survivors' lives and how the positive opportunities for emotional and spiritual healing continue until death.

My 36 years' work with Holocaust survivors has taught me that the immediate physical recovery from severe trauma can mask the deep and on-going emotional impact of that trauma. At the same time the survivors' resilience, strength, will to live and openness to work with me has inspired me to believe in the possibility of healing. This belief has steered my on-going commitment to find new and creative ways of bringing survivors closer to healing the emotional repercussions of their severe pain. Survivors empowered me to fight for the establishment of specialist services to meet their unmet needs, and to share this knowledge with other war trauma survivors. My work has helped me to feel liberated from some of my traditional social work practices, and has changed the way I see the world. As a result, I think I am a more hopeful and positive person.

WHAT DID RECOVERY MEAN IN THE POST-HOLOCAUST EXPERIENCE?

When World War II ended in 1945, the world was in chaos. Those who had been incarcerated in death camps or ghettoes, or in hiding, had spent years living with death, in a world turned upside-down, and in which they had felt abandoned. Survivors were physically liberated from the torture, starvation and inhumane conditions they had been subjected to, but many emerged from this horror only to find that their hope of being reunited with family and friends was shattered by the reality that all had indeed been lost. They had no homes to return to or communities to belong to, as these had been destroyed by the Nazis. Many spent the early post-war years in displaced persons (DP) camps, unable to mourn their massive losses, as their minds were dominated by day-to-day survival. The severe trauma they went through struggled to find an outlet, and any notion of recovery had virtually no meaning. When survivors left the DP camps, many of them experienced additional factors that impeded recovery. First, they were largely met with a wall of silence – virtually no-one wanted to listen to them, and they learned not to speak about their suffering. This response was at variance with their perceived duty to those who had been murdered. They believed that, as witnesses, they needed to tell the world what happened so that it should never happen again. This was their principal *raison d'être* for continuing to live. The enforced silence meant that survivors' traumatic memories emerged endlessly in nightmares but were generally not spoken about by day.

Second, those survivors who did seek professional help often found that they were not understood or even believed. A medical/psychiatric model, based on William Niederland's classification of survivor syndrome (1981), was used to try and make sense of the survivors' unimaginable horror, and to summarise the complexity of their post-traumatic difficulties.

There was a tendency to assume that all survivors had been damaged, physically and emotionally, instead of seeing their condition, as Victor Frankl did in his book *Man's Search for Meaning* (1987), as a normal reaction to extremely abnormal experiences. This assumption then transferred from medical to therapeutic settings. It influenced many professionals to over-emphasise pathology rather than focusing on survivors' past and present strengths. Survivors have told me that this was not helpful to them, and a wide gulf developed between the survivors and those trying to help them. I believe this was a major setback to recovery and healing. I suggest that this should also be taken into account with the current diagnosis of post-traumatic stress disorder.

In response to this lack of understanding, plus the facts that there was no welfare state, and that Britain was recovering from the horrors of war, some survivors got together to support each other, although others continued to feel like outsiders. For most survivors, returning to life after living with death was a major struggle. Survivors needed to concentrate their energy on starting anew. Their emotional recovery seemed to pale into insignificance against the backdrop of their past suffering. Out of necessity survivors tended to focus on moving forward rather than dealing with the past. In fact, with very little help, most survivors adapted remarkably well to life in the UK, establishing new homes for themselves, finding work, raising families to replace those who had been murdered, and learning a new language and customs. Some survivors contributed significantly to the UK through a whole range of professions, including medicine, psychoanalysis and science, as well as through the arts and media. This led to an assumption on the part of non-survivors that a complete recovery had been made. In fact the emotional repercussions of the survivors' severe trauma had only been suppressed, and it resurfaced, often with great ferocity, as they got older and frailer.

THE LONG-TERM EFFECT OF TRAUMA AND ITS IMPACT ON RECOVERY AND HEALING

Thirty to forty years after the trauma the survivors' grief remained inside them 'like a stone', as one survivor described it. This largely unaddressed grief did not allow survivors to heal, but converted itself into emotional vulnerabilities that lay just below the surface of the survivors' skin, waiting to erupt with age. Triggers for re-experiencing past trauma have included retirement, bereavement, loss of health, entering a hospital or residential establishment, or children leaving home. It is also a normal part of aging to remember details from the past more vividly than recent events. With age, survivors tend to become less able to blot out or control their unwanted traumatic memories, especially those with dementia. However, no two survivors are the same and there are many variables that affected their recovery, both then and now.

GOOD PRACTICE POINTS

Many variables can affect recovery. These include:
- the age when the trauma happened
- whether they had good childhood experiences
- whether they were with their families during the Holocaust
- what happened to them during and after the Holocaust.

The overwhelming impact of these resurfacing traumatic memories, both for survivors and those involved with trying to help them, led to a spiral of helplessness that clouded early attempts at healing. Listening to survivors, I came to realise that therapeutic services can only assist in healing when they are able to engage traumatised people and have meaning for them, when they feel helped by these services. However sophisticated the professionals' knowledge and skills may be, they are of little value if they cannot be made use of by the traumatised person. To facilitate healing I had significantly to adapt my traditional ways of working.

KEY ADAPTATIONS IN PROFESSIONAL PRACTICE
TO PROMOTE RECOVERY AND HEALING

To help survivors move forward in their emotional recovery, I had to unlearn some of my familiar social work practices and relearn responses based on what *survivors* thought would help them. The adaptations I developed include the following:

- Listening closely to survivors' experiences over extended periods of time, and learning from them *before* responding, helps pave the way to more meaningful and healing therapeutic services.
- Recognising the vital importance of developing specific and specialist therapeutic services for survivors avoids the pitfall of trying to fit them into existing models.
- Having the courage to go beyond the familiar responses of talking/ counselling to include a wide range of creative approaches and

social programmes offers survivors the freedom to choose which approaches will help them.

- Encouraging mutual support groups as a first response to traumatised people recognises the importance of survivors' power to heal each other. This is often more meaningful to them than one-to-one encounters with professionals.
- A willingness to work in a variety of settings (e.g. café or social centre), and not just in a social work/therapy context, increases the opportunities to reach out to survivors who may feel vulnerable in asking for professional help.
- Focusing on empowering survivors helps to strengthen their coping mechanisms. It changes the familiar practice of being a provider of services into a working partnership with survivors.
- Being facilitators rather than experts helps to avoid a tendency to make assumptions, or make prescriptive responses.
- A willingness to use informal, flexible and more equal relationships with survivors helps to build a bridge to facilitate trust and healing.
- Working beyond the familiar focus of individual/family towards building a community with survivors helps to heal the loss of identity and belonging experienced in the Holocaust.
- Freedom from professional jargon helps us to communicate through a 'shared language', and to reach out to survivors as people rather than clients/patients.
- Focusing on spirituality in addition to the familiar practical and emotional responses provides another healing dimension.
- Ensuring the centrality of hope, and maintaining a belief that something can be done to alleviate emotional suffering, allows a climate of healing to develop.

TRANSLATING ADAPTATIONS IN PROFESSIONAL PRACTICE INTO A HEALING/ THERAPEUTIC SERVICE FOR SURVIVORS

I evolved these adaptations in my practice over a long period of time. They needed to be incorporated into a therapeutic model that would take account of the survivors' specific and particular traumatic experiences. My aim was to make the therapeutic model meaningful to survivors through my on-going consultation with them, and thereby increase its potential to heal.

The therapeutic model that developed consists of a multidisciplinary therapy centre, Shalvata (opened in 1990), adjacent to a social centre, the Holocaust Survivors' Centre (HSC) (opened in 1993). The two centres symbolically represent the two worlds of darkness (the world of death and destruction in the trauma) and light (the world of life before the trauma), which became severed in the Holocaust.

Shalvata's primary focus is to address the dark shadow of the survivors' past as well as working with their current practical and emotional issues. The HSC's social programme predominantly aims at relieving traumatic memory as it emerges in later life, connecting or reconnecting survivors to life-enhancing experiences, and giving them a sense of belonging and community which was taken away from them in the Holocaust.

However, to try and heal the rupture in survivors' lives caused by the Holocaust, it was essential for the two centres to be woven together into one integrated, therapeutic whole in which darkness and light could co-exist. Bringing the two centres together helps survivors to live side-by-side with their trauma, never forgetting it, but at the same time being able to keep one foot in the world of the living through their enjoyment of the social programme.

SHALVATA'S CONTRIBUTION TO RECOVERY AND HEALING
If Shalvata (Hebrew for peace of mind) existed on its own without the HSC adjacent to it, its specialist staff would still be able to offer significant comfort to survivors through practical responses to survivors' physical needs, particularly as they age. Shalvata would also be able to considerably lighten the survivors' emotional difficulties through its one-to-one and group encounters (including groups for former hidden children; for those who came here as unaccompanied children on the Kindertransport; an emotional support group for survivors who speak publicly about their experiences; and a spouses group), as well as through recording their testimonies for posterity.

GOOD PRACTICE POINTS

Key healing aspects in Shalvata's therapeutic focus:
- Empower survivors.
- Give survivors the freedom to choose from a wide range of therapeutic options.
- Strengthen survivors' coping mechanisms.

Empowering survivors rather than fostering dependency helps to aid recovery from some of the negative impacts they experienced as powerless victims.

Consulting with survivors – giving them control over the length and frequency of individual sessions and involving them in decisions about which therapeutic options they feel would be most helpful to them – helps to heal and restore some of the dignity and self-worth that were denied them in the Holocaust. Focusing on the survivors' strengths helps to liberate them from the pathological labels previously attached to them, and opens up a wider range of healing therapeutic interventions.

I shall now illustrate how Shalvata adapted these therapeutic principles by focusing on two common practices, namely professional boundaries and assessment.

Professional boundaries

The survivors' past fear of authority (Nazis) and victimisation meant that any professional, however benevolent, was nevertheless seen as potentially threatening. To help overcome this difficulty, it became clear that Shalvata's specialist workers needed to develop more flexible, informal and equal relationships with survivors of severe trauma. Shalvata's workers needed to understand the boundary, but interpret it in a way that allowed them to be more accessible, and more willing to share appropriate personal information with the survivors. Loosening some of the traditional boundary restrictions allows Shalvata's team to engage with survivors whose trust in others was shattered in the Holocaust. This approach helps to heal some of the survivors' fears of being at the mercy of others.

Boundaries between the two centres also needed to be crossed, to allow staff to get to know survivors in different ways, and to de-stigmatise Shalvata as just a place for 'survivors with problems', as they initially saw it. To implement this idea, Shalvata's team not only work in the familiar office or home-visit environments, but also meet survivors informally in the HSC, sometimes over lunch, on social outings, or facilitating one of the informal groups in the HSC, such as the Hebrew singing or Solo group (for survivors without family or close support). This fluid interaction between staff and survivors has led to a significant increase in survivor self-referrals to Shalvata, many of whom would formerly have shunned the idea of therapeutic intervention, and would have remained unreachable. The result of widening these boundaries has been to extend the range of healing options for survivors significantly.

Assessment

It is common professional practice to make an assessment of a client's difficulties and summarise the possible interventions that would help alleviate those problems. When working with survivors, it is essential to try and understand what it would feel like for them to be assessed by someone who has not gone through such severe suffering. How would survivors even begin to describe the indescribable? Besides, based on past experience, survivors also fear that they will not be believed. Shalvata's initial process is to allow plenty of time and depth to explore the raw, complex and often chaotic world of resurfacing trauma. Shalvata's non-statutory context frees its specialist staff to resist the pressure to prescribe outcomes in order to conclude assessments neatly and quickly. For survivors of severe trauma, assessment is not finite. It is an on-going, open-ended and flexible exploration. In getting to know the survivor, and by asking for clarification when we do not understand, the specialist worker searches with them for the 'spark amongst the ashes', for that is where the trauma lies buried. Together they seek to rediscover the strength that helped the survivor to cope in the past, and which could aid recovery and healing in the present.

The following example illustrates how I adapted the two issues of professional boundaries and assessment in my work with a Holocaust survivor.

‖‖

CASE EXAMPLE 10.1: ENCOUNTER WITH A SURVIVOR – ISAAC

Isaac came to see me when his son committed suicide. Isaac had survived the death camps, including Auschwitz-Birkenau. After liberation he got on with his life. He set up a successful business, married and had two children. He did not talk to his family about the horror he had been through. He had not only endured severe hardship and suffering, but had also lost his teenage years. Isaac was in his mid-60s when I first met him in one of the mutual support groups for survivors that I facilitated. When this latest tragedy occurred the memories of overwhelming loss returned to him, and he was losing the will to live. Getting to know each other informally in the group made it easier for him to come and see me at Shalvata. His sense of hopelessness and despair was overwhelming and it was difficult to see a way forward.

During the course of our meetings, Isaac spoke about his love of art and painting. It was this 'spark' that allowed us to focus on the creative areas in his life. Crossing the boundary between Shalvata and the HSC helped him to develop his artistic skills and share them with fellow survivors in the art group. He also achieved outstandingly in the academic world. Having lost any chance of education under the Nazis, this mastery helped him to cope with the chaos that emerged in his emotional life, triggered by his son's tragic death.

Though problems continued in his life, and he continued to meet the art therapist in Shalvata, this core strength gave him the essential hope to heal some of the raw grief, both past and present, and allowed him to live more positively into old age.

||||||||||||||||||||||||||||||||||||||||||||||||||||||||||||||||||||||||||||||||||||||||||||||||||||||||||||||

One of the challenges of working with survivors like Isaac is trying to keep hope alive long enough to stay with the pain of past and current trauma. It is important to point to the factors that strengthened me to continue with Isaac.

GOOD PRACTICE POINTS

- Work as part of a team, and not in isolation.
- Receive on-going specialist consultation and supervision.
- Have a positive and uplifting counterpoint like the HSC when dealing with trauma of such magnitude.

The time that Isaac spent in Shalvata helped him significantly to begin the long journey towards some healing. However, it could not adequately deal with his deep feelings of isolation, emanating from his incarceration in the death camp, which magnified his despair. The HSC became the catalyst that accelerated the healing process, for Isaac and other survivors. I shall now look at the crucial role of the HSC in complementing Shalvata's work.

THE HOLOCAUST SURVIVORS' CENTRE: ITS ROLE IN RECOVERY AND HEALING

Founding the Holocaust Survivors' Centre (HSC) in 1993, next door to Shalvata, was a key turning-point in post-traumatic healing. My earlier work with mutual support groups for survivors in the 1980s had shown me how survivors can help each other to live positively without needing to talk about their trauma, and where they would not need to ask for professional help, where laughter and enjoyment could co-exist with sadness. These survivors told me that what they needed most was a place of their own, a home from home where they would feel safe. The empty space next door to Shalvata turned that wish into a reality, with funding provided by Jewish Care.

Building the HSC into a community to replace, in some sense, the ones wiped out by the Nazis is the single most important factor in helping to heal survivors. A community creates a feeling of belonging, an identity and a voice, all of which were denied to victims in the Holocaust. The active engagement of survivors in the development and decision-making in their centre, and their empowerment through its elected consultative advisory committee, ensures the appropriateness and meaningfulness of the service to them. Survivors experience the healing effect of 'feeling that they matter', as one survivor put it.

The six-days-a-week social programme, including parties and outings, helps relieve the negative impact of traumatic memories. Survivors can attend the HSC as often as they like, choosing whether to participate in the programme, just eating in the café, or meeting fellow survivors. When they are ill or have a bereavement, they are not left to cope alone. The centre is open on Sundays and Bank Holidays, often an isolating time for older people. For some survivors at the HSC/Shalvata the staff and their fellow members become like a family that takes the place of those murdered in the Holocaust. This helps survivors not to feel abandoned, as they did in the Holocaust, and helps heal some of their past fears about the indifference of the world to their plight.

The staff in a specialist centre of this kind can anticipate some of the difficulties that may arise and try to alleviate or even avert them. For example, understanding the profound impact of past starvation on survivors today ensures that there is nutritious food available at all times, that they can choose what they want to eat, and that there is always a plate of bread available to free them from their past fear of never-ending hunger. Serving a thick, nourishing soup every day provides a healing, positive experience in contrast to their memories of the thin, watery starvation rations in the death camps.

The art and creative writing classes explore new and creative ways of expression as an alternative to returning to the trauma itself or speaking about it. For example, the survivors' positive images in their painting help to lift their mood, and encourage mastery over the dark feelings that may lie deep inside them. The HSC is an uplifting celebration of survival. The survivors' positive feelings are one of the best antidotes to the injustices that were done to them, and allow healing to impact on their lives.

The social programme is only part of the equation in emotionally healing survivors. Significantly important is the centre's work in training survivors to speak publicly in schools and other educational establishments, in prisons, to footballers about issues of racism in football grounds, to the media, etc. The structure of these sessions, the interest shown by their audiences and the positive feedback they receive give meaning to their continued survival. In this sense meaning and healing are synonymous.

GOOD PRACTICE POINTS

Key healing aspects that emerge from the HSC:
- Set up mutual support groups as a first response to trauma.
- Establish the infrastructure for a specialist therapeutic service.
- Offer a safe haven for survivors to meet frequently.
- Focus on building a community in partnership with survivors.
- Empower survivors through their active participation in decision-making.
- Develop a meaningful social/educational programme in partnership with survivors.

HEALING AT THE END OF LIFE

The possibilities for healing continue until the end of life. To let go of their lives, survivors need to feel that all they have witnessed, and all that they have carried for those who were murdered, will be remembered in future generations. To assist in the process of healing, we need to work with survivors to prepare for the end of life, and for them to feel that their suffering and life experiences have not been in vain. We need to ask them how they wish to be remembered, and which are the key issues that would help them to find some peace of mind. In my experience the presence of justice, spirituality and hope, though not exclusively, are healing components as survivors think of their end and of the future after they have gone.

The healing power of justice for survivors may be linked to more recent German Government payments to former slave labourers. The active role of certain survivors in securing the slave labour payments gives them, and other survivors, a feeling of victory over their oppressors, which is in itself healing. Though it is not possible to compensate financially for all the hardship they have been through, the payments nevertheless signify for survivors some public recognition of their suffering, as well as bringing them some physical comfort as they grow frailer. Justice may also be seen in the on-going conviction and trials of Nazi war criminals. The triumph of justice and its healing effect may also be found in each celebration of life including, for some survivors, the joy of grandchildren and great-grandchildren, or even just reaching advanced age (with many over 90 and a few over 100 years old), in defiance of Hitler's plan to wipe all Jews off the face of the earth.

The healing effect of spirituality may be less tangible than that of justice. Spirituality, for survivors, may take many forms, including maximising and enjoying the time they have left. For many aging survivors, spirituality may also have a religious dimension. Some survivors have ambivalent feelings about their Judaism because of the persecution and torture they experienced just because they were Jews. As they grow older, however, many survivors wish to return to their Jewish roots. To help them in this process, survivors can attend the monthly Friday night (Sabbath) dinners at the HSC and celebrations of Jewish festivals. Those who do attend gradually feel connected to the familiar rituals, songs and prayers, as well as enjoying the specially prepared meals. Many say that they experience a feeling of family and of home which they remember from their childhood. This seems to bring emotional comfort.

Other survivors may just wish to come to a Jewish centre, eat kosher food, or find out details about Jewish burial. Over the many years I have worked alongside survivors, I have seen how the centrality of the Jewish/spiritual dimension, which is never imposed, takes on greater significance in healing some of their inner conflicts, including the unanswerable questions to do with faith and the Holocaust, that remained with many survivors in the aftermath of their suffering. This spiritual dimension comforts and prepares many of them for the end of life.

The healing impact of hope in the last part of the survivors' lives is significantly linked to the successful transmission of their legacy to future generations. Despite the establishment of Holocaust exhibitions, the survivors' testimonies and books, the founding of a National Holocaust Memorial Day, and teaching about the Holocaust as part of the national curriculum, survivors continue to fear that all that they have been through will be watered down and ultimately forgotten after they have died. Survivors need other people to carry the details of their lives before, during and after the Holocaust, as well as their rich cultural heritage, which the Nazis tried to eradicate. Reassuring survivors of their continued remembrance brings them hope. Hope was the key to survival in the past and hope needs to be central to the last part of the survivors' lives to maximise the opportunities for healing.

GOOD PRACTICE POINT

Healing can be described as the equilibrium, the balance between negative and positive, between the survivors' horrific memories as victims and their positive life-affirming experiences as survivors.

The key to unlocking the healing process in the latter part of their lives is through intergenerational connections that can be made between survivors and young people who are willing to keep the survivors' memories alive. Involving young people in the centre, helping them to get to know survivors as people who are not defined only by their suffering, seems to bring survivors some peace of mind. For example, educating young people by taking them to visit the death camps in Poland also needs to include debriefing them afterwards in informal meetings with survivors. The survivors' positive message of their strength and coping helps to bring hope to these young people after the horrors of what they have seen in Poland, and the young people in turn bring hope to the survivors by pledging never to forget them.

I shall illustrate the healing impact of justice, spirituality and hope by telling the story of a survivor I worked with – Esther.

||||||||||||||||||||||||||||||||||||||||||||||||||||||||||||||||||||||||||||||||||||||||||||||||||||||

CASE EXAMPLE 10.2: ENCOUNTER WITH A SURVIVOR – ESTHER

Esther was a very young child when her mother was deported to a death camp. Esther was hidden in a convent for three years. Isolated and abandoned, she not only lost her family, her comfort and the security of home, but also lost her childhood. The death of her sister after the war, and her abuse by the family with whom she lived, gave her no emotional foundation on which to build.

I met Esther informally when in her late 40s she attended a child survivor group in Shalvata. At that time she was vibrant and full of life. However, this changed when Esther's son was diagnosed with a life-threatening illness. The powerlessness she felt in relation to her son reactivated frightening memories of the helplessness she had felt 40 years earlier when she was separated from her mother and could do nothing to save her.

Esther asked to see me in Shalvata. We met weekly, and as she began to trust me we started to focus on how we could work together on the resurfacing trauma. When coming to Shalvata Esther started to make connections to her Jewish identity, which had almost disappeared from her life. I asked whether she had ever thought of giving her mother, who was murdered in Auschwitz, a Jewish burial. She welcomed this suggestion. The next nine months were spent helping her to mourn for her mother and sister. Her sister was buried in London, and Esther chose a tombstone that would incorporate both their names. We went to the cemetery with one of my rabbinical colleagues, to recite the ritual mourning prayers for her family. She said that she had been metaphorically 'carrying her mother on her back' for so many years. She felt that justice had finally been done when she gave her mother the Jewish burial which she had been denied in the Holocaust, and by re-uniting her sister with the mother she had always been waiting for.

This small but significant experience helped to heal a part of Esther that had remained untouched since the Holocaust. Esther then felt free to move on in her life.

The healing continued as she maintained a spiritual connection. She began to attend the Friday night (Sabbath) dinners at the HSC, and joined a synagogue. The spirituality fed her positive feelings, and she participated in the creative writing group in the HSC and published a book about her life. She took up painting, went on holidays, and spent more time with her grandchildren.

Esther continued to face major difficulties, including a diagnosis of cancer. Yet she felt that the inner strength and hope she had gained during our work together, and the nurturing she received from her on-going relationship with me over 20 years, helped her to deal with these obstacles.

As I sat with Esther when she was dying, she told me that she remembered the sense of peace and healing she had felt at her mother's 'burial'.

Esther had prepared for the end of her own life, arranged a Jewish burial, made her will, and had her grandchildren with her, even though her son was too ill to be there. Though Esther's life was interspersed with emotional turmoil, the healing that had taken place helped her live positively and die peacefully, aged 70, with courage and dignity.

CONCLUSION

When I compare my early work with Holocaust survivors, many of whom were so traumatised that suicide seemed the only option, with survivors I see today, I can clearly see the positive impact that our services have had. When I see so many survivors living positively into old age, maximising the time they have left, and letting go of their lives more peacefully, I realise that some form of spiritual liberation and emotional healing has taken place.

I have demonstrated how, by listening and learning from survivors, and by having the courage to adapt and develop new and creative ways of working in partnership with them, it is possible to aid their recovery and promote healing. By empowering them, we work together on ensuring that they never again feel like victims.

The healing power that is interwoven into the fabric of the therapeutic model of Shalvata/HSC has become a blueprint for aiding recovery and healing in a much wider context than that which I describe in this chapter. This is demonstrated in the application of the model to my work with other survivors of war trauma from Bosnia and Rwanda, as well as Holocaust survivors in Eastern and Western Europe.

The ending of my chapter is the beginning of a new one in which the positive and healing outcomes I have witnessed and described will hopefully inspire others to accelerate their services in alleviating the suffering of all those who have been traumatised.

REFERENCES

Frankl, V. (1987) *Man's Search for Meaning: An Introduction to Logotherapy.* London: Hodder and Stoughton.

Niederland, W.G. (1981) 'The survivor syndrome: Further observations and dimensions.' *Journal of the Psychoanalytic Association 29*, 413–426.

SUGGESTED READING

Des Pres, P. (1976) *The Survivor: An Anatomy of Life in the Death Camps.* Oxford: Oxford University Press.

Hass, A. (1996) *The Aftermath: Living with the Holocaust.* Cambridge: Cambridge University Press.

Hassan, J. (2003) *A House Next Door to Trauma: Learning from Holocaust Survivors How to Respond to Atrocity.* London: Jessica Kingsley Publishers.

Hunt, L., Marshall, M. and Rowlings, C. (1997) *Past Trauma in Later Life: European Perspectives on Therapeutic Work with Older People.* London: Jessica Kingsley Publishers.

Levi, P. (1989) *The Drowned and the Saved.* London: Sphere Books Limited.

Marcus, P. and Rosenberg, A. (1989) *Healing Their Wounds: Psychotherapy with Holocaust Survivors and Their Families.* New York: Praeger Publishers.

Wiesel, E. (1990) *From the Kingdom of Memory: Reminiscences.* New York: Schocken Books.

USEFUL ORGANISATIONS

Shalvata (Jewish Care)
Corner of Church Road and Parson Street
Hendon
London
NW4 1QA
Telephone: 020 8203 9033

The Holocaust Survivors' Centre (Jewish Care)
Corner of Church Road and Parson Street
Hendon
London
NW4 1QA
Telephone: 020 8202 9844

Jewish Care
Amelie House
Maurice and Vivienne Wohl Campus
221 Golders Green Road
London
NW11 9DQ
Telephone: 020 8922 2000
Website: www.jewishcare.org

CHAPTER 11

GROUP WORK AND THE HEALING PROCESS

JACKI PRITCHARD

OBJECTIVE OF THE CHAPTER

As stated in the prologue, the main objective in editing this book is to promote best and creative practice in helping victims[1] of abuse; first through recovery and eventually through healing. As a social worker I have worked with victims of abuse (children and adults) for the past 31 years and used a variety of methods to help people address their abuse issues. In this chapter I want to focus on a particular methodology which can often be overlooked when thinking about healing – group work. I shall do this by discussing the work I have undertaken through the organisation Beyond Existing.

I shall give a brief historical perspective of how Beyond Existing came into being as a result of a research project, and then discuss the ways of working which have been used in groups during the period 2000–2013 to help victims through the healing process. Beyond Existing's development and work with older people between 2000 and 2002 has been written up in depth elsewhere (Pritchard 2003). This chapter will focus on the organisation's work since 2003, when it expanded its remit to work with any adult aged over 18 years. Verbal and written evaluations are regularly undertaken with members[2] attending the groups; quotes from evaluations will be included in this chapter to give members a voice.

BEYOND EXISTING – THE HISTORY

Beyond Existing is an organisation which works with adults aged over 18 years of age who have been abused in adulthood and/or childhood.

---

1   The term 'victim' will be used in this chapter to describe someone who has not yet gone through the healing process.
2   We refer to people who attend the Beyond Existing groups as members, and this term will be used in the chapter.

The organisation came into existence as a result of a research project which was funded by the Joseph Rowntree Foundation (JRF) between 1997 and 2000 – *The Needs of Older Women: Services for Victims of Elder Abuse and Other Abuse* (Pritchard 2000). The original research project was looking at the needs of older women, but as the research developed it expanded to include male victims who said they also wanted to participate in the project (Pritchard 2001, 2002).

One of the major findings of the research project was that victims of abuse wanted to meet other victims, and consequently JRF funded a pilot study to see whether support groups could be helpful. The pilot study ran for a year and was evaluated; the findings were that victims of abuse did benefit from engaging in group work (Pritchard 2003):

> The findings from the Beyond Existing project support the findings of the original research project; namely that victims *do* want to talk about their abusive experiences and that they may have an on-going need for practical advice, information and support...members of the Beyond Existing groups found it beneficial to meet with each other – not only to share their experiences and work towards healing, but also to help and support each other with past and current problems (not only those directly related to the outcomes of abuse). (Pritchard 2003, pp.193–194)

Although this chapter is focusing on the work of Beyond Existing since 2003, it may be useful for the reader to be aware of the areas of work which were undertaken in the pilot study between 2000 and 2001, because some of them have continued to be important when working with younger adults:

Pilot study

Subject areas addressed during the healing process

- Disclosure about child/adult/elder abuse, domestic violence, abuse in residential settings
- Early life – family, school, work
- Previous relationships – unresolved feelings
- Regrets
- Losses/bereavement
- Loneliness
- Depression
- Power and control
- Building self-esteem
- Assertiveness

- Hobbies/interests
- Illness
- Information about medical conditions
- Alcohol/drug misuse
- Fighting the system
- Housing
- Finances
- Preparation for death
- Working on the future.

Needs met by the groups

- *Feelings and events in the past*
  - to meet other victims and share with them
  - to be believed/understood
  - to talk about abuse – recent and past
  - to vent anger and frustration, and to come to terms with these feelings
  - to build self-esteem and confidence.
- *Seeking a sense of direction*
  - to reminisce
  - to undertake a life review
  - to face up to the future, including in some instances their own death.
- *Practical problems*
  - information about residential care and the choices available to them
  - alternative accommodation when the current situation remains painful
  - how to get a bus pass, and other entitlements
  - information about the legal system – e.g. restraining orders, rights and responsibilities
  - information about health issues, particularly the problems of excessive alcohol use
  - planning for the future in a spirit of independence, avoiding the fears, collusions and panics of the past.

When the pilot study finished, further funding was sought. Beyond Existing has now been providing therapeutic support groups for 13 years. The main difference in what we do now is that we focus solely on recovery and healing. In the pilot study victims wanted to focus on a wide range of problems, as listed above. We make it explicit in the contracts we make with members that we are dealing with abuse issues and cannot get involved in sorting other unrelated problems, which should be addressed by professionals or workers involved with the person. There have been many times when professionals have failed to undertake tasks which are clearly their remit, not those of the facilitators in Beyond Existing.

FROM 2003 ONWARDS

Since expanding the remit in 2003 to work with anyone aged over 18, Beyond Existing has run single-sex groups for men and women. Between 2000 and 2013, 75 per cent of membership has been made up of women, and 25 per cent of men. In the past year we have accepted a 17-year-old woman, who is now our youngest female member; the oldest female who has ever attended a group was 93 years old. In the men's groups the youngest member was aged 19 years, the oldest 65 years. The majority of people who attend have experienced physical and sexual abuse in adulthood, but have also been abused in childhood.

The groups are facilitated by myself and a colleague, Janice Ward. We also have members whom we call co-facilitators – that is, people who have healed and are now ready to help others (this will be discussed further below). At the time of writing there are three such people in the women's group (aged 26, 44 and 83) and one in the men's group (aged 68).

REFERRALS

Referrals to Beyond Existing come through in all sorts of ways. A victim of abuse can self-refer, and the majority of these people have made contact after seeing leaflets in post offices, doctor's surgeries, libraries and shopping centres. Over the years a lot of inappropriate referrals have been received from professionals, who have telephoned asking to make a referral without having discussed it with the victim. These referrals are made because the professionals feel unable to offer the right support themselves, as they do not have the specialist expertise in dealing with abuse. It is absolutely crucial that the referral is discussed with the victim, so that s/he understands what attending the group will entail. Organisations sometimes put the Beyond Existing telephone number on their own leaflets without any description regarding the service offered; the victim is just told to ring the number without any further explanation or discussion. The consequence is that people may get angry that they are being passed around and wasting money on telephone calls to people who cannot help them. It is vital that a person knows what is involved in any service that is being offered.

GOOD PRACTICE POINTS

- Explain what an organisation does and what methods will be used.
- Get consent before making a referral.

TIMESCALES

Every victim of abuse is an individual; they will react to and deal with the abuse they have experienced differently. This is why in-depth assessment is so fundamental to planning the healing process. Assessing how people can be helped through the healing process can take several sessions and may change as progress is made – that is, using new, previously untried methods. Some people just want the opportunity to tell their story in full once and feel that is sufficient. Others can take years to finish the healing process because there are so many issues to work through and/or they get blocked at different stages of the work. We have had people do some work in a group, go away, and then come back literally years later to complete their healing. There are no set rules. This is why open rather than closed groups are run, which is discussed further below. It also has to be acknowledged that some people will not heal; there are complex reasons for this, which are not the subject of this chapter.

GOOD PRACTICE POINTS

- Thorough assessment is key to finding the best method to help a victim through the healing process.
- The length of time for healing will be different for each victim; so time-limited groups will not suit everyone.

THINGS TO BE CONSIDERED BEFORE ENGAGING IN RECOVERY AND HEALING WORK

Beyond Existing has always made it clear that its support groups are not 'tea and sympathy' type groups. All the flyers and information produced state that the groups are therapeutic, with the main aim being to help a person through the healing process. A person has to be at a stage in their life where they want (and are able) to face, relive and address the abuse issues. It is imperative to find the best way of working with someone so they can heal. A victim of abuse can feel at a total loss regarding how to begin, because the feeling of hopelessness (and possibly worthlessness) prevails.

Although most of the work undertaken in the groups is in relation to long-term healing, it is important to say that we do get referrals regarding people who are in crisis and need immediate short-term support – that is, recovery work.

||||||||||||||||||||||||||||||||||||||||||||||||||||||||||||||||||||||||||||||||||||||||||||||||||||||||||

CASE EXAMPLES 11.1: SHORT-TERM RECOVERY WORK

- A local voluntary organisation that supports rape victims only offers support for six weeks. Young women have been referred to Beyond Existing whilst the Crown Prosecution Service (CPS) conducts the evidential tests and decides whether to proceed. We cannot address issues in the pending case, but often there are other recovery issues that we can deal with in the interim.

- Adults who are waiting to go to court regarding historical child abuse need support as sometimes they have had to wait up to two years before they give evidence at the trial. One member has currently been waiting 15 months and still has not got a court date.

- A 40-year-old adult with learning disabilities disclosed to her sister that their stepfather had been sexually abusing her since early childhood and continued into adulthood; he had fathered her two children. While the police and CPS pursued the case, the victim's sister referred her for support. The trial date was set but unfortunately the alleged abuser died very suddenly. Thereafter both women attended the women's group, as they were very angry they had not had their day in court and both had abuse issues to work through.

- A young man in his early 20s who had committed a violent crime and was expecting to receive a custodial sentence was referred by his probation officer, who asked that before he got sent down her client be given the opportunity to talk about the gang rape he had experienced (his stepfather having been one of the perpetrators).

||||||||||||||||||||||||||||||||||||||||||||||||||||||||||||||||||||||||||||||||||||||||||||||||||||||||||

Group work or one-to-one support

Group work is not going to suit everyone because some people find it hard to discuss with other people what has happened to them and to express their feelings. They can feel embarrassed, and a commonality is the fear that they are not going to be believed. Therefore some people will need or prefer one-to-one support. The original JRF research project found that it was important to ask a victim who they preferred to talk to – that is, either someone they knew or a stranger. This has been important to some members in the groups:

> *To be able to talk when I felt ready to but to people who I did not know – so was able to talk freely with no danger of friends, family finding out.* (Female victim of child abuse, age 42)

GOOD PRACTICE POINTS

As part of the assessment it is necessary to find out:

- whether group work is a suitable way of working for the victim
- who the victim feels comfortable with and can talk openly about the abuse experienced and their feelings.

Type of group

Beyond Existing is committed to providing 'open' groups rather than 'closed' ones. This is because people need to be able to heal within their own timescales. In other organisations people can be referred for counselling or therapy for a set period of time (often due to budget constraints) and a person can feel very restricted by being forced to deal with the issues within a set period of time. The Beyond Existing ethos is that there should be flexibility so that a person can address the abuse issues at their own pace. We have had members who have nearly completed the healing process but there is one last issue to be worked on and they cannot face it. These members have continued to attend the group meetings to support other members until they have been ready to do their own last piece of work, or they have decided they are not going to do it at all.

GOOD PRACTICE POINTS

- A victim should never be rushed through the healing process; they should heal at their own pace.
- An 'open' group can help a victim to heal without the pressure of having a set time to finish the healing process.
- A victim should never feel they have to leave a group because they are blocked or not addressing the abuse issues.

Frequency of contact

The Beyond Existing meetings take place once a month for two-hour sessions; this might not suit everyone. Most permanent members have said that for them this is 'enough' because the work is very intense and they feel that they could not do it on a more frequent basis. Members often talk about how they psych themselves up for a meeting during the previous week, and that it can sometimes take two to three days after a meeting to cut off completely. The process of healing can be emotionally and physically draining. Members are offered telephone support in between meetings if required or needed.

Setting objectives

When members attend their first meeting they are reassured that they do not have to speak unless they want to do so. It is fine for them to sit and listen. Once a person decides that they do want to attend on a regular basis, then it is necessary to set objectives about what they want to work on and how they will do this.

Contract

A contract should be made with the person so they are clear about their commitment to and engagement in the work. It is also important not to duplicate work. This has been a recurring problem when a person has been referred to several 'helping' organisations at the same time – the end result being not only that they feel they are being passed around, but also that they have too many people in their lives, which can become overwhelming. It is possible to be a member of a Beyond Existing group and to see a counsellor or therapist in another organisation, but boundaries must be set in order to avoid duplication. Everyone has to be clear about who is working on which issues. It is also important that the victim understands what methods will be used when working on the abuse issues. We have had women join a group having had counselling for up to five years, who complain that they have never talked about the abuse, even though they had gone to the counsellor to address this subject. We have always been able to engage these women within two sessions.

It is made very clear to all new members that they will never be forced to do anything they do not want to do. We state that people can sit and say nothing for their first couple of meetings if they feel they cannot participate; we want them to see what goes on and how we work. It is very rare that a new member says nothing at all. However, there was one person who did not speak in the group for four sessions; at the end of each meeting she was asked if she wanted to continue and she said she had definitely found it useful. After four months we said that she had to make a decision about whether she would interact with the other members, as we felt it was time for her to do so; from that moment on she participated well and was a member for a further five years.

GOOD PRACTICE POINT

A key skill which is required for any helper is to find the right balance between not taking control in the way an abuser does, and being directive with a view to empowering the victim.

When people are in crisis or are anxious, they do not always take in what is being said to them. So it is very important to repeat explanations – in particular about:

- how the group and its facilitators work (covering basic values, beliefs, philosophy)
- the main objective (to work through the healing process)
- methods
- ground rules (see Appendix 11.1 for an example of ground rules used)
- confidentiality and its limits
- consent and sharing information (see Appendix 11.2 for an example of consent form used)
- how records will be kept (paper and electronic) and where.

METHODS OF WORKING

In my own social work practice I use the psychodynamic approach, believing that someone has to address unresolved issues from the past before being able to strive for some sort of resolution or contentment in their current situation. This cannot always be achieved when a victim is continuing to live in an abusive situation; however, s/he may to choose to leave in the future. There are many different schools of thought regarding psychoanalysis and it is not the purpose of this chapter to explain the differences between Freud, Jung, Klein, Erikson, etc. I have never believed that it is helpful to adopt just one approach in one's own practice, hence the reason for using Gestalt methods in my own practice. Beyond Existing functions according to the same principles – that is, every victim is an individual, and the correct method of working must be found in order to help them heal.

GOOD PRACTICE POINTS

- Every victim is an individual and will be unique in their own way.
- It will be necessary to find the correct way of working with the victim.
- Explanation is needed about what the healing process may involve and what methods will be used.
- The length of time to heal will be different for each victim.

Preparation

People are often nervous when they come to a group for the first time; it can be very scary walking into a group of strangers. So it is important to talk to people and answer their questions leading up to the first group meeting. It is not unusual for people to back out at the last minute. Simple actions are important to make someone feel welcomed into the group.

GOOD PRACTICE POINTS

- Offer tea, coffee, water, biscuits.
- Show the location of the toilets and smoking areas; making it clear a member can exit the meeting for a break at any time.
- Give a new member a plastic A4 pack which includes a work book, pen, etc., this gives them a sense of belonging right at the outset.
- Go through the group's ground rules (and amend as necessary) to make people feel safe.

Planning the work to be done

As already said, it is important to find out by undertaking a thorough assessment what methodology is going to help an individual; this is the key objective when a person attends a group for the first few meetings. Sometimes this can be done through talking, but some victims are very muddled, nervous or shy, so engaging in a non-threatening, private, individual exercise can help. An exercise which is used a great deal in Beyond Existing to plan the healing work is 'The Snake Exercise', which is explained in Exercise 11.1.

· ·

EXERCISE *11.1*

THE SNAKE

Objective

In order to move on in their lives victims have to deal with the past. This exercise can be used as a way of finding out more about a person and what past events need to be dealt with in order to heal. The objective of the exercise is to get a participant to do a life review through drawing and writing and to identify events in life which need to be worked on.

Equipment

Flipchart paper and pens.

Time

One hour.

Task
1. Each participant is given a flipchart sheet and a variety of coloured pens.
2. Participants think about the major events (both good and bad) which have occurred in their life.
3. Participants are asked to draw a snake with bends in its body. Each bend signifies a major event in life. Each bend is dated.

Discussion
1. Each participant presents their snake to the rest of the group by summarising the key events and how they feel about those events now.
2. Events are identified for future work.

Notes for leaders
1. This is a very useful exercise to find out more about people and what has happened to them in the past.
2. This exercise can be used to plan future individual or group work.
3. This can, however, be a very painful exercise for some participants, as it may trigger memories and feelings which are difficult to cope with. Leaders should very sensitively ensure that participants are not forced, or do not feel obliged, to talk publicly about such painful memories. Some participants may be in two minds whether to speak. It may therefore be necessary for some individual work to be done in a private area.

(Pritchard and Sainsbury 2004)

. . . .

'The Snake' is mainly used to plan the healing work, but some members have requested to 'do another snake' months or years after the first one because they want to look at what still needs to be done. One member, Tanya, who liked doing the snake initially, much later used it to address something that was bothering her.

|||||||||||||||||||||||||||||||||||||||||||||||||||||||||||||||||||||||||||||||||||||||||||||||||||||

CASE EXAMPLE 11.2

Tanya was aged 52 when she was ill and off work one day and at home on her own; so had some privacy, which was unusual. Tanya has been a victim of child sexual abuse, rapes in adulthood and domestic violence. She had been thinking a lot about the men she had slept with through her life: '*I wanted to count how many men I had slept with. Something I had always wanted to do.*' She was questioning how she viewed herself – '*Was I a slag?*' She decided to draw a snake and thought about all the sexual relationships she had experienced. After doing this Tanya was in a very emotional state and needed to talk about how she felt immediately.

|||||||||||||||||||||||||||||||||||||||||||||||||||||||||||||||||||||||||||||||||||||||||||||||||||||

Tanya rang me because she needed to talk through her negative feelings about herself; she said she felt *'disappointed in myself'*; she was in fact judging herself. This illustrates an important point – that, although it is good that a victim can work on issues at home, there needs to be someone available to talk things through, if the victim becomes upset. Through spending half an hour on the telephone talking things through, Tanya no longer saw her sexual activity negatively but instead learnt from the experiences. Eight months later I asked Tanya to say what she had learnt about herself from doing the exercise:

> *Nice men are boring. I had put myself in dangerous situations. I felt worthless, ugly, empty. The pattern was repeated.*

She has kept both her snakes and is keeping all her work in two boxes; one for things dealt with, the other for things she is still working on.

Group discussion

The main method of working is group discussion. It has already been said that this can be nerve-racking for some people when they first join a group. However, this is the real essence of the work which is done and the support which is given. The main benefit is that people realise that they are not alone and that the way they feel is not unique to them. Members can empathise and explain how they have dealt with situations or particular feelings. Members often form strong bonds with each other because of the experiences and feelings they have in common.

> *Group working – hearing other people's accounts of abuse, I felt I was not alone. I am not sure I would have been able to leave the past behind without the support of the group.* (Female, age 43)

I was shocked and comforted by the stories and emotions that other members were expressing. It was all so familiar. Though what they were saying was different, how they felt about it (in some cases) felt the same. (Female, age 26)

After just one meeting I returned home feeling I had some support at last and more importantly I did not feel alone any more. (Male, age 48)

I cry a lot at the group, which I find healing. I don't cry usually outside of the group. (Female, age 52)

At the beginning of each meeting each member is asked to say how their month has been in general and if they need any 'special time'. As discussed above, objectives have been set for each member, but sometimes things occur during the month so they need extra time to discuss this in the group.

Common subject areas discussed and worked on in the groups

- Abuse by mothers
- Mothers - their failure to protect their children
- Abuse by women
- Violence – how it has been perpetrated
- Incidents of rape
- Sexual acts experienced in childhood
- Nightmares and flashbacks
- Reliving abusive incidents
- Distorted memories – questioning whether something really happened
- Suppressed memories coming out
- Finding the truth about what has happened in the past
- How to find people
- Why abuse happens
- Feelings towards the abuser
- Seeing the abuser (because they live locally)

- Confronting the abuser (when and how to do this)
- Needing to tell parents about abuse by a sibling
- Self blame
- Self harm
- Wanting to die
- Depression
- Effects of medication
- Being stuck
- Lack of trust
- Loneliness
- Use of alcohol and drugs
- Distrust of professionals
- Going to court
- Literacy issues
- Applying to college/getting qualifications
- Getting work experience/a job/ retirement

A strategy that victims can use to cope with everyday life is to suppress the memory of the abusive incidents they have experienced. This conflicts with what is being done through the healing process – that is, reliving and thinking about what has happened. Suppressed memories can come back in flashbacks when a person is awake, or in dreams. Victims commonly fear that they are not going to be believed about the abuse; consequently they question themselves about whether the memories which start to come back have really happened. The media has not helped by publicising the idea of 'false memory' syndrome. In the Beyond Existing groups it is clearly visible that when a member is talking about a particular incident this can trigger a memory for someone else. This is where the mutual support is so effective.

IIIIIIIIIIIIIIIIIIIIIIIIIIIIIIIIIIIIIIIIIIIIIIIIIIIIIIIIIIIIIIIIIIIIIIIIIIIIIIIIIIIIIIIIIIIIIIIIIIIIIIIIIIIII

CASE EXAMPLE 11.3

Rhonda was in her late 50s. She had been raped by different perpetrators in her teenage years; one rape resulted in the birth of her first son. Rhonda constantly said she had a 'rubbish memory' and that everyone in her life told her this. Professionals had labelled her as having mild learning disabilities. When she first joined the group she felt it was 'going to be a waste of time because I can't remember anything'. When other members talked about how they had been raped, this triggered a flashback for Rhonda about being in the back of a van. Once she talked about that memory others came back as well, but Rhonda was scared of forgetting it all again – especially in between the monthly meetings.

Using coloured index cards proved to be a really useful technique for Rhonda. Whenever she disclosed about a particular incident (which usually was in short bursts) key words and sentences about the memory were recorded on a card, which was then given to Rhonda to keep at home. She was also given blank cards so she could write down key things if she remembered anything in between meetings.

IIIIIIIIIIIIIIIIIIIIIIIIIIIIIIIIIIIIIIIIIIIIIIIIIIIIIIIIIIIIIIIIIIIIIIIIIIIIIIIIIIIIIIIIIIIIIIIIIIIIIIIIIIIII

Individual work

There are times when a member who normally has no problem participating in the group actually needs to do some work on their own. So this is when a member can be taken out of the group and work with a facilitator in a one-to-one situation. When running groups it is vital to give some consideration to the venue, in case this situation arises. If the group is run in a large room it may be possible to have the one-to-one work going on in the same room (if this is comfortable for the person and the facilitator). In other situations it may be necessary to have access to a separate room.

||||||||||||||||||||||||||||||||||||||||||||||||||||||||||||||||||||||||||||||||||||||||||||||||||||

CASE EXAMPLES 11.4: WHEN MEMBERS HAVE WORKED OUTSIDE OF THE MAIN GROUP

Example 1

- As Magda started to recall suppressed memories of specific incidents of sexual acts in the bathroom, perpetrated by her stepfather, she wanted to draw the bathroom and what had happened in it. She did not want to do this during the course of a normal meeting. So on several occasions Magda met with one of the facilitators an hour before the start of a group meeting. She drew the bathroom on large flipchart sheets and talked about the sexual acts. She then ripped up the drawings and threw them away.

Example 2

- Ian became very angry whilst trying to explain how cunning his foster mother had been in organising opportunities to sexually abuse him in the house when his foster father was working different shifts. Ian said talking about what had happened was not enough; he needed to do something else, and said he wanted to try drawing the different rooms where she had abused him. Ian went to another part of the meeting room and drew on many flipchart sheets for the rest of the meeting. When he came to the next meeting he said he wanted to continue with his drawings away from the other men. The amount of paper he accumulated indicated to him how much abuse he had experienced.

Example 3

- Three young women (all under 22 years of age) were referred to the group because they had been victims of rape. At that time there were also women in their 50s and 60s in the group. The younger women felt uncomfortable about the age differences and said they would feel embarrassed talking about the rapes because it would be like talking about sex with your own parents. So the main group was split into two mini groups. The younger women met in another room with two facilitators – one older and one younger.

||||||||||||||||||||||||||||||||||||||||||||||||||||||||||||||||||||||||||||||||||||||||||||||||||||

Practical exercises

A whole range of exercises have been used in the groups over the years. Sometimes the facilitators decide in preparation for a meeting that a certain exercise will be used; at other times it is spontaneous because something arises in the group discussion and there is a need to do something other than talking. This is where the experience of a skilled facilitator is invaluable. Exercises can be undertaken by an individual, in pairs, or in a large group (see Chapter 11, 'Exercises for Adult Victims', in Pritchard and Sainsbury 2004).

Relaxation exercises

Many victims find it hard to relax; they live on nervous energy. Some exist on very little sleep and are constantly tired. So a variety of relaxation exercises are taught and members definitely develop their own preferences for which ones they will use. When a member regularly experiences nightmares and wakes up very frightened, it is important to teach them how to go to a 'safe place' very quickly in their own mind – that is, to get away from their terror. Others find it beneficial to learn how to relax in general; some members have actually fallen asleep in the group whilst participating in a relaxation exercise, and have been amazed because normally they have problems sleeping.

||||||||||||||||||||||||||||||||||||||||||||||||||||||||||||||||||||||||||||||||||||||||||||||||||||||||||||||||

CASE EXAMPLE 11.5

Chloe has been a member of Beyond Existing for about six years. She was sexually abused in childhood by her uncle, and has also been a victim of physical and sexual violence in adulthood. She has always had what she calls 'night terrors' (dreams). Chloe has worked through many of the abuse issues related to the sexual abuse in both childhood and adulthood, but as those have been resolved the content of her night terrors has changed. She is now seeing the violence which was perpetrated by her father on her mother. Chloe realises now that she views this from the position she took as a child – hiding behind a door.

||||||||||||||||||||||||||||||||||||||||||||||||||||||||||||||||||||||||||||||||||||||||||||||||||||||||||||||||

Writing and drawing

For people who find it difficult to talk about the abuse they have experienced, writing or drawing can be the way forward. Creative writing has been one of the major methods we have used to help members through the healing process. Every member is given a work book and they are encouraged to use the book when they remember something or when they want to write about a particular person or incident. At a meeting a member will be encouraged to read out what they have written and talk about how they feel. Some members cannot do this and will ask a facilitator or another member to read their work out loud to the group. There have been members who have been prolific in their writing, filled a work book before the next meeting and needed a new one. Some members who have had literacy problems have wanted to write, so have been encouraged to write odd words or sentences. Other members have regularly written poems to describe incidents or to express their feelings. Some of these have been published, which has been very important to the individual members (Pritchard 2003, 2007, 2008). Drawing is another way in which members express themselves, as shown in the case examples above regarding Tanya and Rhonda.

|||||||||||||||||||||||||||||||||||||||||||||||||||||||||||||||||||||||||||||||||||||||||||||||||||||||||||||

CASE EXAMPLE 11.6

Allison had been sexually abused in childhood by her brother and then was a victim of domestic violence. She had difficulty in reading and writing. She enjoyed looking at magazines but wanted to be able to read a novel. She was a very shy person, who lacked confidence and was embarrassed about her literacy problems. The facilitators found some literacy classes at a local college. Allison started to attend regularly and the tutor believed that Allison might be dyslexic. She arranged for a formal assessment to be undertaken and Allison was diagnosed as having dyslexia. With the right support through the local college Allison learned to read and write, and the first book she read properly was *Just a Boy* by Richard McCannn (2004).

|||||||||||||||||||||||||||||||||||||||||||||||||||||||||||||||||||||||||||||||||||||||||||||||||||||||||||||

Use of books
As illustrated in Case Example 11.6 above, it can be helpful for members to read books about other victims' experiences, and we do supply certain books for members. Assertiveness training is also a crucial part of the work we do, to build members' confidence and self-esteem. Exercises are used to train members to become more assertive; they develop and practise mantras to help themselves. A book which is given to members in both the women's and the men's groups is *A Woman in Your Own Right* by Anne Dickson (1982).

There are a lot of self-help books available nowadays. We have had people referred to us after having very negative experiences from using such books. A few years ago a particular community mental health team was promoting the use of a self-help book written by a local professional. We had a number of people come to Beyond Existing after that particular drive, who said they had suffered more harm through trying to do the exercises. The main criticism was that the exercises opened up emotions and fears relating to the abuse and there was no-one around to talk to when they were experiencing the bad effects (many of the victims lived alone). This is a key practice issue.

GOOD PRACTICE POINT

When a person has been working on abuse issues through discussion or exercises, they need support – someone to be around to ensure they are alright after completing the work.

At the end of a group meeting, there is a 'wind-down' session where people talk about how they are feeling. Sometimes a member will say s/he is not alright; at other times the facilitators will know that it is not safe for someone to leave the building. So a member will stay in the venue and the facilitators will work with them until they feel better. We also make 'welfare calls' to follow up; this involves telephoning someone later in the day and the following day (or days) to see how they are.

Role-play/rehearsal

Some members want to confront a certain person in their life – often this is the abuser, a family member or other significant person in their life. Preparing what to say and how to say it can build confidence and help summon up the courage to speak. The member can rehearse by participating in role-play with a facilitator or another member. With agreement, other members will watch, give feedback and make suggestions. The facilitators give feedback but also focus particularly on assessing the use of body language. Another method is to talk to an empty chair. There is often a reluctance to do this because 'I feel stupid', but after watching someone engage in this exercise, members always comment on how powerful it is and some want 'to have a go' themselves immediately. The benefit is that it can be cathartic and is particularly useful when the perpetrator is dead or their whereabouts is unknown.

SOME CONCLUSIONS

At the beginning of this book I wrote about the importance of properly planning long-term work to help victims through the healing process. It seems appropriate to end the book with this chapter (and the following Epilogue), which has illustrated that group work can be a creative method of working to achieve both recovery and healing. At a time of severe financial cutbacks and budget constraints it is imperative that the statutory bodies turn to the voluntary sector to provide long-term support; that is, so that victims can go through the healing process without time-limits being put on the process. Healing through group work has the benefits of providing victims with therapeutic methods from experienced workers; mutual support from other victims of abuse who are healing or who have healed; and, crucially, it gives them hope and ambitions for the rest of their lives:

> *I would just like to say that because of the group I've let go of the past, I'm enjoying the present and I can now look forward to the future.* (Female, age 44)

APPENDIX 11.1: GROUND RULES

1. This group is run for the benefit of its members. Jacki and Janice are present in the role of facilitators.

2. Members are attending the group to help themselves; they are not working through issues to please anyone else. At no time should anyone feel that they are letting anyone else down.

3. At the beginning of the meeting members must say if something is bothering them and they need to talk about it. Members are asked not to leave crucial issues or information to the end of a meeting.

4. Everyone can have their say and equal time will be allocated to members.

5. It is expected that members will be honest.

6. Only one person will speak at any one time.

7. Everyone will respect each other, even if we have different opinions.

8. Members will respect each other's privacy.

9. No-one will be judgmental.

10. No-one will criticise or tell another group member what to do.

11. No-one will be rejected or made to feel rejected.

12. Everything which is said in the group is confidential. Exceptions:
    (i) If we thought you were going to harm yourself or others.
    (ii) If we learnt a child was currently being abused we have a duty to report under the Children Act 1989.
13. It is important not to break a member's confidentiality about the group and not to discuss membership of the group outside of the group i.e. to keep members' anonymity.
14. Mobile telephones will be turned off during meetings.
15. There will be breaks and refreshments.

APPENDIX 11.2: CONFIDENTIALITY, INFORMATION SHARING AND CONSENT

I declare that I understand and agree with the following statements:

- Everything discussed in the group meetings or information given in other ways (e.g. telephone, written documents, e-mails, messages) will remain confidential to the group and its facilitators unless a concern arises about a member of the group who may harm him/herself or another person; or a child may be at risk of harm/abuse.
- Where someone is at risk of harm/abuse this information may be shared with others on a 'need to know' basis.
- The limits of confidentiality have been explained to me and I have had the opportunity to discuss this and to ask any questions about things I do not understand.
- Written notes will be taken by the group facilitators during group meetings.
- Records are also kept in electronic files in the offices of Beyond Existing/Jacki Pritchard Ltd, Provincial House Business Centre, Solly Street, Sheffield S1 4BA.
- Records kept will include details about: members; group discussions; telephone conversations; actions taken.
- All records (written and electronic) will be stored safely and kept in accordance with requirements stated under the Data Protection Act 1998.

Print name of member: ....

Address: ....

Signature: ....

Date: .... **Time:** ....

Witnessed by: ....

REFERENCES

Dickson, A. (1982) *A Woman in Your Own Right*. London: Quartet Books.

McCann, R. (2004) *Just a Boy*. London: Ebury Press.

Pritchard, J. (2000) *The Needs of Older Women: Services for Victims of Elder Abuse and Other Abuse*. Bristol: Policy Press.

Pritchard, J. (2001) *Male Victims of Elder Abuse: Their Experiences and Needs*. London: Jessica Kingsley Publishers.

Pritchard, J. (September 2002) 'The abuse of older men.' *The Journal of Adult Protection 4*, 3, 14–23.

Pritchard, J. (2003) *Support Groups for Older People who have been Abused: Beyond Existing*. London: Jessica Kingsley Publishers.

Pritchard, J. (2007) 'Identifying and working with older male victims of abuse in England.' *Journal of Elder Abuse and Neglect 19*, 1/2, 109–127.

Pritchard, J. (ed.) (2008) *Good Practice in Safeguarding Adults: Working Effectively in Adult Protection*. London: Jessica Kingsley Publishers.

Pritchard, J. and Sainsbury, E. (eds) (2004) *Can You Read Me? Creative Writing with Child and Adult Victims of Abuse*. London: Jessica Kingsley Publishers.

USEFUL ORGANISATION

Beyond Existing
Provincial House Business Centre
Solly Street
Sheffield
S1 4BA
Telephone: 0114 270 1782
Website: www.beyondexisting.org.uk

EPILOGUE
THE MASLOW EXPERIMENT

JACKI PRITCHARD AND HILARY ABRAHAMS

This book started with the prologue explaining how the victims of abuse I (Jacki Pritchard) have worked with over the years have viewed recovery and healing, and what current members of Beyond Existing have to say about those terms. It seems fitting that the views and voices of victims should conclude the book. In Chapter 7 Hilary Abrahams introduced Maslow's 'hierarchy of needs' and in Chapter 11 I have discussed the importance of group work. When I approached Hilary to contribute a chapter to this book we had a verbal discussion about the use of Maslow's work, which many workers in health and social care will be familiar with, or may have heard something about on a training course. Maslow was an American psychologist who wrote a paper in 1943 entitled *Hierarchy of Needs: A Theory of Human Motivation*, which is now available from Amazon as a Kindle book (Maslow 2011), and which I have revisited several times whilst editing this book. Maslow's theory regarding human development through five stages developed over the years and is used to this day in many different organisations.

As a social worker who trained many moons ago I am very familiar with Maslow; as I was talking to Hilary about Maslow in relation to domestic abuse I thought about the fact that I had never utilised the pyramid associated with Maslow's theory in any group work I had undertaken with victims of abuse, and I thought this could be useful. Group work was at the forefront of my mind at this time because of planning to write my chapter about this method of working. So after our conversation I developed an exercise to test out whether using Maslow's theory and the pyramid as a visual aid could help victims of abuse as part of their healing process. The test was undertaken with a group of women who were attending a Beyond Existing therapeutic support group.[1] Following on from this I designed a questionnaire which was sent to women who could not attend the meeting on that day and also to male members[2] who had previously attended a men's group.

PURPOSE OF THE EXERCISE

As discussed in the previous chapter, different types of exercises are used therapeutically to help victims of abuse attending Beyond Existing groups to plan the work they need to do in regard to long-term healing, address their abuse issues and work at their own pace through the healing process. The main objective in designing the new exercise was to see whether using the five stages of Maslow's hierarchy of needs could be another way of enabling victims to identify for healing:

- the current needs they have which have been created as a direct result of having been abused
- what they have achieved so far
- what their hopes and ambitions are for the future
- what work needs to be done
- how this work will be done.

HOW THE GROUP EXERCISE WAS CONDUCTED

The original intention had been that the exercise would be undertaken at the beginning of the meeting, if the members agreed to participate. A group exercise is normally planned to take 30 to 45 minutes, as members find they need to take a break from talking about abuse. The members did agree to participate in the exercise and got so involved with it that the exercise was used for the whole meeting, which lasted two hours.

The exercise was led by myself and co-facilitator Janice Ward. Five women participated in the exercise; their ages ranged from 17 to 83 years. The equipment used was very simple: flipchart stand and paper, pens, blu-tack; and the pyramid had been drawn beforehand on a flipchart sheet.

In his original work Maslow never actually presented his theory of human motivation in a pyramid, but this has become a well-known symbol for presenting the hierarchy of needs. So a pyramid was drawn with the five stages, and I did a very short presentation explaining the theory and stages in simple words rather than the exact Maslow terms:

---

1   For more information about the organisation visit: www.beyondexisting. org.uk.
2   This is the term used for people attending a Beyond Existing group.

1. Basics
2. Safety
3. Belonging
4. Esteem
5. Achievements/goals.

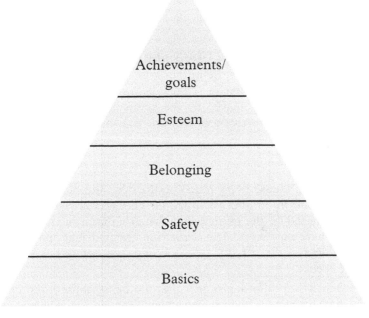

Figure 1: Pyramid used in the exercise

From experience we know that simple exercises work best, and members respond well to being asked to focus on words and what they mean to them in order to stimulate thought and then discussion. So this is what the women were asked to do, having learnt a little bit about Maslow's theory regarding how a human being has needs and develops by having those needs met. The exercise was done in two stages:

1. Each level of the pyramid was considered in turn and the women were asked to consider what their needs were at the time the abuse happened and afterwards.

2. Each level of the pyramid was revisited and the women were asked what they had achieved so far in their own healing process.

Before the discussion started members were asked to think about and reflect on the following questions for each level of the pyramid:

- What have been your needs as a result of the abuse you have experienced?
- Which needs have been met?
- Which needs do you still have?

As the discussion took place the key subject areas and points covered were written on flipchart sheets by the facilitators (and were agreed by the participants).

KEY THEMES FROM THE DISCUSSION

It is not possible, nor is it the purpose, to transcribe everything that was said during the exercise. Listed below are brief observations from the facilitators, followed by the key subject areas which were raised, discussed and written on the flipchart sheets as agreed by the participants.

Basics

The discussion focused very much on the here and now, rather than on needs when in an abusive situation. This was linked to the very first point raised by the participants: denial – that is, a victim denies that they have any needs. The discussion about denial and its long-term impact was discussed for quite a long time before talking about current needs.

- Denial (a victim denies that they are being abused; the feeling that you have no right to expect anything; no needs because you are not worth anything).
- Coffee (it is important to have things which give pleasure).
- Clothes that fit (discussion about weight; how one looks; deliberately changing the way one looks; wearing loose clothes to hide the body; length of hair used to hide face; changing hair colour regularly).
- Money needed for new teeth (poverty; living on benefits; struggling financially; cannot buy basic things).
- Want a job (for money; self-worth; give a purpose in life; feel worthwhile).
- Need experience to get a job (in social care; want to work with children).
- Shadowing (way of getting work experience).
- Volunteering (to gain experience; give something back).

Safety

The discussion was more about 'fear' rather than safety. The women talked about what happens to them when they are scared or frightened – that is, how they feel and how their body reacts:

- Freeze.
- Nausea.
- Need to get away.
- Senses heightened.
- Breathe quickly.
- Panic.
- Cannot breathe.
- Assess the situation – get cigarette.
- Triggers memories of past abuse.
- See abuse everywhere.
- Legs, hands, reminder of physical abuse.
- Mum – hit me in the past.
- Blindness – ([member] gone blind in one eye in the last two years; this eye was damaged during the rape 47 years ago).
- Going to Mum's – fear of seeing abuser (who is a family member).
- Men (constant reminder of male abuser).
- Remembering sentences – things the abuser said: 'I wish you'd never been born'; 'You are useless'; 'You'll never achieve anything.'
- Being on your own is safe; having the space around you (uncle currently staying in house; want to ask him to go; want to be on own; don't know how to tell him to go).
- Sister's avoidance – won't talk about my abuse – feels vulnerable.
- Scared.
- Anxious.
- Tense.

Members said how they manage fear:

- Move away (to another city).
- More confidence now – talking on street (previously had not talked or passed the time of day in shops, etc.).
- Not being on own – making sure people are around me all the time.

- Building trust.
- Making space (not feeling closed in/trapped).
- Pretending/masking; pretending that I am stronger than I am.
- Scarf hiding (always wears a scarf to hide face if necessary or to fiddle with it when nervous).
- Hair (having a fringe; growing long to hide face).
- Finding out who you are.

Belonging

What came out incredibly clearly was that *none* of the women initially believed they belonged to anything or anyone – there was absolutely *no* sense of belonging at all when we moved on to consider this level of the pyramid. A wall was put up immediately. This was even in regard to the group, which was quite shocking at first for my co-facilitator and myself. However, further discussion brought some explanation regarding this blockage, which was related to trust issues. The two youngest members of the group (aged 17 and 22), who had been members for about six months, said that with it being an open group there can never be 100 per cent trust, as people come and go. The older and longer-standing members said they understood these particular comments.

There was a great feeling of sadness during the revelation about not belonging. Participants were persuaded to spend a bit more time thinking about 'belonging' because the reaction to dismiss it had been so immediate. Eventually they did acknowledge that they belonged to or had:

- the group
- mother and kids
- partner
- pets
- personal family
- self
- reliance.

When asked to think about belonging for the future the discussion flowed more easily:

- Scared of losing everyone if I tell about abuse by family member.
- Get rid of the old (self; contacts).
- Workforce.
- Circle of friends.

- Friends who identify with me.
- Some part of the family (sister; sister and brother have not spoken to them for seven years).
- Volunteering (wanted to do it – had a place but could not go through with it; backed out).
- Choir.
- Adult education; taster courses; gathering information.

Esteem

This was the stage that had the least discussion through the whole exercise. As with 'belonging' there seemed to be an instant dismissal of the subject, but this part of the discussion failed to develop as the women struggled to think about esteem and only talked about three things:

- Being a good mother.
- People can talk to me.
- Being creative (writing).

Achievements/goals

The discussion was again negative at first when one member immediately said:

Don't feel I have achieved anything.

However, when asked to focus on what they felt they had achieved since attending the group, positive responses emerged:

- Talk more.
- Confidence increased.
- Recognising things (that I was neglected; mothers do abuse; both parents were as bad as each other; acknowledging that abuse happened; it was not my fault).
- Dropped guard.
- Smiles (never used to smile).
- Laughing.
- Making eye contact.
- Not hiding face any more.

Regarding the future:

- Emotional feelings that it might not be possible to achieve.

- Will explore possibilities from what has been discussed today (e.g. volunteering, shadowing).

The women said they would like to do the exercise again in the future as part of reviewing their objectives, which is done at regular intervals in group meetings as part of the healing process.

As already stated, we knew that members do find it beneficial to participate in an exercise which requires them to focus on particular words or phrases and to talk about what they mean to them. They particularly liked this exercise focusing on the five stages, which was evidenced by the fact that they wanted to carry on talking for two hours without a break. One member said:

I wish we'd done this when I was at the beginning of healing.

THE QUESTIONNAIRE

As some members were absent on the day the exercise was undertaken, a questionnaire was designed and sent to those members who were not present. A man who previously attended a men's group also completed the questionnaire, as he keeps in touch regularly with Beyond Existing. A written explanation was given on the front of the questionnaire regarding:

- the purpose in carrying out the research exercise – that is, to find out whether using a particular model of need is helpful in identifying what needs to be worked on through the healing process
- the model – stages of needs
- how to complete the questionnaire.

The following questions and prompts were used.

- Think of the basic things in life you need when (i) being abused; (ii) going through the healing process.
- What do you need to make you feel safe?
- What, who or where gives you a sense of belonging?
- What do you want to belong to?
- How is your self-esteem/confidence?
- What do you need to increase your self-esteem/confidence?
- What do you want to ultimately achieve in the healing process?
- What have you achieved already?
- What do you need to achieve your goals in life?

Three questionnaires were returned by two women (R1 aged 44; R2 aged 48) and one man (R3 aged 68). Their responses were as follows:

Basics

R1: Without a safe, secure and peaceful place to live I don't think I could have dared to think about the past at all. My priority when I first began to deal with the abuse was to not allow myself to become overwhelmed. As a single person with a mortgage to pay, not getting into debt was of paramount importance to me. I saw keeping my home as the most important thing, and only then everything else could be dealt with. I needed peace and quiet to think, so when I wasn't working I shut myself away from others. I only fully engaged with the healing process when I felt my finances were stable and I could guarantee solitude.

R2: Safe place.
Support.
Understanding.

R3: The need to know that trust works both ways.
The need for truth, honesty, openness so there can be no misunderstandings.

Safety

R1: Having confidence in myself through knowing my own history helps me to feel safe. When I started to think about the abuse my behaviours did at times become ritualised – for example, checking the doors and windows were locked at least three times. I felt reassured by my actions, I felt I was taking control of my own safety. I set time aside when I knew I would not be interrupted to remember the abuse and to try and come to terms with it. I would use some of the safety checks as a way to relax and to try to create a safe atmosphere. I would usually have worked overtime first so I could be financially secure. The more I remembered, the safer and more confident I felt. Feeling unsafe came from not trusting myself and doubting my own memories, which began when I was very young.

R2: Safe place.
Comfortable in my surroundings (locks, bolts and chains on doors and windows).

R3: Feel safe in an environment where there is always someone willing and ready to reassure me should I falter.
Someone to listen to what I have to say, no matter how distressing.
Being non-judgmental.

Belonging

R1: At first I did not want to belong to any group or to socialise, that came later. My sense of belonging came from my home. My safety routine spread to other aspects of my life such as planning a Saturday evening when I wasn't working to follow a certain pattern of familiar events. I did this because I could. It was an antidote to the chaos of my childhood home.

When I began to socialise I quickly built up a social circle which I just as quickly lost again. It took me years to learn how to maintain friendships. Joining a support group helped; meeting other people in similar situations led to me feeling less of a failure socially.

R2: My new cottage.
Friends.
Beyond Existing.
(Previously nowhere. I was trapped.)
Want to be accepted for who I am.

R3: Belong to the real world.

Esteem

R1: The more I have remembered the more stronger and confident I have felt. When I was young my mother told me that I was wrong and that nothing had happened to me. Family members told me that they didn't believe me and that I had either lied out of badness, or worse still that I was feeble-minded and that the abuse had only happened in my imagination. When I started the healing process my counsellor had asked me before I divulged the abuse to other family members what would be the worst scenario. I had said that I feared that I would be accused of imagining it all, which is exactly what happened. But instead of having the devastating effect I expected it to have, it was actually empowering, and that was because I was speaking the truth. Staying true to myself raises my self-esteem. I would feel better still if I could hold onto that resolve when others raise their voices. When people shout, my confidence deserts me.

R2: I still feel it is very low.
People who I trust and friends around me.
Alcohol at times.

R3: The needs for other people's respect.
To accept me for what I am.
To be taken seriously, i.e. my views, ideas and values.

Achievements/goals

R1: Although it was necessary to remember the past there did come a point when I thought of nothing else. I could literally obsess about my past all day. Through attending the support group I came to see that the time for letting go of the past had come. When I did let go I found that there were other things about me that had been hidden away for safekeeping. I find I have a sense of humour and that people do choose me to be their friend, but I have been pushing them away. I would like to turn my tendency to be watchful into something more positive but I am not sure how to achieve this.

R2: To achieve:
Peace – night terrors to stop.
Not to keep reliving the abuse.
Less anxious.
No panic attacks or flashbacks.
The smells to stop.

Have achieved:
Putting my darling firstborn son to rest.
Worked through a lot of my abuse.
Moved home from a prison (flat) where I locked myself in and away from society.
Continuous positive support (friends and Beyond Existing).

R3: To be able to forgive what happened to me in the past. Go forward and get on with life. Try helping others to do the same.

REFLECTIVE THOUGHTS FROM HILARY ABRAHAMS

With the increasing tendency for ever more complex diagnosis, labelling and medicalisation of human behaviour, it can be very easy to forget the need to see people in their own context and, equally, to dismiss the theories of the 1950s as unsuited to modern needs. Yet, as Jacki's 'experiment' shows, Maslow's ideas, expressed in simple words, resonate with individuals who have no professional training, and offer powerful tools to enable them to look at their needs and ways of coping and gain new insights and aspirations for the future.

Early use of Maslow's ideas was in business management and this was where I first encountered them, as a manager in what was a large and stable company. It was only when the company prepared to downsize and rumours grew of redundancy and restructuring, however, that I saw their impact in reality. The threatened loss of safety, of community and identity, reduced cohesive teams to solitary individuals fighting to survive. Only when we knew what the plans were was it possible to re-establish some degree of stability and begin to rebuild team loyalty and identity (and productivity!).

Since then, I have seen both demolition and rebuilding following this pattern in many areas of life, in individuals and families, communities and organisations. Currently I am working as part of a team looking at the needs of homeless women in Bristol, where the loss of home has meant the loss of safety, family and confidence and has pushed many to 'rock bottom' in their lives. In starting to rebuild, however, they talk of exactly the same challenges as Jacki's group – the social and economic circumstances in which they live and the reality of past and current experiences which have damaged or blocked their ability to take action. Like the members of Beyond Existing, these women have found ways to survive and get their basic needs met. They have found a precarious safety on the margins of society and formed slender links to others like themselves. And, like them, these women want to change their lives, but to step into the unknown and challenge the past is perceived as both dangerous and frightening. As Maslow comments, 'growth is often a painful process and may, for this reason, be shunned; [that] we are afraid of our best possibilities in addition to loving them' (Maslow 1987, p.xx).

What can we offer to help this process of rebuilding? Our research shows that this is, inevitably, a slow process. People need to feel safe and build up trust in the agencies and workers who are offering to help them, before they are ready to move on. Those workers who showed an attitude of care and respect, who took time to listen without judging and, above all, did not give up on them, were seen as key in helping individuals to take the first steps into a new life. A further valuable source of inspiration and support can be the voices of those who have taken this path already or are treading it at the same time. Maslow's concepts are a simple yet powerful way for human beings to help themselves and others to be the best they can be, but it needs the imagination and commitment of individuals like Jacki and her colleagues to bring the two together.

REFERENCES

Maslow, A. (1987) *Motivation and Personality* (3rd edition; first published 1954). London: Harper and Row.

Maslow, A. (2011) *Hierarchy of Needs: A Theory of Human Motivation*. (Original 1943.) Amazon Kindle version.

The Contributors

Hilary Abrahams is a research fellow in the Centre for Gender and Violence Research at the University of Bristol. Her work as a Relate counsellor led her to study for a first degree in Sociology/Social Policy, and subsequently a doctoral study of the emotional needs of abused women. Since then, she has worked and written extensively on the support needs and service provision for families where domestic violence is an issue. Violence and abuse are common factors causing homelessness among women and Hilary is currently part of a team looking at their needs and service provision in Bristol.

Sandra S. Cabrita Gulyurtlu is an associate researcher of the Centre for Research on Families and Relationships (University of Edinburgh) where this study was conducted and where she was research assistant to Sarah Nelson. She is an honorary fellow at the University of Greenwich. Her research interests lie in safeguarding children and child protection, children's rights and child welfare, with a specialism in child sexual abuse and exploitation and children with disabilities. She is currently working for the Office of the Children's Commissioner for England as the researcher on the Inquiry into Child Sexual Exploitation by Gangs and Groups.

Amanda Gee (BFA, DTATI, RCAT), originally from the east coast of Canada, is a registered Canadian art therapist living and working in Toronto, Ontario, Canada. She currently works as a Multi Modal Supportive Therapist for Vita Community Living Services and Mens Sana Families for Mental Health. Amanda has been working with individuals with intellectual disabilities for the past 12 years in many different capacities. Amanda also specialises in helping people through grief and loss. With a background in the fine arts, when not at work Amanda is often being creative herself – drawing, painting, sewing, or making soft sculptures.

Judith Hassan, OBE, is Jewish Care's Special Advisor on Therapeutic Work with Survivors of War Trauma. She has a BSc (Hons) in Human Relations and is a qualified social worker. Judith has worked for Jewish Care for 42 years and considers they have always been the vital support for the services for survivors. For 36 years she pioneered and developed specialist services for survivors and refugees, both as a practitioner and as director of the services. She founded the Holocaust Survivors' Centre. She trains professionals and consults internationally on how to work with the effects of war trauma. Her work is widely published. She was awarded the National Care Awards Lifetime Achievement in Care in 2007, and an OBE for Services to Holocaust Survivors in 2008. Judith feels privileged to have been engaged in such rewarding work.

Georgina Hoare, MSc Psychodynamic Counselling/Psychotherapy, PG Dip Music Therapy, BMus (Hons), is currently Clinical Services Manager at SurvivorsUK and in private practice. She is a British Association for Councelling and Therapy (BACP)-accredited psychodynamic counsellor/ psychotherapist, Health and Care Professionals Council (HCPC) registered arts therapist (music) and a qualified clinical supervisor. She has worked as a therapist in learning disability, mental health and forensic services within the NHS, as well as in education and the voluntary sector since 1997, and has worked full-time at SurvivorsUK since 2008, overseeing the strategic development as well as training, counselling, helpline and research aspects of the organisation. Additionally Georgina has been a visiting trainer/lecturer at a variety of settings, including the Royal College of Music, University of Hertfordshire and Birkbeck College, University of London.

Krista Hoffman began her work in the anti-violence movement in 1994. She has worked for the Pennsylvania Coalition Against Rape (PCAR) as their Criminal Justice Training Specialist and has expertise in providing technical assistance and training to the criminal justice system. Her areas of speciality include investigating sexually based crimes, human trafficking, building and sustaining human trafficking response teams, and technology and sexually abusive behaviours. Her work on human trafficking has taken her across the US and internationally. Krista is an adjunct professor in the Masters of Education Program for Cabrini College. She teaches human development, social policy and research.

Ruth Lewis is a research fellow at the London School of Hygiene and Tropical Medicine. She was formerly research assistant to Sarah Nelson on the research study 'Care and Support Needs of Men who Survived Childhood Sexual Abuse' (University of Edinburgh 2009). Ruth's current research focuses on sexual health, behaviour and education, mainly using qualitative methods. She is working on an ESRC-funded study of young people's sexual practices in the UK, and the MRC/Wellcome-funded UK Natsal (National Survey of Sexual Attitudes and Lifestyles) study.

Sarah Nelson, author of the pioneering British feminist analysis of sexual abuse *Incest: Fact and Myth* (1982, 1987), has published and presented widely on sexual abuse issues. These include mental and physical health in both female and male survivors; neighbourhood mapping for child protection; sadistic organised abuse; and the voices of young survivors. Currently a research associate at Edinburgh University's Centre for Research on Families and Relationships (CRFR), she was from 2006 to 2011 a lead professional adviser to the Scottish Government on their national strategy for adult survivors of sexual abuse (SurvivorScotland).

Jacki Pritchard is an independent social worker registered with the Health and Care Professions Council. She specialises in working directly with victims of abuse and was the founder of the organisation Beyond Existing: Support Groups for Adults who have been abused. She is director of the company Jacki Pritchard Ltd, which provides training, consultancy and research in social care, expert witness work, and training products – DVDs, books, training manuals. Jacki has written widely on the subject of adult abuse and other social work topics. She has been series editor of the Good Practice Series (Jessica Kingsley Publishers) for the past 20 years.

Bernie Ryan is a trained nurse (RGN), counsellor and counselling supervisor (MA in Counselling) and also holds training and NVQ assessor awards. She currently manages the St Mary's Sexual Assault Referral Centre (SARC), leading a multidisciplinary team providing forensic medical and aftercare services to victims of rape and sexual assault. Bernie has acted as consultant to a number of police force areas on the establishment of SARCs; advised on operational policies and procedures; contributed to the development of minimum standards for SARCs; and is the chair of the National SARC Advisory Board. Bernie provides training and consultancy nationally and internationally to law enforcement agencies, non-government organisations (NGOs) and health care professionals.

Christiane Sanderson is a lecturer in psychology at the University of Roehampton and at Birkbeck College, University of London. With 25 years' experience of working with survivors of sexual violence, domestic abuse and complex trauma, she has provided consultancy and training to parents, teachers, social workers, prisoners, nurses, therapists, counsellors, the NSPCC and the Metropolitan Police Service. Christiane is an internationally published author who regularly speaks at conferences worldwide. She runs a practice in London, is a trustee of the charity One in Four and is a member of the Catholic Safeguarding Advisory Service committee representing survivor organisations.

Jacqui Smith is service delivery manager for the Young Women's Housing Project in Sheffield, where she has worked for the past 15 years. She started as an admin assistant and made her way through most jobs in the organisation, including Support Worker and Operations Manager. Jacqui has always had a strong interest in issues that affect women. She studied for a BA (Hons) in Women's Studies as a mature student and afterwards was involved in voluntary work for various organisations, which included Victim Support. For the Youth Association South Yorkshire (YASY) she did youth work and also worked on a project which involved developing a young women's group.

SUBJECT INDEX

Author Index

Abrahams, H. 138, 142, 148
Agar, K. 85
Alaggia, R. 85, 86, 87
Allgood, M. 97
American Psychiatric Association 39, 40
Association of Chief Police Officers 63, 138

Balding, V. 64
Barns, R. 148
Benn, P. 74
Berney, L. 87
Binney, V. 142
Bion, W.R. 103, 112
Blane, D. 87
Breuer, J. 103
Bromberg, P. 44, 60
Brown, M. 119
Burgess, A. 65

Cameron, D. 86
Campbell, P. 86
Caprio-Orsini, C. 175, 176, 177
Carlton, L. 132
Casement, P. 104, 108
Chowdhury-Hawkins, R. 64
Co-ordinated Action Against Domestic Abuse 72
Cohen, L. 119
Cole, A. 87
Community Living Ontario 172
Corbin, J.M. 87
Corbis Bright Consulting Ltd 148
Courtois, C. 117
Craven, P. 148
Crown Prosecution Service 78

Dale, P. 82, 96
Day, A. 85
De Luca, R.V. 85
De Silva, P. 82
Denzin, N. 87
Department for Education and Employment 19
Department of Health 19, 20, 63
Dhunpath, R. 87
Draucker, C.B. 82, 86, 96
Dube, S.R. 84, 85

Edmond, T. 97
Estes, R. 119, 120
Etherington, K. 102
Evans-Weaver, E. 117, 118, 126, 127, 129, 132, 133

Faculty of Forensic and Legal Medicine 68, 74
Feigenbaum, J.D. 82
Fick, D.M. 82
Fisher, M. 74
Foa, E. 47, 118
Fowks, G. 87
Frankl, V. 191
Fraser, A. 96
Freud, S. 103
Friedman, M. 118

Gagnon, J.H. 131
Garland, C. 115
George, J. 97
Goldman, J.D.G. 84
Grossman, F.K. 82
Groth, A.N. 50

Hague, G. 142